A HISTORY OF NEV

GW01186394

This is the first history of New South Wales to be published in over a century. From its convict origins to the present day, Beverley Kingston describes the dramatic events and fascinating characters that have shaped the history of Australia's first state. Beginning with the convict colony at Port Jackson and tracing the way New South Wales has been shaped by natural resources that produced both wealth and a home for an ever-increasing population, this book provides a concise chronicle of events from the first fleet to the present day.

Beverley Kingston is an honorary research fellow, School of History, University of New South Wales. Her previous books include *Women and Work in Australia, Basket Bag and Trolley: A Short History of Shopping in Australia, The Oxford History of Australia Volume 3 and My Wife, My Daughter and Poor Mary Ann.*

A History of New South Wales

BEVERLEY KINGSTON

CAMBRIDGE UNIVERSITY PRESS

Cambridge, New York, Melbourne, Madrid, Cape Town, Singapore, São Paulo

Cambridge University Press
477 Williamstown Road, Port Melbourne, VIC 3207, Australia

Published in the United States of America by Cambridge University Press, New York

www.cambridge.org
Information on this title: www.cambridge.org/9780521833841

First published 2006

Printed in China

A catalogue record for this publication is available from the British Library

National Library of Australia Cataloguing in Publication data
Kingston, Beverley.
A history of New South Wales.
Includes index.
ISBN-13 978-0-521-83384-4 hardback
ISBN-10 0-521-83384-1 hardback
ISBN-13 978-0-521-54168-8
ISBN-10 0-521-54168-9
1. New South Wales – History.   1. Title.
994.4

ISBN-13 978-0-521-83384-4 hardback
ISBN-10 0-521-83384-1 hardback

ISBN-13 978-0-521-54168-8 paperback
ISBN-10 0-521-54168-9 paperback

In memory of Henry Kingston, born London, 1882, and Louisa Daisy Short, born Sydney, 1882, who married in Sydney 1908, and their three children, Ronald, Gordon, and Miriam, born Dubbo, 1909, 1914, and 1921

CONTENTS

ILLUSTRATIONS

PLATES

MAPS

ACKNOWLEDGEMENTS

Most friends, colleagues and students with whom I have conversed in recent years have contributed knowingly or otherwise to my understanding of this story, but special thanks for ideas, suggestions, or helping me to find books go to Deborah Oxley and David Meredith, Gary Wotherspoon, Bruce Scates, Paul Tracy, Glen Mitchell, Margaret Bettison, Keith Campbell, Kate Deverall and booksellers David Lennon at Berkelouws, and Tim Peach at the State Library Bookshop, also Jane Keehn.

Following invitations from convenors Nick Doumanis and Marnie Hughes-Warrington, the members of history seminars at UNSW and Macquarie University cheerfully explored possible interpretations with me, while 'Kaz' (M. Kazim) in the UNSW library always knew where the references were hidden.

My colleagues on the New South Wales Working Party of the *ADB* taught me a great deal and those with whom I worked closely on the *ADB* Supplement, Chris Cunneen, Jill Roe and Stephen Garton, were both helpful and reassuring after reading the whole manuscript, as were Julia Horne and Eileen Chanin. One is lucky to have such friends and colleagues. Thanks also to Brian Fletcher, the Department of Environment and Conservation (NSW), and Gloria Zucker for permission to reproduce maps and photographs for which they hold the rights.

I

Introduction

'At daylight in the morning we discovered a Bay which appeared to be tollerably well shelterd from all winds into which I resoloved to go with the Ship' – thus James Cook first saw Botany Bay on Saturday 28 April 1770.[1]

Four months later (on 22 August) he took possession of the east coast of 'New Holland' and set his course westward to Batavia. In the copy of his journal which he sent ahead from Batavia, he named the coastline he had followed north from latitude 38 minutes south to 10½ minutes south, 'New Wales', but by the time he reached England with the *Endeavour*, it had become 'New South Wales'. There was no explanation for the name or the change, but already he had used 'New Hebrides' and 'New Caledonia'. And he had 'New Holland' in front of him.[2] Perhaps his attention had been drawn to the fact that 'New Wales' had already been used for part of northern Canada. Or perhaps Cook was simply the first of many travellers to be reminded of the Welsh coastline near Fishguard by the long white beaches separated by high bluffs which are characteristic of the coast of New South Wales where he made that first landfall in April 1770.

The New South Wales of which Captain Phillip formally took possession on 26 January 1788 was extended to include land known from the charts of Abel Janszoon Tasman's 1664 voyage out of Batavia to be lying as far as 43 degrees 39 minutes south, and west to 135 minutes east longitude. It also included 'all the islands adjacent in the Pacific Ocean' within those latitudes, and may or may not have included New Zealand. The original area proclaimed as New South Wales was 1,584,389 square miles (more than 4.1 million sq km) including New Zealand, or 1,480,527 square miles (over 3.8 million sq km) without it. In 1825, New South Wales was extended by a further 518,134 square miles (more than 1.3 million sq km) to 129 minutes east – which is now the boundary of Western Australia. This was its greatest extent.

During the next hundred years New South Wales was gradually reduced in size. In 1834, 309,850 square miles (802,508 sq km) were carved out to become South Australia. In 1840, New Zealand was explicitly proclaimed a separate colony thus ending the uncertainty about its status. The southern settlements in the Port Phillip district became the colony of Victoria in 1851, and in 1859, 554,300 square miles (over 1.4 million sq km) of the northern squatting districts were designated as Queensland. New South Wales was then roughly the shape we know today, though it still had responsibility for some untidy areas on the borders of South Australia, rationalised by 1863 to become part either of South Australia or Queensland. New South Wales had not yet, however, reached its modern size of 309,433 square miles (801,428 sq km). Between 1909 and 1915 three parcels of land totalling 939 square miles (2,432 sq km) in the Yass–Canberra region and at Jervis Bay were transferred to the federal government to become the Australian Capital Territory; and as well, Norfolk Island for which New South Wales had had responsibility, on and off, since 1788 became a federal territory. Of all the 'islands adjacent in the Pacific' only Lord Howe remained, administered for electoral purposes as part of Sydney (the electorate of McKell).[3] Thus the history of New South Wales from 1788 to about 1860 is also the history, until they became separate colonies, of Tasmania, South Australia, Victoria and Queensland.

Of the Aboriginal people he had encountered, Cook famously wrote:

From what I have said of the natives of New-Holland they may appear to some to be the most wretched people upon Earth, but in reality they are far more happier than we Europeans; being wholly unacquainted not only with the superfluous but the necessary Conveniences so much sought after in Europe, they are happy in not knowing the use of them. They live in a Tranquility which is not disturb'd by the Inequality of Condition: The

Earth and sea of their own accord furnishes them with all things necessary for life, they covet not Magnificent Houses, Household-stuff etc., they live in a warm and fine Climate and enjoy a very wholesome Air, so that they have very little need of Clothing . . . In short they seem'd to set no Value upon any thing we gave them, nor would they ever part with any thing of their own for any one article we could offer them . . .[4]

Both the story of first contact between Aborigines and Europeans, and those years during which the foundations of European settlement in Australia were laid have been extensively studied. It is now quite difficult to do justice to the work of all the historians, archaeologists and anthropologists who have examined these times from many angles, or to isolate the story of New South Wales from that of Australia. In the short space allowed to me here, I have tried to focus on those themes that seem to have a particular significance for what the colony of New South Wales became after it had shed its responsibilities for all its other areas, and settled into the boundaries that are familiar to us today, and to provide a coherent and accessible account of the kind of society that developed within those boundaries. Readers who wish to know more about the land itself before 1770 or the way of life of the Aboriginal inhabitants before they were unwittingly incorporated into the colony of New South Wales should consult the many excellent detailed studies of the pre-1770 period.[5]

While all the other Australian states have managed to maintain a kind of identity, after 1901 New South Wales seemed to be submerged in the federation or to be seen as the Australian archetype. The challenge has been to isolate themes that are specific to New South Wales from those which are common for all Australia. Some are based in geography, climate and the increasing significance of Sydney and the east coast in a world where both America and Asia have become more important. Others relate to the survival of ideas and social patterns that began with the convict settlement and the effect of a longer experience of the Australian environment than in the other colonies. The combined effects of native-born vitality and the liberation of the Irish element in the New South Wales population proved politically dynamic, while the availability of rich and varied natural resources, not only in land and timber, but in minerals too, made for remarkably easy development and wealth

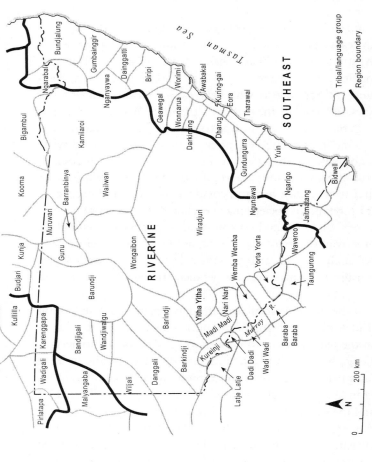

Map 1.1 Aboriginal language boundaries in New South Wales c. 1788, adapted from the map drawn by Norman Tindale in 1974 and D. Horton, ed., *The Encyclopedia of Aboriginal Australia*, Australian Institute of Aboriginal and Torres Strait Islander Studies Press, Canberra, 1994. (Rodney Harrison, *Shared Landscapes: Archaeologies of Attachment and the Pastoral Industry in New South Wales*, Department of Environment and Conservation (New South Wales) and UNSW Press, Sydney, 2004, p. 19)

creation. The constant demand for labour and skills produced a confident working class eagerly embracing both politics and education so that by the end of the nineteenth century New South Wales had become a modern progressive democracy setting the pace for the other colonies. The constraints of federation and closer involvement with the real world during the twentieth century forced a closer scrutiny of both earlier tolerant social attitudes and easy exploitation of natural resources. New South Wales has always had the economic capability to exist independently and its size and diversity give it some of the qualities of an independent nation. At times there has been impatience, if not conflict, with federation. Often the smaller states (with the help of the federal government) have seemed to resent the strength of New South Wales. Yet internal tension, especially between Sydney and the rest of New South Wales, has had a restraining effect. In some ways, the Riverina has always seemed closer to Victoria, and northern New South Wales has much in common with southern Queensland, while the west has always followed the fortunes of the Murray–Darling river system ultimately to South Australia. So Sydney cannot escape the fact that New South Wales has much in common with the adjoining states. Out of this tension has grown an impression of New South Wales as a residual version of Australian history, encumbered with the embarrassment of the first settlement, unable to rise above its origins or shake off its lower class tendencies, permanently enveloped in a cultural cringe. That was perhaps more understandable in the middle of the twentieth century than it is now. But there is more to New South Wales than the historic accidents of its first settlement and gradual dismemberment, as the following pages hope to show.

2

1788–1840, the convict colony

Generations of historians have puzzled over the reasons why the British government chose in 1786 to make a settlement on the east coast of Cook's New South Wales at Sir Joseph Banks' Botany Bay. To describe it as an invasion of Aboriginal land may be accurate, but this does not explain why the settlement was planned or what was intended. It may have been a strategic and economic move, to establish a base to prevent other expansionist European powers like France from claiming the newly charted territory and resources of the South Pacific, such as the flax and ship's masts of Norfolk Island. Certainly the arrival of two French ships in Botany Bay while the first fleet was still there, but about to move to a more attractive site at Port Jackson, is one of the great coincidences of history. And considering the pressures he was under in early February 1788, Phillip obviously took his instructions to lay claim to Norfolk Island as well as New South Wales seriously.

There was probably also some idea of protecting British trade routes to the East and expanding the sphere of influence of the East India Company. For quite a few years after 1788 all trade to and from New South Wales was technically the prerogative of the East India Company, and the religious life of the colony came under the authority of the diocese of Calcutta. So there were strategic and trading considerations for the settlement.

But there were also the convicts, accumulating in hulks round the coast of Britain since the end of the war with the American colonies, unexpectedly lost by Britain. With the loss went the long-standing

2.1 The New South Wales coat of arms decorated by artist
Christina Yandell with a waratah, the New South Wales floral
emblem, and flannel flowers. (E.J. Brady, *Australia Unlimited*,
Geo. Robertson, Melbourne, 1918, p. 143)

dumping ground for the unfortunate ones who were products or victims of the huge social and economic upheavals brought by the agricultural and industrial revolutions in eighteenth-century Britain.[1]

Between 18 and 20 January 1788, miraculously it seems, considering the distances involved, the eleven ships which had left
Portsmouth almost nine months earlier came to anchor in Botany
Bay. On board were 736 convicts (548 men and 188 women) and
294 assorted men, women and children, marines, their commanding officers, a chaplain, a surveyor, a judge-advocate and several
naval surgeons. There were also 27 wives of marines and civil officers and 37 children. Botany Bay, seen by Cook and Banks in 1770
in perfect late April weather, looked less attractive in mid-January
eighteen years later. The water supply especially seemed inadequate,
and Banks' 'meadow' looked more like a swamp. Within a week,
the commander of the expedition, Arthur Phillip, had found a better
site inside Port Jackson and moved the whole operation northward
to the place he named Sydney Cove.[2]

From the beginning the existence of the colony was precarious.
Because of the distances involved, it was an enterprise perhaps as
difficult and as ambitious as now trying to found and sustain a
substantial colony on the moon.[3] Had the newcomers been dependent, as the local Aborigines were, on what was available in the
vicinity of Port Jackson for food, clothing, and shelter, the colony

would have failed. Until Phillip's unenthusiastic settlers were able to clear land, establish productive farms, and ensure the survival of the domesticated birds and animals which had accompanied them on the long voyage from England or the Cape of Good Hope, they lived largely on supplies they had brought with them, or could be gathered from India or the Cape, or could scrounge locally. Those who lived through what later came to be called 'the hungry years' were often close to starvation. Phillip's greatest fear was not that the natives would be troublesome, but that there might be a rebellion among the convicts, or a mutiny among the marines. That neither eventuated until 1804 when there was a convict uprising at Castle Hill, and 1808 when the officers of the NSW Corps led by Johnston and Macarthur mutinied against Governor Bligh's attempts to suppress their commercial activities and especially their trade in rum, is some indication of the real fragility of the settlement. However, Phillip's insistence on as fair and equitable sharing of the available resources as possible set a precedent which was more or less maintained while the hard times persisted. Whether this was also the origin of our idea of a 'fair go' is an interesting question. From that beginning, though, the convicts knew that they had certain rights both as human beings and as British subjects in this strange and remote place.

Competition for the fish and oysters found in the waters of Port Jackson was probably the first intimation for the Eora people of the seriousness of the danger represented by these newcomers. Then there was the incredibly efficient felling of trees with iron axes and saws, the destruction of tubers and fouling of water supplies. The Aborigines saw the mysterious but deadly effect of firearms. They experienced inexplicable and devastating sickness as they were exposed to colds and flu, smallpox and venereal disease. Competition for food and other resources led to conflict, thieving, and murder on both sides. Eventually farms with a plentiful supply of corn and potatoes in the barns and lots of meat neatly herded and enclosed by fences would present both a threat and a snare to the independence of the Aboriginal people. This did not happen for some years, and in the meantime, Europe's diseases and her bad habits were let loose in New South Wales, hunting and fishing grounds were destroyed in desperation or ignorance, and havoc was wreaked on those Aborigines unfortunate enough to live too close to the white settlement.

We tend to forget how desperate the conditions of these years really were, made worse as the Napoleonic wars continued in Europe, and shipping and supplies needed in the colony were withheld or unobtainable. In time the settlement did become secure. Farms hoed out of the bush without the help of ploughs or working animals, towards Kissing Point, more effectively at Parramatta, on the Nepean towards Camden, and then in the upper reaches of the Hawkesbury at Windsor, became productive. It has often been said that the first fleet was ill-equipped and the first settlers badly prepared for the work they had to do. Really it was such a strange undertaking, to settle a place so far away and so little known with a large number of convicts, that no one could have imagined what might be required. Something of this can be sensed in the conscious fascination with which most of the educated or literate members of the first fleet recorded their experiences and set down their observations of the strange flora, fauna, and the local inhabitants. More significant, probably, was the unforeseen difficulty of transforming the convicts into reliable and productive workers. When the first fleet sailed, the debate in England over the merits of physically punishing those who committed crimes (by execution or flogging), or trying to reform them through persuasion or education had already begun. This was tied up with early attempts to transform a rural labouring workforce into a disciplined industrial one. As John Hirst has argued, the early convicts especially were unused to disciplined work, and not keen to do it, even though it was for their own survival.[4]

No question in the early history of New South Wales has been more closely studied than the origins of the convicts. Were they mostly poachers and pickpockets, caught up in a harsh criminal code, or habitual criminals lucky to have their sentences commuted to transportation? Or in the case of the women convicts, hardened prostitutes or poor servant girls led astray by fondness for pretty clothes? The question has mattered because these people were the first two generations of settlers in New South Wales. On their reputations rested the reputation of the colony itself.

Fortunately, by 1788 the British government had begun to develop a recognisably modern bureaucracy and the early population of

New South Wales is remarkably well documented. Over the fifty years and more that the convict system operated, the record-keeping became more efficient, so that by the 1830s the lives of individual convicts could be closely monitored.[5] Good record-keeping meant closer supervision and more carefully targeted punishment for those appearing too frequently before the courts. Computerised convict records have enabled historians to study the origins of the convicts with modern sociological thoroughness. It has been possible to establish for example that more came from the cities than the countryside – though of course how many of these were originally driven from their rural backgrounds to the cities by the growing shortage of rural work is not a question easily answered. It has also been possible to show the kind of work experience claimed by the convicts, the pattern of their ages, and the crimes for which they were sentenced, whether they were literate, and more – or less how they fared while they were still in the system. What happened to them afterwards is more a matter of chance for the family historian pursuing his or her ancestors, as many people now are inclined to do. Whether or not as deliberate policy, these studies have shown that most of the male convicts were relatively fit, fairly young, and generally suitable material for colonisation. Though not necessarily educated in a formal sense, they were probably a bit smarter or a bit more worldly than average. The women too were eminently suited to the kind of life they might expect to lead in the colony, as domestic workers, perhaps as a wife, but almost certainly also in some kind of sexual relationship with one of the men, though relatively few claimed to have been sex workers before they were convicted, usually for petty thieving. They were also, surprisingly, more literate than average servant girls. It seems as if on the whole the women came from backgrounds where they had little to lose by being bold or clever and had learnt to fend for themselves.[6] An ability to cope, not necessarily in a conventional law-abiding way, with whatever life threw at them, and often to make the most of it, seems to have been a characteristic of many of the convicts. New South Wales gave them opportunities where England or Ireland offered none.

Whatever the principles governing their selection, the convicts were used in New South Wales, not always willingly, as labour. From 1788 to 1840 (and beyond), most of the labour to clear and till land, for all building of houses, shops and storage, roads, bridges, and wharves, and most services, domestic and public, was provided by convicts. At first they were mostly required for essential government work, but soon some were being assigned to work privately on land allocated to various officers of the colony. Convict labourers were later assigned to ex-convicts who had taken up the government's offer of farming land, and even to their own wives who came or were brought to the colony to be reunited with their husbands as free settlers. As the number of free settlers who were permitted to emigrate to New South Wales after 1793 grew, so did the number of convicts assigned to them. While there were regulations covering relations between convicts and private employers, their interpretation varied considerably, giving rise on the one hand to greatly improved productivity where there was satisfaction on both sides, and on the other, to accusations of injustice and inequality because there was such variation in conditions. Government work became despised, partly because it was more closely regulated, and there were fewer opportunities to win privileges or make money on the side, and partly because increasingly government work was used as punishment for convicts who had fallen foul of private employers.

Lachlan Macquarie's building plans during his term as governor (1809–21) made considerable demands on the convict workforce to the great annoyance of private employers who had come to regard their assigned convicts as a right, and essential to the prosperity of their farming and other businesses. A long-running argument as to who made better use of, and had more right to the labour of the convicts, government or private enterprise, was resolved by the decision made in London to end transportation altogether by 1840. Thereafter labour had to be supplied from within the colony, or by immigration, invoking new arguments. Whether public works are better managed by government or by private enterprise, and whether immigrant labour is more docile, cheaper and versatile than the home-grown variety became questions often debated and subsequently heavily influenced by ideology. Convict society in New South Wales has been seen variously as a prototype of socialism or communism, a command economy, or a benevolent despotism. Perhaps knowledge of its unusual beginnings has been the source of the pragmatism or the scepticism about ideology that has ever been a characteristic of NSW society. Certainly, a version of the mixed economy was effective from the beginning, and this has been significant ever since.

Phillip's original instructions contained provision for granting farms of up to 30 acres (about 12 ha.) to time-expired convicts so that they could stay and continue to make a living in the colony. Thus a great many former convicts became small-scale landowners. The irony was significant. Many had been victims of the enclosure of agricultural land in eighteenth-century Britain, depriving tenant farmers of their livelihoods. Convicts from Ireland, especially, had suffered the loss of their traditional rural existence. There were convicts who had been convicted for burning hay-ricks, destroying machinery which was putting them out of work, or joining together to resist loss of wages or other customary rights. Now in New South Wales they were awarded land freehold.

Land grants were made also to marines who were willing to stay in New South Wales, partly in the hope that they would constitute a kind of home guard as protection against convict uprisings or Aboriginal attacks. Their officers, however, were not entitled to land grants. It was never imagined that they would want to stay after their tour of duty was over. But the idea of land changed everything. When Phillip left the colony at the end of 1792 to seek medical attention for a hernia, acting governor, Major Francis Grose, began making substantial grants to his fellow officers. They could already see a grand future for themselves in New South Wales.

Through the system of land grants, many small holdings and large freehold estates were created in the area stretching from south of the Shoalhaven to Port Stephens in the north and west beyond Bathurst and Goulburn. Alan Atkinson's study of the Macarthurs' estate and village at Camden shows the extent to which older, almost feudal British farming and agricultural management practices were adopted in New South Wales during these years.[7] Camden had its village, its church, its school, and its tenant farmers working under the supervision of the Macarthurs who were effectively lords of the manor. Many examples of this neo-feudal style of estate management could be found in what were known as the settled districts, from the Illawarra to the Hunter and as far north as Port Stephens. In part the estates were a product of intensive farming in the fertile river valleys, but they were also related to the availability of labour, convict mainly, though the local Aborigines were often encouraged to stay and work on the estates. There was some similarity between the management of convict labour and old feudal-style relations of dependence and responsibility between master and bondservant.

Where they were permitted or encouraged to stay, the Aborigines too found the seasonal nature of most of the work on the estates and their ability through this kind of work to maintain close links with their ancestral lands more congenial than the outright struggle for possession elsewhere.[8] It is probable that the survival of strong Aboriginal communities in the coastal valleys both north and south of Sydney owed something to this early pattern of land management as well as to the rugged nature of the foothills which defied easy settlement by white farmers or stock-owners and provided protection for the local tribes. Much of the farming was experimental. Labour was only part of the problem where it was also necessary to learn the lessons of the climate, what crops did best, and which varieties were least prone to pests and diseases. At Coolangatta on the Shoalhaven Alexander Berry experimented with bees and honey. At Dalwood on the Hunter, George Wyndham tried growing tobacco and in his diary drew up lists of the fruit trees and grapevines he had acquired for planting.[9]

Convicts were technically forbidden to own property, though the fact that so many had to fend for themselves, finding accommodation and food or clothing, meant that they did acquire possessions, even savings. For ex-convicts, access to a small portion of land whether as a farm or as the site for a cottage was deliberately made easy since in this way they could become self-supporting. Accumulating quite large amounts of property was not difficult for anyone who understood the system. Before long some of the wealthiest landowners in the colony were ex-convicts. When the NSW lists for jury service, or later, for voting, were drawn up according to existing British qualifications of property-ownership, many ex-convicts were automatically included as respectable property-owning citizens of New South Wales. So the idea of property-ownership as an indication of respectability or legal status was a poor guide to who was convict or ex-convict in the population of New South Wales.

For the first twenty-five years of its existence the settlement in New South Wales looked to the sea, anxiously, at first, for ships bringing news and fresh supplies, and was confined to the coast near Sydney and to those river valleys to the north and south that could be explored by sea. Whaling and sealing became important early industries, the whales being chased and captured for their oil while the seal populations of the islands in Bass Strait and south of New Zealand were decimated for their furs. American whalers were among the regulars refitting in Sydney Cove while later Ben Boyd established a whaling station on the south coast at Eden.

This land-locked outlook suited the authorities since it made the penal settlement easier to manage; however, many attempts were made to find a way through the barrier of the Blue Mountains, mostly by escaped convicts in the belief that China lay beyond. In 1813, a practical route to the western plains was pioneered by free settlers, Blaxland, Wentworth and Lawson. During the next twenty years the mystery of the rivers flowing north and west was solved and the names of governors and colonial officials liberally distributed as far as the Glenelg in the south, the Darling in the west and the Brisbane in the north. Sydney was becoming a base from which the resources of New South Wales could be explored and its potential as part of the great enterprise which was early industrial Britain slowly exploited. The boundaries of settlement, both official and unofficial, were gradually extended. By 1840, New South Wales was almost as large as it would ever be.

The first official extension of the settlement occurred within a few weeks of completing the move from Botany Bay to Port Jackson, when on 15 February 1788, Phillip sent Lieutenant Philip Gidley King in the *Supply* to secure Norfolk Island, a volcanic peak in an undersea range stretching from New Zealand to New Caledonia. James Cook had landed there, noted its possibilities (his men had cut down one of its pines to repair a broken mast), taken possession, and named it on 11 October 1774 while on his South Pacific sweep in the *Resolution*.[10] Phillip had been instructed to establish a settlement there as well as Botany Bay in the expectation that its tall pines and flax plants might prove valuable for making masts and sails for the British navy.

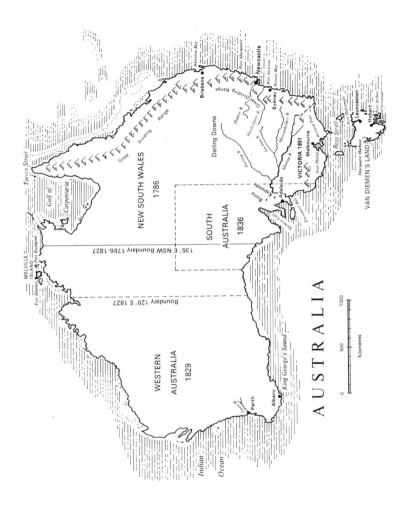

Map 2.1 Boundary changes to New South Wales before 1859. In December that year Queensland was created north of a line running from Point Danger on the coast, through the ranges, along the curve of the Condamine, and west to meet the South Australian boundary near Cameron's Corner. Thus New South Wales achieved its modern shape. (Brian Fletcher, *Colonial Australia before 1850*, Nelson, Melbourne, 1976, p. 2)

King took with him a party of nine male convicts, one of whom
had farming experience and another who had worked with flax,
six female convicts chosen for their good character, and seven
assorted seamen, marines, and medical attendants. These 'Robin-
son Crusoes of the South Pacific'[11] had stores for six months, seeds,
some sheep, pigs, a goat, four hens and a cock, three ducks and
a drake and a four-oared rowing boat to keep them going. The
island was known to be uninhabited, although once farming began
evidence was uncovered of possible previous human visitors. For
the next twenty-six years the convicts and their overseers struggled
to make it a viable settlement though it was conspicuously unsuccessful in fulfilling the original expectations for its timber and flax,
and never self-sufficient. Small adjacent islands, named for Phillip
and Evan Nepean, were found to be neither very fertile nor well
watered. Norfolk was a convenient place for off-loading difficult
convicts (and officials) from time to time, but as other secondary
convict settlements were established, it became less important. In
1814 it was abandoned. The convicts were moved to Van Diemen's
Land, later Tasmania, and long-term residents – there had of course
been children born on the island – were resettled outside Hobart
at New Norfolk. Laboriously constructed buildings were burned to
discourage any other settlers.

In 1825, it was decided to re-establish the settlement, this time,
deliberately as a place of banishment for intractable prisoners.
During this phase, it became notorious for its harsh conditions,
though at least one commandant, Alexander Maconachie, had a
good reputation for his work in reforming both prisons and prisoners. In 1844, however, after transportation to New South Wales
had come to an end and a misjudged plan to re-introduce it had
been volubly rejected by protest meetings in Sydney, New South
Wales handed responsibility for Norfolk Island to Van Diemen's
Land which was still fully engaged in convict administration. When
transportation to Van Diemen's Land also came to an end in 1856,
Norfolk Island was returned to New South Wales and thereafter
became a home for former *Bounty* mutineers and their families from
Pitcairn Island.

For the rest of the nineteenth century New South Wales took
responsibility for the island as a British crown colony though
the islanders largely governed themselves. In 1895 the British

government offered Norfolk Island to New South Wales altogether, though New South Wales was not enthusiastic about acquiring a quasi-colony. So from 1902 the premier of New South Wales served also as minister for Norfolk Island in the NSW parliament until 1913 when it became a federal responsibility.

New Zealand had been vaguely included by Cook in the area he named New South Wales in 1770, though his subsequent encounter with cannibalism among its Maori inhabitants gave no expectations that it would be an easy place to colonise. Indeed, Governor Phillip suggested that any convict who committed murder or sodomy in New South Wales might be sent 'as a prisoner of the natives of New Zealand, and let them eat him'.[12] Until it became a separate settlement in 1841 as part of the Wakefieldian experiment, New Zealand and the adjacent islands were used as a source of raw materials – seals, whales, flax and timber – and a place ships visited briefly after Sydney in the hope of picking up a return cargo. Otherwise only earnest evangelical clergy like Samuel Marsden and Thomas Kendall saw the heathen Maori as a challenge for conversion.

To the north of Sydney, cedar found on the Hunter River in 1791 was first exported in 1795. Coal was found in the Illawarra (at Coalcliff) and on the Hunter in 1797 from where it was first exported to India in 1799. A small convict settlement mining coal as a form of secondary punishment was established at 'Coal Harbour' in 1801, abandoned, and re-established in 1804 when it officially became Newcastle. As well as coalmining, convicts were employed in cedar getting and lime burning. By 1823 settlers were moving into the surrounding areas that had been surveyed along with town allotments in Newcastle itself. It was decided to move the convict settlement further north to Port Macquarie where another convict settlement had been established in 1821. Here too convicts were employed in timber getting, but by 1830 free settlers were fast encroaching. Brisbane River replaced Port Macquarie as a centre of secondary punishment from 1824. These settlements had as their main objective the segregation and punishment of convicts who had proved troublesome, but they had the effect also of creating a presence elsewhere on the coast. Subsequent strategic settlements further extended the official area of New South Wales to cover most of the continent by 1829, but also diminished it by the separation of Van Diemen's Land (1825) and the creation of South and Western Australia in the 1830s.

2.2 Coal Cliff. The site of the first discovery of coal in
Australia in August, 1797. (The cliff is formed of the Upper
Coal measures, overlaid by the Hawkesbury Series.) This
photograph showing the loading facilities was taken by
NSW's government geologist in 1901, E.F. Pittman. (E.F.
Pittman, *Mineral Resources of New South Wales*,
Government Printer, Sydney, 1901, facing p. 307)

Closer to Sydney it was found that much of the mainland was not
obviously suited to or easily converted to European-style agriculture.
The Aboriginal inhabitants had been content to harvest naturally
occurring foods and to fish and hunt the game. Only in the coastal
valleys did the white settlers find land they could plough, plant and
harvest. There were no obvious crops they could adopt as British
settlers in North America had adopted corn and potatoes from the
Indians, or game birds to compare with the turkey. Only the fish and
oysters seemed useable. Soil that had never before seen a hoe was
difficult to till. The seasons were upside down, and though crops like
maize began to flourish, the coastal valleys were too warm and wet
for wheat. Cattle brought from the Cape escaped into the bush and
were not seen for seven years when they were found happily breeding and grazing on what was thereafter known as the Cowpastures
south of Sydney. The farmers had no choice but to persevere and to
adapt. By 1821, wheat growing was established, orchards and even
vineyards were prospering. Sheep-breeding experiments at Camden
and elsewhere produced encouraging results, but it was not until a

road over the Blue Mountains built by convict labour as one of the major public works initiated by Governor Macquarie was opened in 1815 that farming and grazing on a large scale became a reality. The first of two major settlements beyond the ranges was named Bathurst, after the Secretary of State for War and the Colonies. Goulburn a little later honoured one of his successors.

The discovery of rivers rising in the dividing ranges and flowing westward led to hopes that there might be a great system of rivers opening the inland to water-borne transport. However, Oxley's passage down the Macquarie was blocked in 1818 by reed beds and marshes, and promising rivers flowing west turned disappointingly south where they joined the Darling. Though by the late nineteenth century most of these rivers were being used to ship wool and firewood, they were considered unsatisfactory as a major communications system. Their flow was unpredictable and they diverted trade from western New South Wales and Sydney and towards the rival ports of Melbourne and Adelaide.

Coastal shipping on the other hand remained a vital means of transport. At first boat-building was banned because it was feared that convicts would try to escape, as some did, by sea. But the need to maintain contact with the outlying settlements, the growing importance of sealing and whaling as export industries, and maintenance of the existing fleet became more important than the fear of escape. In any case, most of those who did escape went bush. Some joined the Aborigines or lived rough and were known as bushrangers. Others came to an early end. Rugged country to the south of Sydney became notorious, not only for its bushrangers, but also because well-organised and determined Aborigines managed to defend the gullies of the Shoalhaven against timber getters for a decade or more.

By the 1820s families like the Macarthurs had shown the possibilities of producing fine wool in New South Wales for Lancashire's hungry mills. West of the ranges the promise of limitless acres of lightly wooded pasture excited the land hunger of all New South Wales, convict and free. Those who could not secure grants simply took their sheep to squat on crown lands. Unlike ex-convicts and immigrants, young men born in the colony – known as cornstalks, currency, or more problematic for the modern reader, the native-born – were not entitled to grants of land, though Governor Darling was eventually persuaded to change that. In comparison to the neo-feudal pattern of settlement in the settled districts, squatting, perceived initially as a temporary phenomenon, soon required regulation, and eventually became a major cause of conflict between government and the most influential settlers. Squatters were licensed on payment of a small fee to run their flocks and herds on 'vacant' crown land. Commissioners were appointed to collect the fees, supervise the squatters, and adjudicate disputes over rights to grass and water. However, the speed and the distances the squatters covered in search of unclaimed pasture made regulation impossible. More importantly, the squatters became easy targets for the Aborigines whose lands they were invading with their flocks and herds and wagons of arms and provisions. As Aboriginal attacks became common, so too did squatter demands for military or police protection. But the murder of a group of harmless Aborigines, mostly women and children, by stockmen at Myall Creek in 1838 was certainly not in self-defence. The law exacted capital punishment with unfortunate consequences. As in another judgment fifty years later on a gang rape at Mt Rennie resulting also in capital punishment, serious crimes committed both against Aborigines ·(after 1838) and women (after 1887) were driven underground. Police became reluctant to lay charges, and juries to convict, lest the prescribed penalty be imposed.[13]

The squatting movement showed the authorities in London that there was no need to bribe prospective settlers by giving land away. During the 1820s land grants to ex-convicts were discontinued, and, under the influence of the theories of Edward Gibbon Wakefield, in 1831, all land grants were abolished to be replaced by land sales, initially at 5 shillings per acre, rising to 12 shillings in 1839, and £1 by 1843. The relatively high cost of land, of course, made squatting more attractive, though new regulations required a separate licence for every run and fees according to the number of stock carried. Thus New South Wales experienced its first overheated property market. Speculative capital flowed into the purchase of both land and stock. Loans were easily obtained. Credit was overextended. But the years 1838–1840 brought drought, and British capital began to dry up too in anticipation of changes when transportation ended in 1840. By 1843 the Bank of Australia had failed, the Savings Bank of New

South Wales was in difficulty, and the first land boom in New South Wales was over.

The convict system had made New South Wales a rough and callous place, bearable for many only because of alcohol. Spirits, usually described as rum, were imported or distilled locally from sugar and grain, and widely used in barter in the early years when coin was in short supply and other forms of exchange were not trusted. Illegal stills and breweries of dubious quality flourished in isolated spots beyond the edge of settlement. Beer was thought less harmful and brewing encouraged, so that beer might be used to pay wages or issued as an allowance to convicts. However, barley grown in New South Wales was unsuitable for brewing, and until reliable means of refrigeration became available, New South Wales' high temperatures made the fermentation process difficult to control. Even though life grew easier, levels of alcohol consumption remained high, probably because of the high proportion of men in the population and the lack of other outlets for their disposable income.[14]

Average life expectancy was less than fifty. Most families lost one or more children before they turned three. Cruelty to both humans and animals was common. The usual method of disciplining convicts was flogging. Twenty-five lashes with the 'cat', a whip made of nine to twelve greenhide tails sometimes knotted at the ends, could be ordered by a magistrate at the request of an employer for mere insubordination, or for losing a few sheep. Repeat offenders, sentenced to public works such as road making, were shackled at the ankles and formed into iron or chain gangs (though surprisingly this did not stop them absconding). As Roger Therry remembered his arrival in the colony in 1829,

Early in the morning the gates of the convict prison were thrown open, and several hundred convicts were marched out in regimental file, and distributed amongst the several public works in and about the town. As they passed along – the chains clanking at their heels – the patchwork dress of grey and yellow cloth marked with the Government brand in which they were paraded – the downcast countenances – and the whole picture of the men, exhibited a truly painful picture. Nor was it much improved throughout the day as one met bands of them in detachments of twenty yoked to wagons laden with gravel and stone, which they wheeled through the streets; in this and in other respects they performed all the functions of labour usually discharged by beasts of burden at home.[15]

However, John Hirst has warned us to take care in how we read the record of violence and cruelty in the convict system. Most of the accounts detailing unfairness or abuse, he says, were written by those most anxious to bring the system to an end, i.e. its enemies.[16] The records show that during the 1830s about one convict in four was flogged each year. About three and a half million lashes 'were delivered to convict backs'. Most of those flogged were actually flogged several times, constituting a small core of hardened or repeat offenders. But occasionally men were flogged to death. As late as 1854 executions (by hanging) were conducted in public, and there were always plenty of spectators. Between 1828 and 1855 nearly 490 hangings (including 6 women) were carried out, 70 per cent of them before 1838.[17] On thirty-seven occasions, four or more were hanged simultaneously, the largest group being 11 in October 1828. Europeans and Aborigines were hanged side by side, and it is doubtful whether either had better legal representation than the other.

In part this harshness derived from the early naval administration of the colony – the eighteenth-century British navy was notorious for the cruel and dangerous conditions in which ordinary seamen worked, though life for most people in early industrial Britain was not meant to be easy either. Accumulated experience in New South Wales, however, may have led to a kind of institutionalised severity that became more marked as the colony became more prosperous. To extract good work from the convicts it became the custom to bribe them with the promise of free time in which they were 'on their own hands' either to work for themselves or for private payment, or to drink, gamble, or otherwise seek amusement. Not surprisingly, those who did develop a taste for work, especially if combined with a skill, or natural cleverness, prospered, and work became a route not so much to salvation as to freedom and a better life. The gradual shift in Britain towards ideas of reforming rather than simply punishing those who had committed crimes against property or society led to the more systematic use of work as an educative punishment in New South Wales. But the contradiction was there: the evidence was abundant that transportation was effective as a kind of reform, but it had ceased to serve as a threat or a punishment.

Some of the harshness of life in early New South Wales came simply from the uncertainty of existence and the difficulties and dangers of establishing a viable existence under primitive rural conditions. Missionaries working in the Wellington Valley were sure that most of the problems with local Aborigines were caused by habitual violence in the living conditions of convict and ex-convict shepherds. These men had certainly been brutalised by their experience, but living in rough huts without regular female company and only sly-grog shanties for recreation did nothing to improve them. Aboriginal women were eagerly sought as sexual partners and hut-keepers. The pale skinned babies resulting from such unions were often abandoned as defective, though the missionaries tried to rescue them.[18] One of the lasting consequences of the convict system was that there was little need to try to integrate the Aboriginal population into the working life of the colony especially beyond the settled districts. Because there were plenty of convicts available cheaply as shepherds or stockmen (and who were theoretically subject to the discipline of the courts if they were negligent, or their work was otherwise unsatisfactory) there was no need to try to understand the Aborigines or employ them. The most significant encounters between black and white were sexual unions which, because of the close identification of marriage with baptism in the Christian churches, could not be legalised or sanctified even where both partners wished it unless the Aboriginal woman herself had taken the huge step of becoming baptised as a Christian. But there were children and many survived, giving rise to a mixed race population which blended quietly into rural society. No one wished to know too much about where anyone came from, black or white, bond or free.

The general shortage of women, especially marriageable women, added an extra dimension to levels of intolerance and hypocrisy. In 1790 there were approximately six men for each woman over the age of twelve. By 1840 this was down to two men for every woman. However, such figures give only a crude and probably optimistic picture of the real situation. Only a few of the officials brought their wives at the beginning – the marines were forbidden to bring theirs. In the 1790s, on most Sundays, several marriages were celebrated, and baptisms as well. Richard Johnson, the first clergyman, and his wife Mary, gave their daughter, one of the earliest white children born in New South Wales, an Aboriginal name, Milbah. One of the sadder observations was a child's burial following soon on its baptism. Many marriages were bigamous. There was also a great deal of what was called concubinage, men co-habiting, usually with convict women. Officials such as the judge-advocate, David Collins, and diarist Ralph Clark, left wives behind in England but established liaisons of a more or less lasting kind with women in the colony. The men felt no need to disgrace themselves by marrying their convict mistresses and housekeepers, while the women knew they would not be abandoned because they were not easily replaced. There was a sense in which the women could pick and choose among the men, and those men who could offer economic stability and a good home for a woman and her children fared best in the competition for female companionship.

However, the large number of irregular unions made for a degree of difficulty in polite society. Properly married women like Elizabeth Macarthur who had come to New South Wales as free settlers did not approve of convict mistresses at social gatherings. Convict mistresses, even ex-convict wives, and later the daughters of these liaisons knew that they did not belong in the best circles. From the beginning therefore, polite society functioned with a high level of sexual segregation. To make it easier to overlook domestic irregularities, men conducted their business as much as possible away from home and far from female influence. Women attended to women's business – hatching, matching, and despatching – in full knowledge of the precise status of everyone involved, maintaining with great delicacy the boundaries of respectability. A society worthy of Jane Austen's skill in observing the proprieties functioned in and around Government House. Only at the occasional public balls held under vice-regal patronage to celebrate important events such as the king's or the queen's birthday were the frayed edges of this delicate structure visible.

Those settlers without criminal associations became increasingly sensitive about being identified as convicts, ex-convicts or even the children of convicts. William Charles Wentworth, son of a liaison between a surgeon who had become the black sheep of his family sent to Norfolk Island to avoid charges connected with an attempted highway robbery, and a convict woman, was rejected, so the story went, as a suitor to one of the Macarthur daughters because of his murky past. He later married the daughter of a bigamous former convict and though he became rich and powerful, his wife and daughters found many of the doors of Sydney society closed to them. It was easier for them to live the kind of life their wealth allowed in England where the family history was not generally known.[19] Yet the origins of many of the free settlers who claimed to be the elite of New South Wales were known to be ordinary. Wealthy landowners and pioneers of the wool industry, John and Elizabeth Macarthur had come to New South Wales in 1790, he an officer in the less than prestigious NSW Corps, she an orphan before her marriage, dependent on the kindness of relatives, both hoping to better themselves, which they did with grim determination. For many like the Macarthurs New South Wales was a gamble in which they traded second-rate skills or connections at home for a first-rate opportunity in the despised colony, creating a primly self-conscious society in which gossip and innuendo served for currency as much as wealth or achievement.

Further down the social scale it was not possible to maintain such fine distinctions. The cumulative effect of trying to manage social irregularities was mass hypocrisy and eventually a widespread anxious obscuring and careful forgetting of who was, or who had been, a convict. By the middle of the nineteenth century denial of convict origins had become commonplace.

Before 1856 NSW society was dependent on Government House for leadership. The fact that Phillip had come without his wife tended to emphasise the naval-style masculine nature of his administration. Hunter too was unmarried. By the time Governor King arrived with his wife, Anna Josepha, it was possible to think about more than matters of survival, and Mrs King was also inclined to take an interest in the welfare of the women and children in the colony. After the Kings, Bligh brought his daughter Mrs Putland and her husband who was on Bligh's staff to live with him at Government House. But she added to rather than diminished dissatisfaction with Bligh. By contrast the Macquaries seemed a modern, benign liberal couple. She ably complemented her husband's interest in planning and building by adding her sense of style and interest in architecture.

Macquarie found the contradictions of managing the penal colony and maintaining authority in a society which was coming every day more to resemble a part of provincial England impossible to resolve. An increasing number of free settlers began to complain that they should not be subjected to the regulations of the penal colony, and especially that they should not be required to pay the taxes introduced by Macquarie to help pay for the civic amenities he was constructing. By 1810 if New South Wales was to become more than a penal colony, it needed a different kind of administration. The town of Sydney, for instance, needed cleaning up. The streets were a mess. They were narrow and crooked where buildings had grown without proper alignments or building plans. Macquarie thought to set an example with buildings and streets designed to provide a sense of dignity and self-respect. By 1827 the main streets of the town were lit from sunset to sunrise by 100 oil lamps. The map James Maclehose included in his 1839 Sydney street directory and tourist guide showed the neat order of the business side of town west of the Tank Stream, and to the east, the more expansive residential area centred on Government House and the Domain. Contemporary paintings show kangaroos, emus and Aborigines wandering in the extensive gardens of private houses built on the heights overlooking the town in what is now Kings Cross. Among Maclehose's illustrations were many buildings, public and private, in harmony with architect Francis Greenway's Georgian designs for Macquarie, and ideally suited to the warm golden sandstone being quarried in and around Sydney.[20] The sandstone buildings of the old New South Wales would become one of its most enduring characteristics for they were both sturdy and naturally at ease with their environment.

By Macquarie's time there was a sizeable population who called New South Wales home. Some were former marines or officials who had taken up land and prospered. Others were ex-convicts who had also taken up the land they were offered, found they could practise their former professions profitably in New South Wales, or had been able to turn their talents to trade. Many had long since married, become the fathers of respectable families, in all respects, good citizens. The Scottish laird in Macquarie recognised that they and their families were the future of New South Wales. Yet the problem remained of how the convict settlement was to be administered in such a way that the necessary authority was maintained but not hijacked as it had been by small cliques of ambitious individuals, first during the interregnum after Phillip's departure and before Hunter's arrival, and more recently after Bligh had been deposed.

When New South Wales was first settled in 1788, France was about to explode in revolution. As a result of that revolution and the subsequent Napoleonic wars, England too experienced intense dislocation leading eventually to major social reforms including the management of crime and the justice system. As part of this process the convict system in New South Wales was subject to three major inquiries. The first in 1812, based on evidence collected in Britain, concluded that though convicted criminals were shipped to New South Wales in order to dispose of them as efficiently as possible, there was little or no suggestion of reforming them and no idea that the punishment should fit the crime. In 1819 the British government appointed former judge John Thomas Bigge to carry out another inquiry into the future of New South Wales. By this time it was becoming clear that despite the perceived iniquities of the system, New South Wales was too promising a place to be left forever to convicts. Bigge spent more than a year travelling around New South Wales with his secretary, interviewing the residents, and collecting evidence about the state of the economy and society. Bigge's report added urgency to the need already perceived by Macquarie to change the basis on which New South Wales was administered.

By the time of the third inquiry, the Molesworth Select Committee of 1837–38, it was almost a foregone conclusion that transportation to New South Wales would cease although it continued for another ten years in Van Diemen's Land and was introduced by request in Western Australia when that colony was desperately in need of cheap labour in the 1850s. These three inquiries between them produced an immense amount of evidence and opinion concerning the convict system. When added to all the court, shipping, and individual records of transportation, New South Wales has uniquely detailed archives of its early history, so detailed, in fact, that historians can still find evidence which may not have been taken into account, or become absorbed in analysing the detail.

Until 1823 each NSW governor was responsible only to the Colonial Office in London for his administration of the colony. This made him, depending on his personality, background, and

experience, an autocrat or a benevolent dictator. Increasingly, however, the laws and the regulations that were necessary for the order
of the colony impacted as much on the free settlers as on the convicts. Resentment of the quasi-military nature of the government of
New South Wales grew, especially in the civil courts which were de
facto courts martial. When the legality of taxes levied by Macquarie
for public works was also questioned, the British government was
obliged to pass an annual bill protecting all measures introduced by
the governor of New South Wales against legal proceedings.

The New South Wales Judicature Act of 1823, devised as a solution to these problems raised by Macquarie's administration and
outlined in Bigge's report, was a modest first step on the long road
to self-government. To modify the military power of the governor in
relation to the free settlers it set up a court structure presided over
by a chief justice, and foreshadowed the establishment eventually
of civil trial by jury. As well, a council of between seven and five
members was to be nominated to advise the governor. Though the
governor still remained responsible for both initiating legislation
and carrying it out, if a majority of the council withheld consent
from proposed legislation, the chief justice would be called in to
give his opinion on the validity of the law in relation to English law.

Early councils consisted mainly of senior government officials and
the occasional prominent settler who would probably have advised
the governor informally anyway. Even so, Governor Brisbane
(1821–25) never got around to constituting his council and it was
1826 before a council was summoned by his successor Ralph Darling. In 1828 the size and scope of the council was extended to
include between ten and fifteen nominated residents in the colony
who were not government officials, and the council itself was
enabled to initiate legislation. To the growing number of free immigrants and the cornstalks this hardly seemed adequate participation
in the process of government. So much still depended on the skills
of the governor and his ability to translate the needs of the colony
into terms that were acceptable in London.

While Ralph Darling and his wife Eliza set a fine example to the
colonists of a close, affectionate, Christian family – during their time
in New South Wales (1825–31) they were rearing six children aged
between 13 and a few months – they were not loved.[21] Eliza showed

significant leadership in her work among the poor and especially in the founding of the Sydney School of Industry to train poor girls as domestic servants. She was probably also involved in Darling's experiment in town planning when he arranged land grants along the ridge of what later became Darlinghurst. There, senior government officials and leading men of Sydney were invited to build 'villa residences' – according to plans which the governor himself had to approve. But Eliza was thought to be too close to her Dumaresq brothers who had come to the colony with the Darlings and were visibly prospering with Darling's support. Darling himself had risen through the administrative ranks of the army because of his capacity for thoroughly and efficiently performing his duty in carrying out the instructions of his superiors. In New South Wales this meant showing how Bigge's recommendations could be applied to make the colony more efficient as a place for punishing the convicts (and more profitable for landowners who employed them). He succeeded as no previous governor in imposing a tough administration on New South Wales. With his fondness for order and formality, an ad hoc public service was remade. Before Darling, Brisbane's lack of interest had encouraged the autonomy of the increasing number of administrative officials appointed from London – the colonial secretary, treasurer, engineer, surveyor, superintendent of convicts, and chief commissioner of police. Darling paid close attention to their responsibilities and the performance of their departments. He also did his best to replace all convict clerks in the public service with free settlers at increased rates of pay. He appointed boards to inquire into persistent problems and make objective determinations, for example about the many applications for land grants. However, he also made enemies, most notably because of his attempts to control the fledgling local press. It had become critical of his administration and outspoken on behalf of the rights of the 'currency', eventually mounting a campaign to have him recalled. His successor, Richard Bourke, took a gentler approach. It had also become clear to the authorities in London that Darling's direction, effective though it may have been at maintaining order and discipline, was repressive rather than productive for the colony.

Inherent in New South Wales' convict origins was a contradiction in the role of law and order. From the beginning it seems that the

British government had assumed there would be a normal British system of criminal and civil courts in the colony,[22] but the absence of qualified lawyers at first meant that the only courts were staffed by officers of the NSW Corps and were in effect courts martial. But increasingly the cases coming before the courts involved civil disputes and were brought by free settlers. After the departure of the first military judge-advocate, David Collins, his successors turned out to be weak, incompetent, or under the influence of the dominant officer clique led by Macarthur and Johnston. Having alienated this officer clique Governor Bligh found himself reliant for legal advice on George Crossley, a London solicitor and attorney for twenty-five years who was transported to New South Wales in 1799 for perjury. Crossley paid dearly for assisting Bligh. As soon as Bligh was deposed, Crossley was charged, probably falsely, with acting improperly as a lawyer, and sentenced to seven years in the coalmines at Newcastle. With the arrival of Governor Macquarie he was reprieved and even though he continued as a clerk for a lawyer who was officially qualified to work in the courts of New South Wales, there was always a cloud over Crossley, his fate a warning to other ex-convict lawyers who might be tempted to practise in the colony.

The appointment of Jeffrey Hart Bent, brother of Judge-Advocate Ellis Bent, both of them fully qualified lawyers from London, as chief justice in 1814 promised a more independent judiciary. Jeffrey Bent's extreme interpretation of his responsibility, however, meant he refused to accept any former convicts as lawyers or magistrates. His court rarely sat for lack of qualified lawyers to appear before it. His successor Francis Forbes, appointed chief justice under the terms of the Act of 1823, was, however, able to negotiate a liberal, reforming and independent role for the law in New South Wales. He decided, against Governor Darling's interpretation, that criminals in New South Wales should not be treated more harshly than in England, and also that it was time for the promised jury system to be introduced. However, if there had been uneasiness about ex-convict lawyers returning to practice, this was nothing in comparison with determining what qualified a man to serve on a jury and as a magistrate.

The Anglican Church was from the beginning expected to serve as the moral and educational arm of the convict administration. Not surprisingly, the convicts proved discouraging material for salvation, and there was not much enthusiasm for ministry or mission work in New South Wales. There was, however, some hope that the children born in the colony might be saved, and a considerable effort by both the church, beginning with Rev. Richard Johnson, and the state, when Governor King imposed the first taxes in New South Wales to fund the female orphan school, was devoted to the education of girls and boys alike. In order to win recruits, the Colonial Clergy Act of 1819 allowed that men only partially trained could be ordained for service in New South Wales. The notion henceforth that all NSW Anglican clergy were second-rate was very hard to shake off.[23] However, clergymen like Samuel Marsden were not different from their counterparts in England, evangelical by conviction but in practice more interested in power, status, and material prosperity, access to which indicated that they had found favour with God. Through men like Marsden, those values of the eighteenth-century Anglican church which were passing in England became embedded in New South Wales. More use to New South Wales were the Methodist and Presbyterian clergy whose outlook was closer to the lower class, earnest, hard-working Anglican chaplains and with whom they had more in common than with their high-minded superiors. However, the problem was not so much the clergy themselves but the fact that a large proportion of New South Wales' convict population was neither Anglican nor non-conformist but Catholic.

Almost one in three of the convicts who arrived in New South Wales between 1788 and 1840 came from Ireland, with the numbers rising after 1816. In the closing years of the system, 1836–40, six out of every ten convicts were from Ireland. The proportion of Irish convicts and their religious needs only gradually dawned on the authorities. And though the number of women included among the Irish convicts was relatively high – in some years the Irish women convicts outnumbered the women coming from the rest of Britain – they still provided less than a quarter of the Irish male convicts with possible wives.[24] It should not have been surprising when Caroline Chisholm perceived this as a problem and set about recruiting young women who would come as assisted immigrants from Ireland with a view, eventually, to matrimony.[25] At the time her activities were viewed with alarm and suspicion and denounced by rival immigration promoters such as Presbyterian clergyman John Dunmore Lang as part of a plot to turn New South Wales into a Catholic colony.[26] From this distance Lang's fears seem paranoid and sectarian. At the time, however, the Irish Catholic population of New South Wales was clearly gaining both strength and confidence and this was to have a lasting significance for the history of New South Wales. By the late 1830s Catholics accounted for 28 per cent of the NSW population. And under the benign influence of the Anglo-Irish Governor Richard Bourke, they experienced a level of tolerance unknown hitherto. It was clear to Bourke that the existing church-sponsored arrangements for education in New South Wales were not adequate. The churches could not afford to provide their own schools on the scale required, and would not agree on how the state should be involved, so education suffered. Bourke's solution was to introduce the non-denominational Irish national system of state-run schools. Naturally his plan was resisted, especially by the Anglican bishop Broughton, a man whose conservatism 'ran counter to the mainstream of Australian history' on this and many other issues.[27]

Attitudes to Catholics in England were changing as the English Catholic Emancipation Act of 1829 (adopted in 1830 in New South Wales) opened all civil and political posts previously denied to Catholics. This led quickly in New South Wales to the appointment of John Herbert Plunkett, a graduate of Trinity College, Dublin, who had worked with Daniel O'Connell's Catholic Association for Catholic emancipation in Ireland, as solicitor-general in 1832.[28] Along with Roger Therry, a lawyer from Cork who arrived in 1829 to take up a legal post in New South Wales, Plunkett is credited with influencing Bourke's administration in the direction of religious tolerance and democracy. But here too, New South Wales reflected the reforming spirit at large in Britain with the election in 1830 of the first Whig government after half a century of Toryism. Among significant developments in New South Wales was the Church Act of 1836 by which the Anglican church was disestablished and the existing churches, Anglicans, Catholics, Presbyterians and later Methodists, placed on an equal footing in relation to government support and funding. Plunkett was later active in the creation of municipal government in Sydney and Melbourne and the extension of legal and civil rights to emancipists, He also worked amicably with the liberal Scots colonial secretary, Edward Deas Thomson and the no-nonsense Governor Gipps in drafting the new constitution of 1843. Plunkett's sense of justice coinciding neatly with that of Gipps had ensured the eventual conviction of the perpetrators of the Myall Creek massacre in 1838.

Until 1820 when the first Catholic priests were officially allowed, there can be no doubt that Catholics among the NSW population were badly served in the observance of their religion. Father John Joseph Therry who ministered to them from 1820, on and off, until his death in 1864 was a most unusual man. Loved and respected by Catholic and protestant alike for his selfless humanity, passionate, idiosyncratic especially when it came to mundane things like money, he helped to create a climate of religious tolerance in which the position of the Catholic church improved in New South Wales. But thereafter its fortunes fluctuated according to the political and pastoral skills of its leaders. Increasing prosperity and independence among the Irish settlers and their offspring challenged unquestioning obedience to the church. It was by no means the case that the interests of the NSW Irish population and those of the Catholic church always coincided. James Waldersee has argued that the Irish convicts and settlers were not as poverty stricken and ignorant as they were portrayed, especially in Ireland, by the likes of Bishop Ullathorne, for political or fund-raising purposes.[29] Nor were the Irish convicts illiterate as was usually assumed, though it is probable that many spoke Gaelic rather than English. Indeed from 1839 when W. A. Duncan became founding editor of the *Australasian Chronicle*, the Irish community was generally able to support some kind of newspaper, though the *Chronicle* itself did not last long. Duncan was in fact too sophisticated for 'the ex-convict parvenu Irish who dominated the Sydney laity'.[30]

Irish rebels transported for their involvement in the Wicklow rising of 1798 settled at Camden, Appin and Campbelltown. According to Patrick O'Farrell, they were in reality 'conservative middle-class farmers with a keen eye . . . for good land, high farm prices and the extraordinary opportunities offered by free land grants'.[31] They quickly appreciated the advantages of being in New South Wales and were able to prosper. With the help of compatriot surveyor James Meehan, other Irish families followed their example, so that the concentration of Irish settlers to the south-west of Sydney towards Yass became quite marked.[32] By contrast, though a good proportion of the population of Maitland was Catholic, there was a relatively thin distribution of Catholics north of the Hunter. Towards Scone, Tamworth and into New England, Scots settlers were very much in evidence.

Waldersee analysed the continuing significance of the Catholics of the south-west down through the censuses of 1891 to 1961. In 1891 south-west counties showed 40 per cent Catholics while those north of the Hunter had less than 20 per cent. 'Boorowa (53%) was definitely a more Catholic town than Taree (9%).' 'Even as late as 1961, there was still a remarkable contrast between the comparably sized municipalities of Gloucester (9.6%) and Boorowa (47.3%).' In general the southern tablelands still had a 36.4 per cent Catholic population in contrast to only 20 per cent in the Hunter and Manning.[33]

The census of 1841 showed that of a total population of 130,856 (87,298 male, 43,558 female), 29,449 (14,819 male, 14,630 female) were currency, i.e. born in the colony. By the 1830s those born in the early years had become middle-aged and were beginning to assert themselves in colonial affairs. The currency are usually lumped with convicts and ex-convicts because most of them were children of former convicts. However, contemporary comment was almost always surprised by their vigour and wholesome approach to life. The currencies saw themselves as a group apart too, different because they were born in the colony. Unlike all immigrants, both they and the Aborigines were of this place. (Though there is no evidence that they identified with the Aborigines.) They knew their numbers would grow just as the numbers of convicts and former convicts must surely fade away.[34]

It had become the custom to observe Anniversary Day on 26 January every year with a flag-raising ceremony, a salute, a function perhaps at Government House or a regatta on the harbour. Anniversary Day in 1838 marked fifty years of European settlement in New South Wales. It was a very warm day, tempered on the water by a brisk easterly. A large crowd taking advantage of the public holiday gathered on the foreshores to watch the procession of decorated sailing craft. A local poet produced 'An Address' for the occasion in which 'The youthful patriot' hopes to behold 'the isle that gave him birth/Enrolled among the empires of the earth'.[35] The real hope lay in the immediate future, however, with the scaling back of the assignment system and the recommendation of the Molesworth Committee that transportation to New South Wales should end by 1840.

In its origins as a convict settlement, the experience of New South Wales was unique, shared only in part by Van Diemen's Land. In years to come, other settlements elsewhere in Australia would try to distance themselves from these origins, and New South Wales would itself become deeply ambivalent. The society emerging from this unpromising beginning was callous, hypocritical, legalistic, but good at making the most of anything, whether native grasslands or human weakness. It was self-reliant, enterprising, with a kind of cocky confidence partly Irish, partly native-born, masculine and energetic. Though a product of eighteenth-century British attitudes to property, with convicts and their guards as sturdy peasants and yeoman farmers, yet the bands of Aboriginal raiders descending on remote farmsteads and melting away into the bush might have been Picts or Welsh tribesmen from the mythic past. A land thought suitable as an open prison because it was so empty and unwanted proved rich in ways no one had imagined. By 1840 it could no longer be considered a place of exile or punishment. Its wealth and the variety of its natural resources were only beginning to be uncovered and exploited.

3

1841–1864, horizons and boundaries

The end of transportation to New South Wales brought immense and dramatic changes. Two new colonies, Victoria and Queensland, were carved out in 1851 and 1859. Wool was almost supplanted by gold in the economy. A partially elected Legislative Council, instituted in 1843, was replaced in 1856 by a parliament of two houses, the upper nominated, the lower fully elected on a broad franchise, further widened within a few years to include most adult males. Land policy ceased to be controlled from Britain through the governor and became a powerful political and economic tool, both shaping the nature of government and underwriting development in New South Wales.

No more convicts were sent to New South Wales after 1 August 1840. The last ship, the *Eden*, with 270 males, arrived in Sydney on 18 November. As we have seen, some aspects of the convict system had already become almost impossible to manage as the free enterprise economy grew and the numbers of free settlers increased. It took a long time, however, for the machinery of the convict system to be dismantled, and longer still for the 'convict stain' to fade from New South Wales.

Those convicts on the *Eden* had at least seven years to serve. In a total population of 114,386 in 1839, 38,035 were convicts of whom about 25,000 were assigned to private employers.[1] A decision to phase out assignment had been taken in 1838, so several thousand ex-convicts each year joined the ranks of the wage-earners as sentences were completed. By 1842 the last penal station on the mainland, that at Moreton Bay, was closed, access to its hinterland became possible and squatters quickly sought it out, taking their sheep as far north as the valleys of the Mary, Burnett and Dawson rivers.

The transition from a convict workforce largely controlled and paid for by the British government to one comprised almost entirely of free and independent labourers was not easily achieved. A small group of influential employers had profited hugely from the labour of subsidised and disciplined convicts. In an attempt to maintain control, a series of masters and servants acts were imposed on free labourers in the 1840s as if they were convicts, but they were resented and evaded. Shearers were recruited in China and Ben Boyd brought labourers from the Pacific Islands,[2] but attempts to re-introduce convicts with tickets-of-leave or conditional pardons as 'exiles' from Britain were vigorously resisted, especially by local workmen who feared the loss of their jobs or their high rates of pay. Eventually a large crowd of Sydney residents gathered at Circular Quay in 1849 to prevent a consignment of 236 'exiles' landing from the *Hashemy*. After that demonstration, the reality was accepted. Convict labour was finished.

Ex-convicts, free immigrants, and the increasing number of locally born children, some of them already parents and grandparents, shared similar ideas about the future of New South Wales. They all saw it as a place of opportunity where they could prosper and improve life for themselves and their families. The official image of post-convict New South Wales laid emphasis on opportunities for investment, especially in sheep and wool, though the scope for very simple enterprises requiring no capital, little skill, but plenty of initiative and hard work, was great. Work of all kinds was widely available (though subject to seasonal fluctuation), and skills were very much in demand. Skilled workers like typographers, cabinet-makers and coach-makers were able to enhance their value by organising themselves. As early as 1841 the term 'scab', often thought of as quintessentially Australian, but in fact imported from the United States in the early nineteenth century, was being used to describe Sydney bootmakers who accepted very low rates of pay.[3] (Perhaps an outbreak of scab among sheep at the time gave the term special resonance.)

Manufacturing on a small scale had been carried on of necessity since the early days. The supply of raw materials, timber, bricks, stone, thatch, slate and the construction of public buildings and houses became major industries. Ironworks, tanneries, and rope works using locally grown and imported New Zealand flax and Indian hemp were established. Boat-building for the coastal trade developed at Cockle Bay on the harbour, on the Hawkesbury, and by the 1830s also on Brisbane Water.[4] Breweries and illegal distilleries, flour mills and salt works processed raw materials, as did early textile mills producing coarse woollen cloth, blankets, linen and canvas. Windmills to generate power for grinding wheat to flour appeared on the heights of Millers Point and Darlinghurst. There was a water-mill in Barcom Glen near Rushcutters Bay, though as soon as suitable machinery could be imported and reliable labour hired to operate it, steam power was preferred to both wind and water. There was a continuing demand for locally made soap, candles and leather goods, and for hats, caps, and clothing. Emancipist entrepreneur Simeon Lord had established a woollen mill in 1816 near where Shea's Creek ran into Botany Bay. He was at various times also engaged in glass and paper manufacture.[5] Furniture makers taking advantage of the red cedar and other fine timbers being cut from the coastal river valleys found a steady market for their quality products, also regular work as upholsterers and undertakers.[6]

As the landscapes of artists like Conrad Martens and George Edwards Peacock show, Sydney was beginning to grow into its natural beauty, and to develop something of the style which has characterised it ever since. According to G. B. Earp's handbook for immigrants published in 1852:

The heights of Woollomolloo [sic], rising above the city, are crowned with the truly elegant villas of the elite of Sydney society – composed of men who have, for the most part, become so by their own efforts, aided, it is true, by the luck of circumstances, which, however, often casts them down, even from the Woollomolloo [sic] heights, only to find their way back in the course of a few years, for there is nothing on earth so elastic as a Sydney merchant. You may cast him down, but it is impossible to keep him down. He will work day and night to gratify his love of display; and in this he rarely fails, however thwarted for a time. From this passion spring the elegant suburban edifices which crown picturesque Sydney, as seen from the harbour.[7]

Down by the water at Circular Quay and the Rocks, the harbour was crowded with ships' masts, merchants and chandlers, oil and paint and hardware shops, accommodation houses and taverns for the crews, and warehouses and bond-stores for the increasing variety of imports which the colony could now afford.[8] Further up George Street were shops selling everything from tea to musical instruments, books and stationery, jewellery, silks, laces, fine clothing and riding boots. Visitors were usually impressed by the range and quality of goods available and the evidence of such civilised life (though they almost always found the roadways bad and the footpaths execrable). Nothing could be further from the idea of a convict settlement or even an English provincial town than the sight of the Sydney market.[9] Here the extent and variety of fruits and vegetables available and the quality and cheapness of meat and fish caused astonishment. In the benign climate of New South Wales it was possible to grow peaches and pineapples, melons and lemons, grapes, bananas, nectarines, plums, all in abundance, all within reach of the pockets even of poor people. The orange groves of the north shore had raised hopes that here was a possible export industry. Local vineyards were already producing wine of drinkable quality. Colonial Secretary Deas Thomson was certainly not the only immigrant who came reluctantly to what he hoped was a lucrative short-term job in New South Wales and was won by the climate and the excitement of the new society.[10]

The defects of Sydney's climate were seasonal. When it was hot and dry, dust mingled with dried manure from the hundreds of horses which pulled carriages and wagons rose in filthy clouds from the streets. When it rained, all turned to mud. The Tank Stream had become a virtual underground sewer, and all drainage was directly into the harbour creating a run-off problem always evident after rain. In 1850, although good water was available through a system of underground pipes and reservoirs near the Lachlan Swamps, less than 12 per cent of houses had water laid on. The rest relied on buckets filled at standpipes on street corners or purchased from water carts at a halfpenny a time. This meant that water closets were confined to a small proportion of houses (and as there was no treatment for sewerage, it too flowed into the harbour). Most houses relied on an outdoor privy, often shared with others, and emptied only when necessary. The smell and the flies in summer can scarcely be imagined now.

In other respects, Sydney was proud of its modernity. In 1841 gas lighting was introduced to the streets. Since November 1838 it had been possible to buy stamped envelopes at 1 shilling and threepence per dozen for posting letters within the town itself. This innovation by the NSW postmaster-general James Raymond gave New South Wales the first pre-paid stamped letters in the world and predated the famous British penny post by two years.[11] By 1849 letters could be posted anywhere in New South Wales for 2d, and the next year the first adhesive postage stamps were introduced.

Communication between Sydney and the rest of New South Wales, however, was still difficult. Coastal shipping was vital and after the introduction of steam in 1852 became much more reliable. Steamers ran regularly to the Hunter with Morpeth as terminus, also north to Port Macquarie and south to the Shoalhaven and Eden (Boydtown) and thence to Hobart. When in 1856 a young gold assayer at the Sydney Mint, the future economist W. S. Jevons, took advantage of a long weekend to take a trip to Morpeth and Maitland, he had a choice of two rival steamer companies, both leaving Sydney at 11 pm and racing to arrive at Morpeth about 9 am the next morning. It cost him 15s in fares plus meals one way with the older Australasian Steam Navigation Co., and 12s 6d (meals included) coming back with the Hunter River New Steam Navigation Co. Both fares, he thought, were insufficient to be profitable while the parallel timetables were hardly convenient for the traveller.[12] (Maitland he found rather dull, though 'there was much letting off of fireworks by the juveniles' and a great deal of drinking to celebrate the holidays for the Queen's birthday and the opening of the first parliament.)

Three main roads had been planned to reach the interior of New South Wales. The Great North Road, constructed at great expense by convict labour, ran from Sydney to the Hawkesbury where there was a ferry (still is), then through the valley of the Wollombi to Maitland. It proved difficult and expensive to maintain and was no competition for the sea route. By 1850 maintenance had lapsed and it was barely passable. The road west from Sydney to Parramatta was opened in 1811 as the first of many future toll roads. (By 1865 there were thirty-four returning an income of £22,000 annually.) From Parramatta and Penrith the west road climbed 4,000 feet (about 1220 m) to Mt York in the Blue Mountains and thence to Bathurst and the Wellington Valley. This was the road traversed by the gold seekers of 1851, much of it still little more than a rough track. The alternative route, thought to follow an ancient Aboriginal pathway down the mountains via Mt Tomah and Richmond, and pioneered by Archibald Bell in 1823 (hence its name, Bell's Line of Road) was even rougher.

To the south, James Meehan had surveyed a road through Liverpool, Campbelltown and Berrima to Goulburn and Yass attracting the settlement of his Irish compatriots. There were known crossings at the Murrumbidgee and Hume (Murray) rivers but further south, nothing but a wagon track. Surveyor Major Mitchell had passed that way in 1836 and, to his amazement, found settlers already established on the northern shore of Bass Strait at Portland. The drive to claim all that land with stock required great organisation and not a little courage. In January 1838, John Stuart Hepburn had set off with his wife Elizabeth (aged 35 and pregnant), their 7-year-old daughter and baby son to travel with ten convicts, some cattle, and about 1,700 sheep from Braidwood via Goulburn and Yass to Gundagai, and thence across the Murray to take up land at Smeaton Hill, north-east of Creswick. Elizabeth and her children rode in a covered horse-drawn cart. They had only three other horses with them, so the men must have walked most of the way. It was three months before they arrived at Smeaton Hill, fending off attacks from hostile Aborigines all the way. Their slab huts were scarcely built when the baby arrived on 22 July.[13] The experiences of the Hepburns were replicated many times as the squatters spilled out during the 1840s.

In the interior, roads petered out into mere tracks through the bush linking fords where creeks and rivers could be crossed. They were kept open mainly by the passage of horsemen, stock, and carriages. Wool was brought immense distances along the tracks made by bullock drays to the coast for shipment, or after the inland rivers had been cleared of snags, by barge and paddle steamer. One of the great attractions of wool was that it was relatively tough and light. It did not deteriorate if delayed for months at a time by floods or otherwise impassable roads. And it could wait indefinitely in a wool store near the quay for shipment to London.

For everyone, men, women and children, horses remained the most widely used form of transport. Sensing the possibilities, however, for his light flexible horse-drawn coaches, James Rutherford brought Cobb and Co. to New South Wales from Victoria in 1862. Coach routes flourished, especially west of the ranges where they had most of the mail delivery contracts. Bathurst became Cobb and Co.'s head office in 1865. Workshops building and maintaining coaches became important sources of employment in Bathurst, Goulburn and Hay, while inns at staging posts strung along the coaching routes served as booking offices, and provided refreshment, accommodation, and fresh teams of horses. It is hard to imagine those intrepid journeys, especially by night with only coach lamps or the moon to guide driver and horses along rough tracks. Though coaches were subject to frequent delays when equipment failed or heavy rain turned tracks into bogs and river crossings into torrents, their cheapness and flexibility kept them in business into the twentieth century.[14]

In the midst of the railway-building mania in England in the 1840s it was decided that New South Wales too needed railways, three lines, like the roads, one to the north, one to the west, and another to the south. But it was not easy to raise the necessary capital or find suitably skilled workers or managers with adequate engineering experience. In 1848, however, a prospectus was issued and two years later, the first sod turned, by Governor FitzRoy's daughter-in-law, Mrs Keith Stewart. The directors of the Sydney Railway Company, quite a few of whom happened also to be members of the Legislative Council, were able to secure government assistance in the form of land grants and a government guarantee of a 5 per cent return on all shares purchased in the company. This was expected to cost no more than the £6,000 p.a. already committed to subsidise the mail service from Sydney to Europe (now carried by steamer). But it was not enough. Rising prices and labour shortages, aggravated by the discovery of gold, sent costs spiralling. Five hundred 'navvies' were recruited in England in 1853 to work on the railway in New South Wales, their passages paid by the government. Further government assistance was necessary before an order could be placed in

England for 3,776 tons of iron rails, four locomotives, eight first-, twelve second-, and twelve third-class passenger carriages, and sixty assorted goods wagons and vans.

'New South Wales . . . has her own railroad' the *Sydney Morning Herald* proclaimed on 20 August 1855, 'she has taken the main step to greatness'. In fact the line ran only from Sydney to Parramatta and was slowly extended to Richmond, Penrith and Picton. By the time it commenced operation, the government had acquired full ownership and responsibility for its management. Another line from Newcastle to Singleton enabled the Brown brothers, James and Alexander, to begin coal exports from their Minmi mine through Hexham. Yet by 1865 only 143 miles (230 km) of track had been built altogether.[15] Government involvement was inevitable, if only because of its power over the disposition of crown land, but the shortage of local capital as well as interlocking relationships in the political, entrepreneurial and managerial elites brought the government in at every level, thus committing New South Wales to one of its largest and longest-lived enterprises.

Behind all this expansion, the roads, coach routes and the move into railways, lay the squatting movement and the rising value of sheep and wool to New South Wales. From 50,000 in 1813, the number of sheep had risen to 2.75 million in 1838. By 1851, before the loss to New South Wales of the land south of the Murray, there were 7 million. Many of these sheep were of poor quality and the wool they produced coarse with short fibres.

There was no security in an industry that relied upon the temporary occupation of large tracts of grasslands, and no incentive for the investment of capital in breeding better stock or permanent improvements. The sheep were still yarded or shepherded to protect them from Aboriginal or dingo attack. They were washed prior to shearing, usually by driving them through a wash pool created in a creek, then shorn by hand. In the more closely settled districts, washing and shearing facilities were built and shared by neighbours, but squatting beyond the settled districts meant makeshift and temporary shearing arrangements, which produced wool of inferior appearance. Dry years in the early 1840s demonstrated the need for more extensive investment in dams or other permanent watering facilities. So there was pressure from the powerful squatting lobby in New

South Wales as well as their influential friends in London for greater security of tenure, also for compensation for improvements when leases changed hands. A government suggestion that the squatters might pay more for their occupation licences in return for greater security was angrily rejected. The profitability of the wool industry depended on the fact that access to land and grass cost practically nothing. The government was actually subsidising the cost of wool production. In 1847 Governor Sir George Gipps, despairing of how he was to finance immigration (to maintain labour supplies), and also to pay for the police and prisons which the British government thought now could be supported from colonial revenues, set out a scheme whereby squatting licences were replaced by slightly more expensive crown leases for seven years in the intermediate districts and twenty-one years in more remote areas. As well, it became possible to purchase homestead blocks and to apply for compensation for buildings and other improvements when leasehold land was surrendered. Along with the ability to borrow on the security of stock or a wool clip, these measures transformed squatting in New South Wales to a pastoral industry which continued to grow in value, power and sophistication into the twentieth century.

The package of security measures Gipps designed for the pastoral industry included a border police force to protect settlers and Aborigines from each other. In 1839 Gipps had proclaimed the Aborigines 'human beings partaking of our common nature'. As such they had 'an equal right with the people of European origin to the protection and assistance of the Law of England'.[16] Gipps failed, however, to convince the Council to pass a law that would allow Aborigines to give evidence in court. (A further attempt in 1849 failed also, and it was not until 1876 that Aboriginal evidence given under affirmation was accepted in New South Wales.)

However, Gipps also felt that the annual May Day blanket distribution to Aborigines, begun by Governor Bourke, was demeaning, and gave instructions that henceforth blankets should only be distributed as a reward for services rendered or work well done. There were already laws requiring that Aborigines in the towns should be clothed, and by the 1840s, part of the growing mood of respectability was to complain of the unsightly appearance of ill-clad or naked Aborigines on the streets of Sydney and the larger towns. Government-issue blankets provided a decent covering and were at least a substitute for the possum skin cloaks that were no longer so easy to get. But the Aborigines themselves had come to see the blankets, not simply as a decent cover and a protection against cold, but as a form of recompense for the loss of their land, a kind of official payment in recognition of their prior occupation. Though abandoned by Gipps the blanket distribution was later resumed. During the 1850s and 1860s the manufacture of blankets became a minor industry in New South Wales. The official returns showed that in 1861, for example, 4,720 blankets were distributed at the cost of £1664 18s 0d and of these, 1,624 were manufactured in the colony at 7s each.[17]

With the end of transportation there was no longer any reason for Britain to maintain many of the services it had supplied to the colony. There were, however, significant institutions, set up or subsidised to service the convict system, from which all citizens had benefited. The churches, for example, by 1840 were all receiving some government assistance for the work they did among the convicts. Education was provided by the state through grants to the churches to enable the children of convict parents to grow up into a better world. The state subsidised the hospital, also asylums to care for aged and insane former convicts who had no families to whom they could turn for care. The obvious benefits these institutions provided to the people of New South Wales, and the expectation that they would continue, was rather different from the self-help ethos underpinning most economic and political development in England at this time. It was not that there was no self-help in New South Wales. Indeed, the establishment of a savings bank, an insurance society (the AMP), a benevolent society, and temperance organisations showed a strong enthusiasm for self-help. But in New South Wales it was not unusual for these organisations to approach the government for assistance or support, often in the form of some land on which to build. Thus a belief in the desirability of government provision of certain services and subsidy to others survived in New South Wales. As the accountant of the Sydney Savings Bank put it in 1841, even banks in New South Wales needed more official support than their British counterparts because 'In a new country like this, society is very different, no division of it is fixed; a great proportion of the population are recent arrivals, and the only permanent body is the Government.'[18]

One of the significant institutions carried over from the convict days was the colony's police force. Gradually the police had taken over from the military the main responsibility for keeping order in the penal settlement and maintained a quasi-military function beyond the settled districts. They were recruited mainly from among the ex-convicts and former soldiers, many of them from Irish backgrounds and poorly paid. Both officers and men were notorious as heavy drinkers. Attempts to recruit for the police force in England in the 1850s produced a better class of policeman but the new recruits were handicapped in comparison with the rest of the force by their lack of local knowledge.[19] Unruly behaviour in frontier and sparsely settled districts among convicts, ex-convicts and the Aborigines was attributed often to general lack of respect for the police, though in fact they had greater powers than Robert Peel's newly instituted police force in England. The New South Wales police were expected to compensate for their low pay by earning rewards for capturing wanted criminals and informing on crimes for which they received a portion of the fine, leading naturally to corruption, or at best, suspicion of police motives in making arrests. Under the Bushranging Act of 1834, in force until 1853, any person suspected of being a runaway convict could be arrested and detained until he proved who he was. Travellers found it necessary to carry identification. Even so they were subject to accidental or mischievous arrest. The police were often criticised for being too zealous in their surveillance of free citizens while paying too little attention to the real causes of public disorder. Gipps' Border Police who were funded largely by a levy on livestock spent a disproportionate amount of their time counting stock and collecting the levy. By their harassment of small settlers, they helped create the bushrangers they then pursued. For example, Wheogo stockman Ben Hall, born 1837, the son of two ex-convicts, embittered by the desertion of his wife with their infant son and the loss of his home and stock while he was in custody on false charges, taunted the police for several years with his superior horses and bush lore while he masterminded hold-ups in central western New South Wales. He was shot dead in 1865 in an ambush on the Lachlan plain.

In Sydney and the other closely settled areas, the police were increasingly called upon to maintain law and order at rowdy political demonstrations like the anti-transportation meetings still the only way for the people to express their views before they had elected representatives. New South Wales' first election was in 1842, to elect aldermen for the newly created municipality of Sydney. Dominated by tradesmen, merchants and professional men from the 'Australian' party, i.e. those born in New South Wales, it was relatively peaceful. Though elections the next year of twenty-four representatives for the new Legislative Council 'went off very well' according to Governor Gipps, there were riots in both Sydney and Melbourne with considerable damage to property and two men were killed. The demonstrators, known as 'the cabbage-tree hat mob' because they wore hats locally woven from the leaves of the cabbage-tree palm as protection against the sun in preference to less useful formal headgear, were mainly currency and working class. Among those arrested were youths under 15.

The boldness, early maturity and readiness of the currency lads to assert their rights in relation to land grants has already been noted. 'The Australian boy is a slim, dark-eyed, olive-complexioned young rascal, fond of Cavendish [i.e. tobacco], cricket and chuckpenny, and systematically insolent to all servant girls, policemen, and new chums', wrote visiting English journalist, Frank Fowler.[20] The mobs demonstrating earlier against the re-introduction of transportation and later the notorious riots where Chinese diggers at Lambing Flat were scalped were largely currency. Later in the nineteenth century Sydney became notorious for groups of youths lounging on street corners who formed themselves into 'pushes' according to their locality and engaged in 'stoushes' with each other. It is tempting to see some continuity from the well-nourished and possibly underemployed cabbage-tree hat mobs of the 1840s to the gold fields rioters of the 1860s and the pushes of the 1890s, even to the qualities most admired in the Anzacs and the noisy crowds on the Hill at cricket and football matches through most of the twentieth century. Organised sport and more serious education in part solved the problem of young men with too much energy and too little to do. It also helped to reduce the need for a large police force.

A contemporary observer thought that the convict system had laid the foundation for an enterprising society. Business in New South Wales, according to G. Butler Earp, was 'more enterprising than scrupulous'.[21] He also observed sardonically that litigation was more fashionable among all classes than honesty, a reminder perhaps of the way in which the convicts had become adept in their use of the courts to secure their rights or to seek restitution for injustices, real or imagined. 'Citizens brought personal and minor disputes before the courts for adjudication.'[22] Francis Low's *City of Sydney Directory* published for 1844–45 included a list of fees to be charged in the courts, and included copies of the forms and rules to be used.[23] What had been a shortage of qualified lawyers during the days of Bent and Forbes was by 1850 an oversupply. As well, W. & F. Ford's 1851 *Sydney Commercial Directory* listed 48 honorary magistrates or justices of the peace for Sydney and over 700 for the country districts.[24]

The law had been one area where Irish immigrants with professional skills could do well in New South Wales. There seemed to be little sectarianism. Solicitors' offices served as a route to education and an avenue for advancement for able young men, especially those born in the colony of convict or former convict parents who found entry to other well-paid or respectable jobs denied them. Future Premier and Chief Justice James Martin, who arrived in New South Wales from Cork with his parents in 1821 as a baby but always identified himself as currency, was typical. Having joined the law firm of native-born 'radical reformer' George Robert 'Bob' Nichols, he supported Nichols' political campaigns on behalf of the native-born in the thousands of words he contributed to the radical press, married the daughter of a successful emancipist, and while his parents retained their Irish Catholicism, Martin gradually let his fade away.[25]

The lawyers provided a nucleus for an intelligentsia. A key figure, Scots Presbyterian Nicol Drysdale Stenhouse, arrived in 1839 and was admitted as a solicitor the next year. An enthusiastic book collector, he made the library in his home, Waterview House, Balmain, available to friends and colleagues like J. L. Michael and W. B. Dalley, and his articled clerk, Daniel Deniehy.[26] He also supported the publication of aspiring local poets like Charles Harpur,

Henry Kendall, and Henry Halloran, James Martin and Henry Parkes.

By 1850 Sydney had a subscription library, a museum, a botanical and horticultural society, all established with government assistance, usually in the form of a land grant, and sustained by the respectable elite. The centre of self-improvement, however, was the Mechanics' School of Arts founded in 1833 also with government assistance. With its library of several thousand volumes it provided a public meeting place for readers and writers, and it subscribed to a large selection of contemporary newspapers and periodicals from England and Europe. Its debating society was a nursery for aspiring politicians like the 15-year-old George Reid who became a member in about 1860. Public lectures were held there and well after the establishment of the university it continued as a cultural and intellectual centre.[27] Stenhouse served on its committee till his death in 1873. He also befriended John Woolley and Charles Badham who were among the first professors appointed to the new University of Sydney and played a part in the establishment of the Free Public Library in 1869. After his death, Stenhouse's library was purchased by wealthy merchant and banker, Thomas Walker of Yaralla, Concord (who disapproved of elaborate and showy bank premises as unnecessary and intimidating to poor people), and presented to the university as a start to its collection.

Stenhouse had a passion for books and literature both of which he thought should be easily available to all. But a squatter's wife observed in 1860,

with a few exceptions, the public of Sydney is not a reading public. It is far too practical to waste much time on general literature. Those whose time is not wholly taken up by money-making pursuits, give all their leisure to politics . . .[28]

The idea of a university was both ambitious and utilitarian. In 1849 it seemed that to establish a university in Sydney would symbolise the achievement and the aspiration of the colony yet it was also needed for the practical purpose of training future professionals and public officials. Wealthy citizens might send their sons 'home' to educate them at one of the old prestigious universities of Britain. But training for lawyers, doctors, engineers took place on the job in what was really an apprenticeship. It was expensive and slow, so there was a move towards general training for these professions. Though the government sponsored and supported university offered a basic secular education with guaranteed professional skills, what was to be done about the training of clergy? All churches had problems with the quality of the clergy they were able to recruit for work in New South Wales, and needed to train men locally. In order to win church support for the secular university, denominational residential colleges were permitted to offer specialised theological training while also providing a suitable moral environment for residential students.

As early as 1840 the separation of both the Port Phillip and Moreton Bay districts from New South Wales had been suggested in England and rejected at public meetings in Sydney. While various groups manoeuvred for power in the partially elected Legislative Council of 1843, the separation movement gained force. After the first elections for that Council, one of the six members representing Port Phillip, Rev. Dr John Dunmore Lang, pointed out that the income generated by Port Phillip greatly exceeded government expenditure there.[29] Next year he moved for its separation. The statistics certainly showed a growing population, an even more impressive set of stock numbers, and substantial revenues. Furthermore, the residents of Port Phillip had become very uneasy about the agitation of the Moreton Bay squatters for some kind of renewed transportation. They felt themselves to be seriously disadvantaged by their distance from Sydney. It was difficult to find men willing to accept nomination to the Council from Port Phillip. To be present at a sitting required a long, difficult sea voyage. Lang had become one of the Port Phillip members simply because, though a permanent resident of Sydney, he offered to represent them. In 1848, to highlight their difficulties, the southern districts nominated and elected Earl Grey, Secretary of State for Colonies in London, as their representative in Sydney. Grey saw the point and acted, though not so efficiently as to inform the residents of Port Phillip who first read 'The news of the impending creation of the colony of Victoria . . . in a copy of a London newspaper, on Monday 11 November 1850.'[30] Asked to recommend a suitable boundary, Surveyor General Thomas Mitchell suggested the Murrumbidgee River as he thought the course of the Murray too ill-defined. Needless to say his advice was rejected in Sydney.

The creation of Victoria meant that there were now five separate colonies in Australia. For a brief period (1851–61), the governor of New South Wales was designated governor-general with the idea that he should give leadership in solving intercolonial differences.[31] However, with the implementation of new constitutions in 1856, ideas of co-operation were replaced by competition, except when intercolonial matters, usually customs, communications or immigration, became troublesome.

The discovery of gold in 1851 first in New South Wales, then Victoria, confirmed the competitive relationship between the old colony and the new. Gold briefly challenged the dominance of sheep and wool in New South Wales and heightened the question of immigration.

On 12 February 1851, Edward Hammond Hargraves and the 18-year-old son of his landlady at the Guyong Inn washed some specks of gold from a few pans of earth scratched from Lewis Ponds Creek, a tributary of the Turon River near Bathurst. The existence of gold had been known since at least 1823 when surveyor McBrien noted some in his field book. It was of no use to the Aborigines, so it weathered from the ancient rocks and lay in the ground. Convicts and shepherds had occasionally quietly sold small quantities they had collected to Sydney jewellers, though legally all gold in the ground belonged to the crown.

While New South Wales remained a convict colony there were good reasons for discouraging gold discoveries. As the effort to control squatting and sporadic outbreaks of bushranging had shown, law and order were hard to maintain, especially beyond the settled districts. Nor was there much need of the economic stimulus which gold might bring. But in 1848 news of gold discoveries in California reached Sydney and about 6,000 would-be gold seekers embarked for San Francisco.[32] Among them were Hargraves and James Squire Farnell, 22-year-old grandson of James Squire, a first fleet convict who had prospered as a brewer and landowner in New South Wales. In 1877, Farnell would become the first

3.1 Facsimile of a page of Surveyor McBrien's field book, recording the discovery of gold in 1823. (E.F. Pittman, *Mineral Resources of New South Wales*, Government Printer, Sydney, 1901, facing p. 1) convict-descended premier of New South Wales. Though Hargraves found little gold on the Sacramento, when he returned to Sydney in 1851 he claimed that the gold-bearing country of California reminded him of parts of New South Wales to the west of Bathurst. Between February and May 1851 he tried to get enough people panning for gold to locate gold fields for him. In Bathurst he lectured on gold and wrote about it in the local papers. Within a few weeks he had a small crowd, including Aboriginal workers from nearby stations and the Apsley Aboriginal Mission, actively searching.

By 15 May Hargraves was ready to announce the discovery of 'Ophir', the biblical city of gold, on Summer Hill Creek, another tributary of the Turon, and claim a reward. At first he was suspected of faking his rush with Californian gold, and the recently appointed government geologist, Samuel Stutchbury, was sent to make an official assessment. Stutchbury reported from Ophir (in pencil, since there was no ink available) that about 400 people were digging along a mile of the creek and that they were finding plenty of gold using only tin dishes to wash it out. He recommended immediate action to ensure order. There were already too many people involved for the government to stop them, so a licensing system, not unlike the system already used to license squatters to occupy crown lands, was devised to regularise what was technically the theft of gold belonging to the crown. With 'masterly commonsense' Colonial Secretary Deas Thomson instructed John Richard Hardy, police magistrate at Parramatta, to take command at the diggings as gold commissioner. Hardy moved quickly to mark out claims, issue licences to dig and settle disputes.

Hardy was a good appointment. He had played cricket for Cambridge and is said to have introduced round-arm bowling to New South Wales. He had taken up land near Yass, but needed an income, so had joined the public service. As gold commissioner at Ophir he proved 'a sympathetic and yet efficient administrator'[33] marking out claims so that access to the creek and the rougher hillsides, as well as the water available for sluicing, were distributed equitably. He thought the licence fee, set at 30s per month, neither too high nor too low. The land was capable of returning enough gold to justify it, though the digging was hard for any but men who were fit and accustomed to heavy labour. Hardy permitted diggers to try their

3.2 'Men, women and children on their way to the gold diggings from Sydney, 1851.' (*The Roadmakers: A History of Main Roads in New South Wales*, Department of Main Roads New South Wales, Sydney, 1976, p. 38)

luck for a few days to earn their first licence fee, a practice that was later disallowed, with consequent disturbances and rioting on other fields. The Turon, he was able to report in June 1851, was as orderly as 'the quietest English town'.[34]

Orderly management of the early gold rushes in New South Wales was assisted by the fact that itinerant Anglican clergyman and enthusiastic amateur geologist William Branthwaite Clarke had already mapped likely gold-bearing areas. Newly arrived diggers were quietly directed to suitable unallocated claims. Despite fears that crime would increase, that there would be famine because the harvest was neglected, or that there would be a terrible outbreak of gambling with too many of the lower orders earning too much money too quickly, none of these things happened. The Turon was a 'poor man's diggings' though a boon to the business people of Bathurst and those engaged in supplying lodging, equipment and transport on the road from Sydney, and in Sydney itself. Most of the diggers came from within the colony, though there were some from ships anchored at Sydney and some overlanders from Victoria. When rain flooded the valley many of the diggers returned home to resume their ordinary occupations. Some moved to a new field on the Araluen River near Braidwood. By the time the news of gold was heard abroad, Victoria's more exciting rushes had begun and 'Ophir' returned to legend. More testing times were to come in 1860 with miners struggling in inhospitable snowbound conditions at Kiandra. In 1861 at

Lambing Flat (Young) the presence of large numbers of Chinese diggers combined with idleness in the mines caused by water shortages led to rioting. Troops were needed to restore order.

The reform of the British parliament in 1832 had allowed the exploration of new ideas, some of which like agitation to end the tax on bread imposed through the corn laws and enthusiasm for manhood suffrage reached New South Wales with idealistic immigrants like Henry Parkes (who arrived in 1839). Notions of egalitarianism and opposition to the old aristocracies in Europe culminated in the 'glorious revolutions' of 1848. The end of transportation, the shift to immigration to boost labour supplies, and the dramatic impact of the quantities of gold arriving in England from Australia after 1851 were all significant in Britain's decision to grant the colonies responsible government in 1856, though it seems obvious from the lack of urgency about Victoria's separation that the management of the Australian colonies was not a high priority in London. Perhaps the procession of lobbyists promoting their own causes convinced the Colonial Office that the sooner the colonists were responsible for their own affairs the better.

Discussion of a new constitution in New South Wales assumed that it would follow the British model with two houses in the parliament (the experience of a single partially elected house from 1843 had shown that there were too many levels of disagreement to be resolved all at once with just the one chamber). It was also assumed that the lower house would be elected on a male franchise much the same as that already established for the Council (i.e. the possession of freehold worth £100 or paying rent of at least £10 p.a.), and that the lower house would provide the executive and most of the legislative initiative as was the case with the British House of Commons. Because of the low property threshold, voting rights were already widely available in New South Wales (so widely, in fact, that Therry was sure that by 1856 there were some 'half-caste natives' on the electoral roll).[35] Inflation of property values in Sydney as a result of the gold rushes further lowered the voting threshold. Hirst has calculated that by 1856, 95 per cent of adult men in Sydney qualified to vote, though less valuable property elsewhere in the colony reduced the average to 55 per cent.[36] By 1856, then, there was already a workingmen's vote to which Sydney politicians could appeal. But to balance the radical tendencies of Sydney, rural electorates huge in area contained quite small numbers of voters.

Most constitutional debate centred round the role and composition of the upper house in New South Wales. Clearly it was impossible to replicate the House of Lords, though there were those, led by W. C. Wentworth, who argued for the creation of a baronetcy in New South Wales comprised of the owners of large landholdings who had demonstrated their sense of responsibility by hiring tenant farmers, building churches and schools on their estates, and generally trying to behave like English landowners. A few noisy public meetings and editorials ridiculing the idea as a 'bunyip aristocracy' put an end to that. Egalitarian sentiments, on the rise everywhere, were easily aroused in New South Wales. The squatters and the wealthy landowners were an obvious target as a pretend aristocracy. Everyone knew of those whose origins lay hidden in the convict record or somewhere nearly as bad. In the end, however, a relatively cautious means of appointing the upper house was chosen. Members of the upper house were to be nominated for life.

The relative orderliness of the transition of New South Wales to responsible government was partly the work of Edward Deas Thomson, colonial secretary from 1828 to 1856. Though his position was redefined under different governors and through several experiments with the shape and function of the Legislative Council, Deas Thomson himself maintained a steady pragmatic and liberal view of the colony and its future requirements. He drew initially on his Scottish education and his experience as a young man working in America. Gradually his accumulating experience of government and administration in New South Wales became a major resource for the governor, the Council and the Colonial Office in London. With the 1856 constitution, his original appointment as colonial secretary, i.e. secretary to the governor of the colony and clerk of the Council, came to an end. The position to which he had been appointed became elective and it fell briefly to Stuart A. Donaldson to form the first responsible ministry as 'prime minister' and colonial secretary. Donaldson was succeeded after three months by the more effective Charles Cowper, known as 'Slippery Charlie' for his ability to make and re-make his views as required to hold his prickly cabinets together.[37] (Though the term premier is now used to describe the head of the government, from 1856 to 1901 it was prime minister though not much used. It was not until 1920 that 'premier' was formally adopted.)

The new parliament replicated the British one albeit on a lesser scale. Its franchise was wider and the members of its nominated upper house were in no way hereditary peers. Unlike Victoria which had decided on an elected upper house with a narrow franchise, it was felt in New South Wales that the forces of democracy would be content with their power in the lower house while the nominated upper house could stand apart, maintaining its authority by the wisdom of its deliberations on potentially divisive legislation. This distinction became more significant after 1858 when the lower house abandoned its property-based franchise for adult male suffrage based merely on a residence qualification. The only sanction against a recalcitrant nominated upper house was the threat of swamping (appointing enough new upper house members willing to support the government to pass legislation previously rejected). It was soon invoked. In 1861 the Council refused to pass free selection legislation agreed to in the House of Representatives. Charles Cowper persuaded the governor, Sir John Young, to appoint an additional twenty-one members to the Council in order to pass this legislation. It was designed by John Robertson, a member for the Upper Hunter, to allow small farmers to select land by squatting where a piece of crown land seemed suitable for use as a small farm. Robertson believed that the only way to ensure employment and develop agriculture was to enable some of the better land tied up as pastoral leases to find its value in an open market. The hypocritical outrage against this legislation from squatters who had themselves only a generation before appropriated land whether from the original Aboriginal inhabitants or the crown, on the basis of its suitability for running sheep, was remarkable. It also showed how the squatters had come to believe that their short-term leases amounted to ownership over huge tracts of land. For years they had argued that they deserved special access and economic assistance because they were making productive use of otherwise 'waste' land., i.e. turning grass into lambs and wool. But when confronted by the logic of similarly turning lightly grazed land into more intensively productive farms, they were appalled.

The insecurity generated by free selection anticipated what was to happen more than a century later with another assault on ideas of land ownership in native title legislation. In the 1860s, squatters and selectors both accused each other of harassment and skulduggery to obtain access to land. Blatant abuses of the legislation were promoted in the press. Litigation and blackmail flourished, while the idea of free selection itself became a kind of sacred cow, jealously guarded by all of Robertson's considerable political skill from careful scrutiny or serious amendment. As is so often the case, when the rights of one group in society were upheld, it was at the expense of the rights of others.[38]

The combined effects of manhood suffrage and free selection legislation considerably diminished the power of the squatters, though it would not have been possible to introduce either without the economic and social impact of gold on the colony. Gold and the growing demand for coal diversified the economy, its exports, employment patterns and social structure. It became clearer that the squatters were but a small group representing nothing but themselves and their sheep. Though wool continued as the major New South Wales export for many years, there was increasing economic strength in a growing population of miners, farmers and urban workers who all needed a myriad of locally produced goods and services. As part of the package of land reforms aimed at making it easier for as many people as possible to participate in the prosperity generated by development, in 1862 New South Wales adopted from South Australia the Torrens system of recording land titles, so urban building blocks could be quickly, cheaply and reliably bought and sold. Firms like Richardson and Wrench began to turn their attention from wool broking and pastoral property to suburban land sales.

An upper house appointed for life was bound to exhibit backward-looking views as its members aged. Before long, those who had drafted the 1856 constitution sometimes felt that New South Wales would have been better off with an elected upper house like Victoria. The next fifty years, however, showed Victoria's elected council to be an impressive defence of squatter-led conservatism. Remarkably, New South Wales managed to avoid the disputes and deadlocks which dogged Victorian politics, and the threat of swamping the New South Wales Council with new members was unusual and carried out only a few times before 1900.[39]

By 1861 it was calculated that there were only 514 convicts still serving their sentences and another 190 holding tickets-of-leave – a total of 704 or 0.2 per cent of the population.[40] (In 1840 it had been 29.7%.) Clearly the gold rushes had diluted the convict population, though because of the superior attractions of Victorian gold it proved necessary to maintain immigration programmes all through the 1850s. Immigrants were subsidised by the government's land fund, by friends, family or prospective employers (as when Henry Parkes recruited compositors for his *Empire* newspaper from among the Eurasians of Madras), and by British charities devoted to improving the prospects of the poor. Natural increase was also very important. Just under half of the population of New South Wales in 1861 was currency, and more than half of those, girls and young women. Most of the women available as marriage partners were, in fact, currency. Like their brothers they grew up early. It was common for currency lasses to be married at 16. Often their husbands were rather older, especially men who had come to New South Wales as immigrants or gold seekers. They needed to establish themselves before looking for a wife. There was some anxiety about the wisdom of marrying these girls, many of whom would have been daughters of convict parents. The shortage of women, a legacy from convict days, and exacerbated by the gold rushes, remained a matter for concern. Violence and lawlessness in remote rural areas were attributed to the absence of women's civilising effect. But even in the towns New South Wales was a notably masculine society. Because women married young and had large families (an average of six or seven children) their lives were lived as daughters, then wives and mothers. It was difficult for them to pursue interests outside the home. At the same time the male-dominated public sphere was confident, energetic, individualistic, acquisitive. Among immigrants and currency alike there was vigour to spare and impatience for success and power.

A rising generation of lawyer-politicians and businessmen, immigrant and currency, was jostling to take control. After 1856 Government House became less important even as a focus for 'society'. The role formerly exercised by the governors' wives and the leading ladies of the colony declined. The churches struggled to maintain moral and social values but were fully stretched by their self-imposed responsibility for the provision of elementary education. The pupil–teacher ratio in all schools was about 1 to 50. About half the teachers were untrained. Charles Cowper's attempts to rationalise education and move some of the burden to the state were frustrated through the 1850s and into the 1860s by inter-church rivalry.[41]

Most significantly perhaps, the shortage of labour which had been a feature of the convict period and which continued through the gold rush and beyond, produced a confident working class capable of organising in its own interests. By the 1860s an eight-hour day had become a reality in most of the building trades – the argument being that it was too hot to work longer. And after work the people of Sydney had time and energy to walk in Hyde Park, go to the theatre, listen to the band in the Botanic Gardens, play cricket (New South Wales had first beaten Victoria in 1856), or swim in the crystal clear baths of Woolloomooloo Bay. Every Sunday coaches to Botany Bay, Cooks River, Parramatta and South Head carried crowds to enjoy the seaside or the country. The promise of prosperity and the opportunity for a better life had ensured the end of the convict system. With continuing prosperity and some experience of the possibilities of self-government the prospect for New South Wales had never looked better.

4

1865–1889, freetrading

In contrast with the pace of change in the previous twenty-five years, after 1865 New South Wales experienced fairly steady prosperity largely untroubled by internal upheavals or events in the world outside. There were drought years, some severe, and periods of what was described by contemporaries as 'dullness' in business and trade, but until the late 1880s, in most years the lambing was good, wool sales continued to bring satisfactory prices, and NSW coal was increasingly in demand in the other Australian colonies.

As well, the population continued to grow. Between the census of 1861 and of 1871 it increased by about a third, and from 1871 to 1891 it doubled so that there were now 1,123,954 people in New South Wales (608,003 males and 515,951 females). By 1891 New South Wales had almost caught up with Victoria's dramatic gold rush population growth. Nearly half of the NSW population now was made up of children under the age of fourteen so that the native-born now had the numbers to dominate. Only about one person in twenty was over sixty, and about three-quarters of these were men, yet New South Wales had more old people than any of the other Australian colonies, and during the 1890s would be the first colony to bring in an old age pension for them. It also had the most people who had been born in Australia with Australian grandparents. The proportion of girls and young women in the population was growing faster than that of young men. This was partly because older men continued to dominate in immigration and therefore to outnumber women in old age and in the death statistics, but also because young men were accident-prone and suffered more violent deaths than young women.

In the 1860s only about one-sixth of the NSW population lived in Sydney. Country towns like Bathurst and Goulburn accounted altogether for more people than Sydney, and the rural population living in the bush away from towns was nearly four times as great as Sydney's. Though in 1891 Sydney was still larger than all the other towns in New South Wales put together, the total rural population exceeded Sydney's. This dominance of rural New South Wales began to alter only in the 1920s. It was not until 1954 that the census showed marginally more people in Sydney than in the rest of the state.

More important than the growth of population in the eyes of many was the growth in the number of livestock. From just over 8 million in 1865, the number of sheep in New South Wales increased to 50 million by 1890. (There were 85 million for the whole of Australia.) Victoria's sheep numbers had exceeded New South Wales' during the 1860s, and wool production there was twice to three times New South Wales'. During the 1870s, however, New South Wales began to pull ahead and in 1889 produced 134 million kilograms of wool compared with just over 30 million kg in Victoria. From the 1880s New South Wales was producing roughly half of Australia's wool. Furthermore, the quality of flocks was improving. New South Wales had about 2 million beef and dairy cattle in 1865, but their numbers declined when dry years made it difficult to keep fat stock in many districts, and by the late 1880s were down to about 1.3 million. Unlike cattle, sheep continued to thrive and to keep producing wool from dry stubble – the dire consequences for both the grass and soil only gradually became apparent when during the prolonged drought at the turn of the century, over-grazed properties were literally blown away by wind.

Canning works to preserve meat for export were established at Ramornie on the Orara River near Grafton and near Homebush in Sydney in the late 1860s, though the canned meat produced was thought unappetising. Experiments with refrigeration during the 1870s by auctioneer and entrepreneur Thomas Sutcliffe Mort and Eugene Nicolle, who operated an ice works in Paddington on a site now hidden within St Vincent's Hospital, eventually made the export of frozen meat a viable proposition.[1] By 1890 this had become part of the regular trade out of Sydney. Refrigeration contributed also to the expansion of dairy farming on the south coast. By 1875 the NSW Fresh Food & Ice Company was supplying Sydney by rail with refrigerated milk from the south coast and butter and cheese from T. S. Mort's Bodalla estate, while on the north coast an export trade in butter was developing with the help of refrigerated shipping.[2]

Horse breeding was already a major industry in 1865 when with 282,587, New South Wales had more than twice as many as any other colony. Australian horses exported to India as remounts for the cavalry had become known as 'Walers'. But horse-racing flourished too, from the first race meeting at Parramatta in 1810, then at Randwick after 1833. By the 1870s New South Wales horses were being bred, it was said, too much for speed and not enough for endurance and Victorian 'Walers' led the export figures.[3]

The increasing population and its relatively widespread distribution during the late nineteenth century meant a rising demand for goods and services, some of which could be locally produced. Hence much of the coal mined at Lithgow was consumed nearby. Brickworks, potteries making agricultural and sanitary pipes, flour mills, butter factories supplied local markets as well as selling their produce in Sydney. In 1866, the enterprising New South Wales statistician, Theodore James Jaques, drew up a list of items, all imported, which he thought could be manufactured in the colony, including blankets, hats and stockings, confectionery, dried fruits, musical instruments, olive oil, and paper products.

Perhaps because of its adoption of protective tariffs, Victoria has often seemed the colony most committed to industrial development during these years. However, both in the number of manufacturing establishments and people employed in them, New South Wales was the most industrialised of the Australian colonies. A great many of the factories were, not surprisingly, devoted to processing raw materials, foodstuffs especially. Flour mills, cheese factories and a soft-drink factory in every suburb and country town (nearly 250 in total) led the lists, while brickworks, sawmills and joineries dominated employment in the building industry. After food processing and building, a major source of employment was the printing industry (where there were some 3,000 employees). Iron rails from

Eskbank near Lithgow were used in railway construction, while Hudson Brothers in Redfern, and Ritchies, the carriage builders of Parramatta who by the early 1880s became part of the Hudson empire, used Eskbank iron to make their railway trucks.

To the dismay of the workers they employed, many of these manufacturing enterprises were short-lived, and most did not require much skill. Indeed the proportion of skilled work available was declining due to mechanisation in trades like building.[4] Piece work was common (i.e. workers were paid according to how much they produced). In 1871 a celebration of the achievement of the eight-hour day, won first by stone masons in 1855, and subsequently by brickmakers, carpenters and some general labourers, was begun, partly to fuel a campaign for a more general forty-eight-hour week. For many workers, however, the reality was casual labour on the wharves and on building sites, or seasonal labour moving between Sydney and the bush. But when there was work, rates of pay were considered good, especially for skilled workers. The working people of New South Wales were said to be well dressed, well fed and contented looking, though the rents they paid seemed high to new immigrants and visitors. The fact that the number of women in the paid workforce was declining was seen as a sign of prosperity and high living standards, though this really meant that in contrast to Victoria, New South Wales had fewer factories producing clothing and textiles. It also overlooked a hidden economy of arduous unpaid domestic work and a high level of female dependency. However, rising standards of comfort and security encouraged men to think more confidently about the future, and to see their wives and children as more than mere dependants. And so there was increasing interest in questions affecting the welfare of both women and children.

Free selection had not produced the revolution some had feared. There was no dramatic leap in the quantity of land being cultivated after 1861, though there was a steady rise from 246,000 acres (close to 100,000 ha.) in that year to about 800,000 (some 324,000 ha.) at the end of the 1880s. One of the consequences of selection was that those who used their land mainly for grazing reassessed the management of their runs in order to find money to invest in freehold homestead blocks and water reserves. During these years most of the great squatters' runs of the Riverina and western New South Wales were re-organised on sounder and more permanent foundations. (An unforeseen consequence was the more effective exclusion of the remnant Aboriginal owners who were forced onto missions and reserves.)

A great many would-be selectors also learned by trial and error that New South Wales was no place for farming on the peasant-sized blocks originally permitted by the free selection legislation. Most successful selectors combined farming with a grazing lease where they could run some stock to supplement their income with a few bales of wool, some fat lambs or a small dairy herd. The Morris–Ranken report on the effects of the free selection legislation in 1884 suggested that the main beneficiaries after twenty years of free selection were the banks and Sydney lawyers. Both Morris and Ranken, however, were inclined to sympathise with squatters whose management skills did not always match their mortgages. As well, years of over-grazing were beginning to show in the degradation of soil and grasses, while water shortages and that 'fiend in a fur jacket' (the rabbit) had become chronic problems.[5]

Selectors in New South Wales had, with some exceptions, sought out land that was suited to agriculture. The more dramatic forms of confrontation between squatter and selector that occurred in Victoria were avoided, mainly because unlike their Victorian counterparts, most NSW squatters owned some pre-1831 freehold that was both protected from selectors and also security against which they could borrow to finance yet more freehold. Most of the best land in the coastal valleys and within the old nineteen counties was held by those to whom it had been granted as freehold before 1831, or had entered the market where it was in steady demand. On many of these old estates there were opportunities for tenant farmers. Share-cropping arrangements could be attractive to aspiring farmers since the need to risk time in clearing and capital in fencing land was avoided. So in practice both squatters and selectors in New South Wales had ways of acquiring land apart from selection. This lessened conflict. There were, however, enough failed or mischievous selections to cause concern. Some were simply too small; others were badly chosen. Some selectors were seriously undercapitalised. Others knew too little about what they were doing. A proportion had no intention of farming, intending only to blackmail a squatter by isolating a dam or waterhole. In some cases farming seemed too arduous and it was easier to make a living by selling water from the well to passers-by at a shilling a bucket.[6] Charles Lyne who made this observation during the course of his extensive investigation of the industries of New South Wales in the early 1880s was continually troubled by the fact that the most profitable rural activities were basically extractive – the production of sheep and wool, and the mining of gold and coal. There was too little of adding value, he thought, either through intensive agriculture or intelligent manufacturing. This theme and the idea that more education and training were needed especially for farmers and workers in industry would be taken up much more seriously during the 1890s when the economy faltered and drought became a permanent fact of rural life.

Mining in New South Wales during the 1850s and 1860s had been dominated by gold. Both the idea of gold and its value to the economy had been important in liberating New South Wales from its convict past and in encouraging the flow of free immigrants. Though gold production began to decline, rich alluvial tin was uncovered in the granite of New England in 1872, and ten years later, silver at Boorook also in New England. More silver was found at Sunny Corner near Bathurst, and in the Barrier Range in the far west at what became known as Silverton. Nearby in 1883 Charles Rasp, a boundary rider on Mt Gipps station, came across silver ore on the Broken Hill and, despite the difficulties of remoteness and lack of water, by 1887 the Broken Hill Proprietary Company had a smelter on the site and 680 hands in employment producing silver and lead almost the equivalent in value to the gold produced in that year. Other mines along the Barrier Range, the Umberumberka, the Day Dawn, and The Pinnacle helped to contribute to a boom in NSW silver-mining shares, though canny South Australian railway builders were quick to extend a line east to capture traffic from the mines for Adelaide. Sydney and Broken Hill were not linked by rail until 1927, and even then it was cheaper to send freight by sea to Adelaide thence by rail to Broken Hill.

Alluvial tin helped to bring both new settlers and the railway to northern New South Wales. There, for a decade or so, from the early 1870s, tin rivalled gold as the most valuable and sought-after mineral by individual prospectors. Many of the tin miners were Chinese who were willing, as they had been earlier on the gold

fields, to rework low-yielding claims abandoned by more impatient diggers. In towns like Glen Innes, some of these Chinese
diggers opened stores that became a resource for the community.
Others soon found livelihoods growing fruit and vegetables in places
as distant as Bourke and Louth on the Darling where there was
a steady local demand. According to the census of 1891, New
South Wales then had the largest Chinese population of any of
the Australian colonies, about 14,000. As individuals they were
generally accepted though often in a patronising way, because of
the services they provided. As a race however, they were resented
for their tendency to work hard and make a living in circumstances which the average miner or selector thought beneath his
dignity.

All this time, the coal beds of the Sydney basin that were so visible on the surface near Newcastle, Wollongong, and Lithgow had
been providing regular employment in mining and constant value
for export. Brown's Wallsend coal was highly regarded in San Francisco, and New South Wales coal was shipped to China as well as
to Melbourne and Adelaide. Welsh miners and seamen arriving in
the 1860s bestowed names like Cardiff and Swansea on familiar-
looking cliffs where they settled in New South Wales. By the 1870s
a Welsh-speaking community had become identified with coalmining and there were seven Welsh chapels in and around
Newcastle. The first Newcastle eisteddfod was held in 1875. At the
first Sydney eisteddfod in 1879, a young Welsh immigrant called
William Morris Hughes carried off the debating section.

The availability of coal within an easy distance of Sydney had a
huge impact on the kind of industrial development occurring in New
South Wales. Much of the subsequent history of New South Wales,
as we shall see, has been intricately woven out of the coalfields on
the Hunter, in the Illawarra, and at Lithgow. In the late nineteenth
century coal was New South Wales' most valuable export after wool
and gold. At times there were more ships calling at Newcastle to load
coal than coming into Sydney Harbour. South of Sydney, coal was
dug out of cliffs rising above the sea and tumbled down to loading
wharves constructed below. Lithgow coal was a great incentive for
the construction of a railway line to Sydney. In the Hunter Valley
where the conjunction of water-borne transport and coal proved

4.1 'Twenty-two feet of first-class coal without a band. Greta
coal seam in the Stanford-Merthyr Colliery, Kurri Kurri, near
Maitland.' Pittman's own photograph illustrates his report.
(E.F. Pittman, *Coal Resources of New South Wales*,
Government Printer, Sydney, 1912, facing p. 14)

an economic combination, flour mills, biscuit factories, brick and pottery works sprang up.

The role of government in New South Wales during the second half of the nineteenth century was to foster circumstances favourable to the growth of trade, the continuation of investment, and ongoing prosperity. This meant maintaining law and order, providing transport and communications where private enterprise found them unprofitable through a 'spirited policy of public works', and ensuring the labour supply both through immigration and, increasingly, education (a form of investment in human resources generally welcomed by both parents and employers). The needs of the population were seen as relatively simple and fairly uniform. It was generally believed that progress came as a result of individuals making the most of their abilities and opportunities. Personal health and welfare were family matters. Moral behaviour was strictly regulated through the churches. Gradually, however, there was more expectation that government would take responsibility for public health and safety in the form of, for example, clean water, rubbish removal, and the imposition of minimum safety regulations in mines and factories.

New South Wales was divided into fifty-four electorates in 1856, some of them very large – leading to the regular quip that sheep had more votes than humans. This had become seventy-two electoral districts in 1880, some entitled by the size of their population to return up to four members. Voters were entitled to vote in every electorate in which they owned property as well as where they resided. For a time, graduates of the University of Sydney also were able to elect their own special representative. After nominations had been called, elections were held, though not always on one day, so it was possible for an elector to vote wherever he had property, and for a candidate to lose in one electorate and stand later in another. Though adult male suffrage had been introduced in 1858, the residence qualification meant that itinerant workers like shearers, seamen, and some agricultural labourers were not able to vote. This seemed more inequitable as the number of rural workers grew and their conditions of employment became harsher. So too did the multiple votes attached to property.

Elected candidates were expected to represent the views of their constituents and to be answerable to them. The idea of a fixed allegiance to a party was despised, as it was in Britain at that time, as weakness, a sign of a man's inability to think for himself on important matters. Every vote in parliament was ideally the product of all representatives acting in the interests of their constituents. In practice, however, small informal and shifting groups of politicians voted together and in fairly predictable ways on matters that had been thoroughly canvassed before and during elections or according to known alliances or old debts. The art of government was to assemble support from enough of these groups (known as factions) to produce a majority. So ministries were frequently constructed by bringing together the leaders of factions, and held together by concessions in return for support. The faction leaders themselves often found their hardest job was retaining the votes of their members since often they had little to offer in return for support – some patronage by way of desired public works or jobs in, say, the post office, or on the railways. Sometimes factions formed round a specially attractive or capable leader. Sometimes they had a regional identity. Occasionally they were committed to a particular view or policy.

Parliament was originally elected for five years, but this was changed in 1874 to three. Even so it was unusual for a government to see out its term. The average length of time between elections was in fact about a year and a half. During the period from 1865 to 1889, there were eighteen changes of government in New South Wales. Eight different men served as premier. It has been argued on the basis of these statistics that the faction system was not a stable form of government. But since government was concerned mainly with economic management on which there was a fair amount of general agreement, and more like local government as we know it now, than national government, this may have not mattered.

New South Wales was supposedly committed to free trade in contrast to Victoria's policy of protection. Free trade meant a minimalist government financed from traditional sources, land revenue, customs, exports, and overseas borrowing. There were protectionists in the New South Wales parliament, though few of them seemed to espouse the liberal social reforms protection had brought to

Victoria. And since New South Wales actually earned more revenue from customs duties on imported goods than did Victoria, protection in New South Wales seemed little more than a label adopted by those who wished to signify that they were in opposition. By the 1880s, however, as government responsibilities expanded and became more expensive and complicated, the protectionists began to argue for diversification of the revenue base by fostering local industry and employment opportunities. They became more organised to argue for their ideas. Whereas the free traders had been reluctant to interfere with market forces (apart from providing most of the economic infrastructure), the protectionists argued for tariffs targeted to encourage local industry, and more vigorous legislation to promote better working and living conditions, actively intervening in the direction of economic and social development in New South Wales as they had in Victoria.

It is sometimes said that the style and tone of politics in New South Wales were set in these years of pragmatic government without much adherence to principle, and that New South Wales politicians, lacking ideological substance, have only ever been concerned with power (or just rude and abrasive).[7] Perhaps the small size and now relatively cramped conditions of both chambers in the NSW parliament may have something to do with the personalised and sometimes undignified quality of parliamentary debate in New South Wales. It used to be thought that the tone had been lowered by the early arrival of the Labor Party; however, it may be simply that the size of New South Wales has given an immense amount of power to governments without the constraining need to present a dignified face to the world.

The faction system emerged naturally from what was then a fairly simple and limited kind of democracy, in which the number of players actually involved either as voters or as their representatives was relatively small, and the issues with which they had to deal were narrowly conceived. Even in the 1880s there were only about 2,000 voters electing each MP who then represented about 8,000 men, women and children (or sheep). After the active constituency was opened, not only to the male population over twenty-one, but in 1902, also to the adult female population, thereby doubling the number of voters in each electorate, the relationship between a politician and his

4.2 New South Wales Parliament House in 1884. The
Legislative Assembly Chamber is on the left and the Council
on the right. At last in 1974 extensive re-building was
commenced at the rear of this historic building to provide
long-needed additional accommodation and facilities, while
the front section containing the two legislative chambers was
carefully restored to reflect its nineteenth-century origins.
(*The Cyclopedia of New South Wales Illustrated. Under the
Patronage of Vice-Royalty, the Government of New South
Wales and the Lord Mayor of Sydney. An Historical and
Commercial Review. Descriptive and Biographical, Facts,
Figures and Illustrations. An Epitome of Progress*, McCarron,
Stewart & Co., Printers, Sydney, 1907, p. 68)

constituents necessarily became more distant and formal, and the
issues became more varied. Before the 1890s, private life based on
home and family was considered completely outside the realm of
politics. Personal problems were left entirely to private initiative or
charity. There was no special protection of wages or working conditions or consumer-oriented legislation. Perhaps conscience, reputation, or the criminal law still worked to inhibit most misdemeanours
on the part of employers and producers or there were fewer opportunities for consumers to be harmed or exploited.

Of the men who governed New South Wales as premier before the
1890s, only two, Farnell and Dibbs, had been born in the colony,
though another four (Cowper, Forster, Robertson, Martin) arrived
as children and therefore had a colonial education. Donaldson and
Parker, the first and third premiers after self-government, were both

men of the old order, colonial officials who retired to England as soon as it was clear that their services were no longer needed in the colony. Charles Cowper, the second premier, had family roots deep in the NSW establishment (both his father and his brother served as Anglican Dean of Sydney). Cowper, himself, was for a time secretary of the Church and Schools Land Corporation. Long known as the 'Member for the Church of England', in 1863 he amazed his critics by abolishing state subsidies for the churches, though his policies were also related to his need to stay in power for his ministerial salary had become his main source of income. This was also partly the reason for his encouragement of a patronage system whereby the sons and nephews of his supporters were appointed to lowly paid jobs in the public service. But before the existence of recognisable political parties, this was also a way of ensuring some kind of voter base at election time.[8] To continue on the New South Wales payroll, Cowper eventually returned to England as agent-general. He died there in 1875.

The first Catholic (and the only non-labour Catholic until Nick Greiner in 1988) to become premier of New South Wales was Patrick Jennings (1886–87) though William Bede Dalley, acting premier 1884–85 was Catholic, and James Martin had abandoned his childhood faith for Anglicanism on his way to power.[9]

With William Forster (1859–60) it seemed as if the new generation of colonial politicians had come into their own. Though born in India, Forster belonged to the third generation of his family in New South Wales for his mother was a daughter of Gregory Blaxland, who with Wentworth and Lawson had pioneered a route across the Blue Mountains in 1813. Educated in New South Wales, Forster took up land on his own behalf and gained considerable experience as a bushman before entering politics. An attractive character, given as much to writing poetry as to making speeches, his persistence, independence, and honesty earned him great respect if not a long term as premier. He served in many governments subsequently, trusted for his experience and good sense.

If Forster seemed an ideal type of the generation who had grown up in New South Wales, John Robertson was the most perceptive. 'No other politician', says Nairn, 'had such a sympathetic insight into the texture and subtleties of the radical needs of the times'.[10]

Having arrived in New South Wales in 1822 as a child just start-
ing school, Robertson like Forster had grown with colonial politics,
observing and understanding the competing claims of convict and
non-convict, and rise of the native-born. He knew why the squatters were so insistent about security of tenure but also saw that this
was at the expense of the colony as a whole. Unlike Deas Thomson,
Donaldson, or Parker who belonged to the past, Cowper who was
hampered by his family and church connections, Parkes with his
background in English politics, and Martin led astray by social ambition, Robertson could appreciate the radical forces in New South
Wales at this time. A keen sailor as a young man, he gave up a sea-
going career to work on his father's property in the Hunter Valley.
Perhaps only Forster had anything like Robertson's outback experience or his feel for the role of land in politics and the economy.
While politics brought him to live in Sydney (though his house by
the sea at Clovelly was some compensation for the former yachts-
man), Robertson never lost his rough countryman's image. He could
and did swear and drink. Tall, good-looking with sharp blue eyes, a
reddish glint in his long hair and beard both of which turned white
as he grew older, his clothes always looked as if he'd just got off his
horse.

Nairn judges Robertson's partnership with Parkes between 1878
and 1883 one of the most productive and effective governments during this period, though it was not an easy relationship. Where Parkes
was self-consciously ambitious, Robertson was wryly amused.
Parkes thought Robertson devious or too calculating, whereas he
was often just simply willing to make small or strategic sacrifices in
order to gain greater objectives. He seems not to have cared much
what others thought of him, a consequence, perhaps, of learning as
a child to live with a cleft palate. This perhaps is also the judgement
of history where Parkes has dominated, in part because of the great
wealth of his personal records preserved for posterity. Robertson
seems to have given little thought to history. He left no memoirs,
published no poems, and the only biography we have is Bede Nairn's
superb miniature in the *Australian Dictionary of Biography*.

By the late 1880s, New South Wales railways were considered
a blessing, but building them had been slow and expensive, and
meanwhile the wealth of the Riverina and the west was being
lost. Wool shipped through Echuca or to Adelaide was handled by

4.3 The first river steamer on the Darling River viewed from an Aboriginal camp on the bank. (*Town and Country Journal*, 10 October 1874, p. 588)

southern agents. Supplies brought up river came originally from Melbourne.

When John Whitton arrived in 1856 from Yorkshire to become engineer-in-chief of the NSW railway he wanted to scrap the 23 miles (37 km) already constructed at 4'8½" (approx. 1.44 m) and move to a 5'3" (1.6 m) gauge, the same as Victoria and South Australia. In this he was supported by John Rae, then under-secretary for public works and commissioner for railways, another of the able, imaginative and dedicated public servants who have served New South Wales. But they were defeated by politics. Indeed Whitton had to fight off later plans for even lighter, narrower tramways. His real goal was to build a soundly engineered railway that would last even though he was stuck with its 4'8½" gauge.

The railway reached Goulburn in 1869 partly because, as with the earlier southern road, that was the route most easily built. Thereafter there was considerable political pressure to meet the Victorian line when it reached the Murray at Wodonga in 1873. Express trains with sleeping cars then took only eighteen hours to cover the distance between Sydney and Melbourne, carrying both passengers and mail. Still, in 1875, only 437 miles (about 703.5 km) of railway had been completed, a construction rate of 45.9 miles (almost 74 km) per annum. The railway arrived in Bathurst in 1876 following the construction of elaborate zig-zags at Lapstone Hill and Lithgow to cross the range. Work was stepped up in the 1880s and the railway reached Bourke on the Darling. By 1886, 1,889.5 miles (about 3,042.1 km) of track were open representing an investment of a quarter of a million pounds, mostly raised by government loan.

Until 1889 when the Hawkesbury bridge was opened, there were really two railway systems in New South Wales, one operating out of Sydney to the south and west, the other focused on Newcastle and covering the north-west. From its terminus at Newcastle, the northern railway followed the main road parallel to the Hunter before climbing the New England ranges beyond Muswellbrook, linking to Queensland's 3'6" (approx. 1.37 m) gauge at the twin settlements of Jennings and Wallangarra by 1888. When it seemed that trains from Sydney to Brisbane might bypass the main Newcastle station, there was briefly an intense decentralisation campaign. In Bathurst, where loss of both railway employment to the new Eveleigh workshops in Sydney and Cobb & Co.'s coach factory to Queensland was threatened, and in Goulburn, campaigns to save railway-related employment flared as well.[11]

The new chief commissioner of railways appointed in 1888, Edward Miller Eddy, a manager rather than an engineer, had a British background in designing timetables. With a bridge across the Hawkesbury, Eddy planned an express service, Sydney to Newcastle in $3^1/_4$ hours demanding huge effort from his men and their machines. The bridge did more than link New South Wales' two railway systems. It was now possible to travel from Brisbane by rail through Sydney to Melbourne and Adelaide, albeit with several changes for breaks of gauge. The opening of the Hawkesbury bridge on 1 May 1889 was celebrated with Moët and Chandon Dry Imperial 1884 vintage. Henry Parkes spoke of 'the crimson fluid of kinship pulsing through all the iron veins', a metaphor echoed later in Henry Lawson's iron rails by which 'the mighty bush is tethered to the world'. Parkes had been aware for some time that intercolonial communications must eventually bring about some kind of union between the Australian colonies. Returning to Sydney by rail from a meeting in Brisbane later that year, Parkes reworked his image in a speech in Tenterfield and the rails became veins carrying the crimson thread of kinship.

Despite New South Wales' expensive railway building, Victoria managed about as many miles, giving much better coverage per head of population. Parts of New South Wales were still hard to reach. The south coast railway was inching towards Bulli. On the north coast, the rivers still provided the main form of transport but their shifting sand-bars confined the coastal trade to small ships. Though there were ferries and punts, most rivers were not bridged until the second half of the twentieth century making the north coast nearly as remote as the coast south of Wollongong.

Compared to the cost and effort of building the railways, a telegraph system covering most of New South Wales was constructed relatively quickly and inexpensively. The first line from Sydney to Liverpool was opened in January 1858, but within months there was a link to Melbourne through Albury. Brisbane had been connected by late 1861.[12] By the end of the 1880s, there were more than 20,000 miles (over 32,000 km) of telegraph wire and over 400 telegraph stations throughout the colony with links through Darwin to India and Europe, used mostly for news and commercial communication. Furthermore, unlike the railway, the telegraph promised to pay for itself. The combination of railways and telegraphs made it possible to administer most of New South Wales directly from Sydney and, in combination with horse-drawn coaches, provided an enviable postal service, though the more it was used, the more it cost to run. In the 1880s it was being subsidised by the government to the extent of several thousands of pounds a year. In part, this was because newspapers were carried free, a service thought worthwhile in the interests of a better informed and educated population.

When in the early 1880s two of Sir James Martin's children as well as his sister-in-law (W. B. Dalley's wife) died one after the other from mysterious illnesses, his wife blamed the bad smells which blew up to their Potts Point waterfront home from the harbour. She moved the rest of their family to semi-rural Vaucluse. Railways enabled many others to move to more spacious and healthy conditions on the outskirts of Sydney. In the 20 years from 1865 to 1885, fares were reduced and passenger numbers doubled. Cheap semi-rural land along the railway and tramlines was easily developed with modest housing to attract owner-occupiers. As the sale books of wool brokers turned estate agents and suburban developers Richardson and Wrench show, an impressive number of the purchasers were women for whom investment in real estate provided security as well as economic opportunities. They paid off their suburban cottages by taking in lodgers, washing or sewing, keeping poultry and growing fruit.

Suburban railways also enabled factories to move to more convenient and less expensive sites outside the city and to draw their workers from ever more remote suburbs. Among those catching the 6 am workman's train in 1884 to Hudson Brothers carriage works relocated from Redfern to Clyde was a seventeen-year-old apprentice carriage painter called Henry Lawson who set his alarm in time to walk from his home in Phillip Street, Sydney to Redfern station, experiences he later recalled in his story 'Arvie Aspinall's Alarm Clock' and poem 'Faces in the Street'.[13]

Paving on Sydney's main streets became essential to combat the dust and mud, otherwise great deterrents to business. Gas lighting lessened the fear of crime in public places and reduced the hazard of fire. But for those without the option of moving to semi-rural suburbs, in increasingly overcrowded and unplanned inner suburbs where much of the housing was rented, problems with smells, sewerage and the water supply could not be avoided.

There were many like Lady Martin who believed that the smells generated by rotting garbage, refuse from butchers and slaughterhouses, overflowing sewers and cesspits were a health hazard. Sydney's first sewer, constructed in the 1850s, drained directly into the harbour. As the city grew so did the number of outlets. As early as 1866, a report on the condition of the harbour recommended that sewerage should be carried further out to sea, either at Bondi or through Botany Bay. Growing quantities of domestic and industrial waste also flowed into Darling Harbour and Port Jackson. In 1875 it was reported that the water in the harbour 'is always in a black and stinking state' and 'a strong smell is nearly always apparent by day and constantly by night'. Poor drainage, sewers that were badly designed, primitively constructed, and either short of water to flush them adequately, or overflowing after too much rain, added to the problem. So did the number of houses relying on cesspits or on nightsoil collections. Meanwhile the foreshores of the harbour were being visibly extended, by rubbish flushed out during heavy rain or dumped deliberately by those seeking to extend their land. Upgrading the sewerage system so that it no longer drained into the harbour became a priority. Silt-traps and dredging round harbour outfalls did little to solve problems too great for the proliferating local authorities whose responsibility they were. Eventually, the Metropolitan Sewerage, Water and Drainage Board with representatives from government and all municipalities involved was established, and legislation for the deep-ocean outfall at Bondi was agreed to, though it was not functioning until 1894.[14] In theory, ocean tides and currents were to disperse the sewerage, and this they did, until the volume became too great. As well as the Bondi outfall, a sewage farm was established to the south of the city, on the shores of Botany Bay, and another for the west at Arncliffe.

Surveyor General Sir Thomas Mitchell had noted in 1850 that Sydney's unreliable water supply was a fundamental weakness. First the Tank Stream, then Busby's bore tapping the Lachlan Swamps had provided the city with fresh water, though it often dwindled to a trickle in the public pumps or dried up altogether in long dry spells. Then the water carts servicing those parts of the city without standpipes at so-much-a-bucket were unable to operate. Mitchell had earlier suggested building a 40-mile (approx. 64 km) long aqueduct from the Nepean River near Penrith, but in the 1850s it had been decided to pump water from the Botany Swamps to a series of reservoirs in Crown Street, Paddington, and Woollahra whence it flowed by gravity into the city.

Water shortages threatened health and general cleanliness. Clean water was essential for drinking and the preparation of food. It was sprayed to lay manure dust in the streets. Water closets could not be installed without a reliable supply. Industries such as brewing using large quantities of clean water were limited in their operation by recurrent shortages, especially in dry years. Before the Botany Swamps scheme was even completed, engineers were looking once more at a dam near the junction of the Nepean with the Cataract and Cordeaux rivers, and a large new reservoir at Prospect 195 feet (nearly 60 m) higher than high-water level in Sydney Harbour, with water carried though conduits and iron pipes into existing city reservoirs. Construction of the Nepean scheme became one of the major public works of the 1880s. By 1890, 71,501 houses and 343,204 persons in Sydney were being supplied from it with piped water at the rate of 24.70 gallons (112.3 l) per day.[15]

Once reliable water was available, laying pipes to connect individual properties was not as difficult or expensive as installing sewers, and the principle was established that if piped water was available in a street all houses would be connected and pay rates accordingly. At first, the cost of connection per house was high. Eventually however, both water and sewerage became more affordable, and legislation for compulsory connection came into force. Though it was the quality of drinking water that was most important for public health, the preoccupation with bad smells, hence the need to flush away sewerage and remove garbage, meant a continuing heavy level of expenditure in the provision of services. Ocean outfalls proliferated until the vile condition of the beaches began to cause concern. Outside the metropolitan area, most major towns including Albury, Bourke, Balranald, Lismore, Orange and Wagga Wagga had, with government assistance, embarked on the construction of water supply systems by the 1890s. The construction of dams and public provision of wells and tanks along stock routes not only made water available in dry areas, but also provided employment in construction and maintenance.

In contrast with Melbourne's late-Victorian grandeur, Sydney retained its early Georgian charm to which was now added a kind of subtropical lushness as parks and gardens matured. A visitor from India in the 1870s, Henry Cornish, was particularly impressed by 'a large-leafed, dark foliaged tree called a Moreton Bay fig, a tree admirably adapted for shading purposes' which had become 'a marked feature in the parks and avenues about Sydney . . . both picturesque and useful in the hot weather'.[16] The figs were a favourite of Charles Moore, director of the Sydney Botanic Gardens from 1848 to 1896 and under his influence impressive avenues became an enduring part of the Sydney scene. Another keen gardener, Sir James Martin, planted Brazilian 'dream trees' from William Guilfoyle's Exotic Nursery in Double Bay in the garden of Clarens, his home in Potts Point. Soon every garden in Potts Point had a jacaranda whose delicate purple haze now welcomes summer all down the NSW seaboard[17] while the scent of frangipani, also a Guilfoyle favourite, spreads on the warm coastal air. The architects of Sydney's new public buildings were designing colonnades and balconies to suit the climate (and the sandstone) and to take advantage of the many beautiful water views. Cedar joinery and locally made furniture complemented elegant and delicate wrought-iron work and masonry. Above the handsome colonnade of the new General Post Office in Martin Place, created from the chaos of lanes and alleys and named for Sir James, Italian sculptor Tomaso Sani (1839–1915) carved scenes showing the people of New South Wales at work. They can still be seen in the building, now incorporated into a modern tourist hotel. But the 'Garden Palace' constructed of lightweight materials as the centrepiece of a grand international exhibition, and spread during late 1879 and early 1880 over most of the Macquarie Street frontage of the Domain, succumbed to fire early on the morning of 22 September 1882 taking with it among other things the records of the 1881 census of New South Wales on which only preliminary processing had been done, art work, and a large part of a collection which was intended for a technological museum. Out of those ashes came the Board of Technical Education, Ultimo Technical College and eventually, the Powerhouse Museum.[18]

Builders were turning increasingly to iron and steel for construction in preference to wood and stone. By the 1870s, the need to conserve timber was already apparent and a number of forest reserves had been established. Most of the magnificent cedar, the 'red gold' of the 'big scrubs' of the Clarence River district, had been cut out. The first forest ranger was appointed in 1875 and in 1882 a Forest Conservation branch was attached to the Department of Mines, though the emphasis was still more on securing adequate supplies for pit props and mine workings than on ensuring conservation.

Given the high proportion of children in the population it is not surprising that education emerged as a major question at this time. The children of the convict generation had been carefully educated to become useful law-abiding citizens, but despite this promising start, elementary education sank into sectarianism, more concerned with maintaining church numbers than providing essential schooling in reading, writing and arithmetic. By the 1860s, church schools were unevenly distributed both in regard to geography and denomination, the quality of teaching was dubious, while content was old-fashioned and sadly lacking in practical knowledge. Under the guidance of William Wilkins who had been working to modernise education in New South Wales since 1851 when he became head of Fort Street Model School, Parkes carried education legislation in 1866 setting minimum goals for elementary education and establishing training, classification and inspection for teachers.

Visiting English novelist Anthony Trollope thought the consequences of education already significant in the 1870s. 'Teaching produces prosperity: prosperity achieves decent garments; and decent garments are highly conducive to church-going', he wrote.[19] Many men in public life, however, had prospered and accumulated property without the benefit of education, products of 'their own native energy and intelligence', inclined to believe simply that whatever was good for them was good for the country as a whole. Even conservative landowners and businessmen in New South Wales' politics were not always well educated by English standards. Unlike Victoria where well-educated gentlemen immigrants with capital to invest were attracted, both before and after the gold rushes, immigrants to New South Wales were of a more prosaic quality. There had never been much pretension about high intellectual achievement among the oldest families, and the narrow vein of quality contributed by reluctant, impoverished professionals sent out to 'govern New South Wales' was resented and resisted after self-government. Some of the native-born when young aspired to education and culture, as we have seen with poets like Harpur, Kendall and the Stenhouse circle, and it was Parkes' hope that the university would produce a local intelligentsia with the advantage of an education gained under 'patriotic influences'. Twenty years after its foundation only a handful of graduates had been produced by the University of Sydney, though they did include lawyers and future politicians like Edmund Barton, Joseph Carruthers, and Samuel Griffith who returned to Queensland, and bibliophile David Scott Mitchell. Technical and vocational education as advocated by engineer Norman Selfe, however, was deemed more appropriate to the needs of New South Wales at this time than other forms of higher education.

Further legislation in 1880 was intended to make primary education free, secular and compulsory, though parents continued to make small weekly payments for their children until the end of the century. The cost of maintaining denominational schools was rationalised and basic religious instruction arranged within the state framework. The Catholic Archbishop Roger Vaughan would have nothing of this, famously attacking Parkes' secular state schools as 'seedplots of immorality'. 'I must say that I do strongly resent the statement that the system under which I have grown up is calculated to produce infidelity, immorality, or lawlessness', remarked Barton, one of the younger members of parliament and an old boy of Sydney Grammar.[20] Parkes dismissed Vaughan's attack as 'the lust of the priestly mind for authority over parents through the training of the children'.[21] But in Vaughan's determination to maintain a separate Catholic school system he identified the Irish heritage of New South Wales as Catholic, often to the dismay of increasingly successful educated and sophisticated Irish-Australians. Catholic parents were torn between their desire for free, modern and vocationally effective education and loyalty to their church and its teachings. And as the cost of teachers was defrayed by Irish teaching orders, it became increasingly difficult to disentangle Irishness from education in the Catholic school system.

Parkes was confident he knew about education, but he sought expert advice on other problems. He tackled the hospital by writing to Florence Nightingale, the heroine of Crimea and great exponent of modern effective health-care. With her help, Lucy Osburn and her group of Nightingale-trained nurses were engaged to reform the management of Sydney Hospital. Osburn had a massive task in overcoming entrenched interests and attitudes, but the effectiveness of the care provided gradually carried the necessary message beyond the confines of Macquarie Street. When English authorities on the care of neglected and abandoned children, Florence and Rosamond Hill, were on a private visit to New South Wales, Parkes sought their opinion on another policy area dear to his heart, the naval training school for delinquent boys on the ship *Vernon*, and Biloela, the less successful home where delinquent girls were supposed to learn the rudiments of domestic service in 1867.

In February 1885, acting premier William Bede Dalley offered troops to support Britain's military campaign in the Sudan. His wilful action produced a four-month farce for what was often then described as N. S. Wales. At first he was wildly supported. There was no shortage of recruits. Four times as many men volunteered as the 700 who were needed. But N. S. Wales promised to pay them 5s a day plus allowances for a wife and children compared with the basic 1s paid to British soldiers. A crowd estimated at 12,000 attended a meeting to launch the New South Wales Patriotic Fund for the relief of probable widows and orphans of the volunteers, and at least £40,000 was pledged, ranging from squatter James Tyson's £4,000 to thousands of pennies collected from school children after carefully orchestrated publicity of an initial contribution from a 'little boy at Manly'.[22]

Then there was criticism. Some like Parkes opposed Dalley simply on political grounds. He had acted without the authorisation of either cabinet or parliament, but with the contingent already at sea, it was too late to refuse permission. And by the time it arrived in Suakin, there was little for it to do apart from some railway construction. Two men died, 'the first men to die overseas while serving in an Australian expeditionary force', but they died of dysentery. Within a month, it was decided the railway was no longer needed. Dalley tried in vain to have the contingent redeployed to fight the Russians in Afghanistan, but the troops themselves were unwilling to go. In late June they returned, to quarantine and North Head – there were several more fatal cases of dysentery and typhoid – before a belated welcome-home parade held on a cold wet Tuesday. The men were hungry having had no breakfast and their khaki uniforms never worn before in Australia, though well suited to the Sudan, were too thin to cope with the cold and drenching rain. One, Private Martin Guest, died as a result of the soaking he received while listening to interminable speeches.

New South Wales remained divided about the worth of Dalley's adventure. When the next opportunity came, in 1899, to join in Britain's war against the Boers in South Africa, there was only token interest. Most of the cost of the contingents sent from New South Wales to the Cape was raised by a group of businessmen who thought they were likely to profit from war contracts or sales of equipment and supplies. The government's contribution was small, perhaps a tenth of what it cost to fund the police force.[23] The

Patriotic Fund survived, however. In 1902 it still contained some £32,000 and became the basis of a disaster relief fund.

Dalley symbolised the successful native-born Catholic intelligentsia. In his study of the Sudan campaign, Ken Inglis noted that much of Dalley's support came from those who were keen to show their loyalty to Britain despite their convict and/or Irish parentage. These were details many preferred to hide.[24] Dalley's opponents were less convinced of the benefits that would flow to N. S. Wales from the 'mother country' through this display of loyalty. Most strident among the critics was the relatively new Sydney *Bulletin*. Its delight was to expose the extent of hypocrisy in New South Wales about its convict origins while enthusiastically promoting the cause of the native-born.

Two young journalists, John Haynes and John Feltham Archibald, had begun publishing the Sydney *Bulletin* in 1880. Their paper fitted easily into a lusty tradition reaching back as far as the 1830s with W. A. Duncan's *Chronicle*, Horatio Wills' *Currency Lad*, and Garrett and Pickering's *Bell's Life in Sydney*. Haynes and Archibald planned a 'smart weekly with a Catholic flavour' and the first issues were printed at the *Freeman's Journal* press, though they soon parted company with anything resembling church support.[25] Haynes, then aged thirty with a tempestuous career in New South Wales' politics ahead of him, took his inspiration from the San Francisco *Bulletin*. Archibald at twenty-four had recently arrived in Sydney after a time working in Queensland, greatly influenced by this experience. He had as his model a Sydney paper called *The Stockwhip* that had flourished in the 1870s, and he wanted to call this new venture *The Lone Hand*, but it would be twenty-seven years before he could use that name. Instead it became *The Bulletin* with an old-fashioned sketch that might be Circular Quay under the title on the masthead. Soon it acquired its characteristic pink cover, providing literary editor A. G. Stephens with his 'Red Page'. Its slogan, 'Australia for the Australians', was later extended to 'Australia for the White Man'.

Despite a fraught early publishing history – Haynes and Archibald were gaoled in 1881 for their inability to pay costs in a libel case arising from an editorial by W. H. Traill – the *Bulletin* survived to provide a high-spirited commentary on life in New South Wales written largely by 'contributors' who were also its readers. It caught

4.4 *The Bulletin's* original masthead with its stylised port
which could be Sydney but isn't. (Patricia Rolfe, *The
Journalistic Javelin: An Illustrated History of the* Bulletin,
Wildcat Press, Sydney, 1979, facing p.1)

the wave of literacy fostered by the educational policies of the 1870s.
It also appealed to an emerging sense of Australian identity as the
proportion of the native-born residents in New South Wales climbed
steadily. And in encouraging writers like Will Dyson, Price Warung,
Barcroft Boake, Henry Lawson and A. B. 'Banjo' Paterson it established the relationship between Sydney and the bush as an Australian
archetype. Images of rural New South Wales developed by Lawson,
Paterson and the many literate, itinerant contributors personified in
Joseph Furphy's 'Tom Collins' who enjoyed seeing their own yarns
in print were matched by clever cartoons which captured not only
wry aspects of rural and urban life, but explored the universal puz-
zles of gender, religious and racial differences.

    After Haynes' departure to pursue his political career, Archibald
became the dominant presence transforming his name to Jules
François. More sophisticated than many of his readers knew or
cared, in those years he, along with others of the Sydney intelligentsia, came under the spell of fin-de-siècle France and the revital-
ising culture of a modernising Germany. While such interests provided serious ballast to the *Bulletin*, it vividly promoted images of
Sydney and of outback New South Wales as the real Australia. With
the *Bulletin*, and other illustrated weeklies like the *Sydney News*
and the *Town and Country Journal*, there was plenty of work for
writers, cartoonists and black and white artists. Lively opportunities

lured other artists like Arthur Streeton from Melbourne to paint in and around Sydney and on the Hawkesbury, or Tom Roberts whose work on Brookong station in the Riverina captured the perfect image of Australia's 'golden fleece'. Through the children of second- and third-generation families in the Monaro, the Hunter Valley and New England like Miles Franklin, Patrick White and Judith Wright, the history of white settlement in New South Wales would be reinforced as quintessential Australia.

To mark the centenary of European settlement in New South Wales in 1888, there were ambitious plans for an official history. It was not delivered in time, however, because of the rivalry of the two authors, G. B. Barton and F. M. Bladen, and much uncertainty as to what was then the most up-to-date and acceptable way of approaching history. The whole project became bogged down in collecting, transcribing and analysing documents in the archives, and only ever reached the 1820s.[26] A popular version of history was emerging anyway in the stories published in the illustrated weeklies. Louisa Atkinson's fiction was based on the experiences of her parents' generation as settlers west of the ranges. Price Warung (William Astley) had been working through the written records already available in the State Library and interviewing and noting the recollections of survivors of the convict days for the sketches he began publishing in the *Bulletin*, reinterpreting the convict system for a contemporary audience.[27] In his immensely popular *Robbery Under Arms*, 'Rolf Boldrewood' (in ordinary life, police magistrate and mining warden at Dubbo, T. A. Browne) explored not only stories of the bushrangers, but also some of the themes underlying the sense of achievement in New South Wales after a hundred years – i.e. what had been the outcomes of a society brought up in the shadow of crime, the possibly inherent criminal propensities of currency lads like Boldrewood's Marston brothers, and the likelihood that under colonial conditions even the best-bred gentlemen might turn to crime like Captain Starlight.[28] Later, Louis Becke captured the wild times when the Pacific trade was more important, and, closer to home, his childhood memories of Port Macquarie when it was still a convict settlement.

For the official celebrations in 1888, the now superseded Lachlan Swamps catchment area for Sydney's water supply was reclaimed, named The Centennial Park, and dedicated with great ceremony in the presence of the governors of all the colonies of Australasia.[29] But where, demanded the *Bulletin*, was the commemorative poem, the specially commissioned painting, the university scholarship to further achievement in the next generation? Instead a statue of Queen Victoria was unveiled. It cost '£5000 or so, and has, no doubt, been paid for out of loan-funds or sales of the lands belonging to the people of the hard-up colony of NSW'.[30] At the official banquet, 'a tremendous feed for those who are apoplectic and overfed' (according to the *Bulletin*), the gentlemen present having toasted the queen and other members of the royal family, eventually raised their glasses to the ladies of Australia who of course could not respond because they were only permitted to observe the proceedings from the galleries.

Around the colony there were other celebrations in which the people themselves could participate. Tamworth managed to install the first electric street lighting into the country to mark the centenary. (Electric light was installed two years later in Newcastle too, fourteen years ahead of Sydney.) For the people of Sydney there was a regatta on the harbour, of course, but for those in need, the highlight of the centennial celebrations was the distribution of food parcels in the days leading up to 26 January. Some 10,000 brown paper parcels containing packages of tea, sugar, flour, raisins, currants, fresh meat, vegetables and cheese from Bodalla, as well as tins of jam and sardines were distributed to those recommended by clergy and welfare workers. With each there went a pat of butter and some fresh milk if the recipient brought a jug or other container. Adults received a fig of tobacco, and there were lollies for the children. It was estimated that the food parcels were worth about 7s each and that as each member of a family was entitled to one, in some cases they might be carrying away 30 pounds (approx. 13.5 kg) of food.

In fact since the mid-1880s the economy had been in decline. High wages and employment based on land sales and public works peaked in the years 1882–85. After that employment became harder to find. Many of those collecting their centennial food parcels were recent victims of unemployment. The late 1880s had seen the completion of some major public works with the loss of perhaps 12,000 jobs and nothing new to replace them. As well there was increasing industrial unrest, much of it related to the need to extract more work for less pay in undertakings no longer as profitable as they had been. Strikes in the southern collieries in 1886–87 were followed the next year by strikes in the north.[31]

Underemployment, however, was probably more prevalent than unemployment. That it could be borne was certainly related to the relatively high level of home ownership, though many of the 'homes' were mere shacks or humpies. The wooden cottage that Thomas Dobeson built for himself and his family on land he had bought in Ney Street, Botany, during the 1880s was probably typical of the owner-occupied houses in outer-metropolitan Sydney and rural New South Wales at that time. It provided basic shelter, nothing more. Yet, there was room for expansion as his family grew, also space for a vegetable garden, some fruit trees, a shed for his cart and horse and a workshop for his various construction activities.[32] Dobeson, a pattern-maker and millwright, had arrived in Sydney as an assisted immigrant in 1883, when such labour was in demand, to work for Hoskins Bros engineering. By 1887 he was 'Out of work again. I consider it harder to look for work than the work itself'. He found occasional jobs, but survived on the self-sufficiency of his house and garden.

Henry Lawson (b. 1867) was thirteen years younger than Dobeson, and missed the chance to establish himself similarly in the prosperous 1880s, and had few illusions about the world he had grown into. 'As the "elder son" of a poor selector on a worn-out goldfield', Brian Kiernan writes,

he had known the back-breaking, heart-breaking life of the selection districts. In his youth he had experienced the cultural transformation that was occurring in his generation when he moved to the city – a disturbingly different world of anonymous faces in the street, larrikins, streetwalkers, haggard mothers of large families, lonely men in boarding houses. This reality was the obverse of the democratic optimism he proclaimed in some of his early verses, and he became the imaginative historian of these social changes.[33]

Yet his romanticised memories of 'The days when the world was wide' captured the optimism of the post-gold rush years, and in the early 1890s, like many others, he believed unionism was 'a new and grand religion'. That belief was to become more important in the shrinking economy of the 1890s.

5

1890–1914, the challenge
of federation

When introducing his chapter on industrial progress in the 1890–91 edition of *The Wealth and Progress of New South Wales*, the government statistician T. A. Coghlan wrote: 'There have been everywhere signs of industrial unrest and of the determination on the part of the labouring classes to take a large share in governing the country.'[1] The year 1890 had been marked by strikes, riots and demonstrations. Then in June 1891, thirty-five labour candidates were elected to the NSW parliament. Amazingly they held the balance of power between the free trade and protection parties, and declared their intention of supporting whichever party was willing to make legislative concessions. But there were difficult times ahead. The newly elected Labor Party had massive problems working out its own identity and ways of coping with the new parliamentary environment. The economic climate continued to deteriorate coming to a crisis in 1893. And drought intensified over New South Wales from the early 1890s well into the new century.

The question of federation, revived by Henry Parkes in an expansive mood in the 1880s, became part of the fin-de-siècle agenda, and a convenient political distraction from the teething troubles of the infant Labor Party, for it enabled New South Wales to focus publicly on economic policy. This meant exploring at length the relevance of free trade or protection to industry in New South Wales. Gradually it became clear that of all the Australian colonies, only New South Wales was strong enough to sustain a semblance of free trade, though with the faltering economy of the 1890s, even that looked uncertain. By 1898 the pressures on New South Wales to give way and enter a protectionist federation had become intense. But as well, time was running out if Edmund Barton's 'nation for a continent' was to be achieved for the new century.

Histories of federation have tended to focus on these economic pressures and the difficulties of preparing a constitution in time for 1901. However, in New South Wales especially, nationalist sentiment may have been growing in importance. As the oldest colony, New South Wales now had the largest Australian-born population. Many families were into their second and third generation. Both Barton who led the federal movement in New South Wales and Alfred Deakin in Victoria were native-born and drew immense loyalty from the 'cornstalks' and 'gumsuckers', popular names for the native-born of New South Wales and Victoria respectively. As well, in New South Wales there was a history of local pride superseding older ethnic and religious differences. There were specific reasons, too, for certain regions of New South Wales like the north coast and the Riverina to welcome the idea of federation, all adding to acceptance by 1899.

After that, the first decade of the twentieth century became a period of adjustment to the new political and economic world of federated Australia. When the Commonwealth adopted protection, the debate about protection and free trade ceased to be relevant. The free traders tried redefining themselves as liberals in the classic individualist sense, but became hostage to protestant extremists unduly agitated by the political ambitions of the Catholic church as detected in Archbishop Moran's decision to stand as a New South Wales candidate for the 1897 federal convention. Though Moran was not elected, fears of militancy in the Catholic working class were aroused, ironically strengthening it as the official opposition.

By 1910, Labor was able to win government under the leadership of J. S. T. McGowen with William Holman as his deputy. Labor, however, was neither working class, nor Catholic, nor even socialist. Though articulate socialists had been prominent in some of the 1890s debates, the necessity of maintaining a united front in parliament had produced a great many compromises on ideological questions, and driven out those who were unwilling to sign a 'pledge' to vote in accordance with caucus decisions. Labor's main objective was, in the words of Bede Nairn, 'civilising capitalism'. Its support came as much from farmers with small holdings as from the unions in mining towns and industrial suburbs. McGowen, a devout Anglican, was for thirty years the Sunday school superintendent for temperance advocate Rev. Francis Bertie Boyce at St Paul's in Redfern. He had worked as a boiler-maker for Russell's engineering works in Balmain, then at Eveleigh railway workshops. Holman too was Anglican, though by no means as committed as McGowen. Trained as a cabinet-maker in England, he became a newspaper proprietor in Grenfell and, after realising the need for legal expertise in the labour movement, studied to become a barrister.

There is a history of trade unionism in New South Wales reaching back to at least the 1830s, with many ideas and experiences arriving from England among convicts transported for defying existing anti-union laws and immigrants with experience of campaigns for workers' rights. In the early years, skilled tradesmen formed themselves into unions to protect their qualifications and rates of pay. On 25 May 1871, delegates from six of about fifteen trade unions then known to exist in Sydney met to form a Trades and Labor Council (TLC).[2] Their chief interest lay in establishing a common policy on working hours, and the eight-hour day, which had already been achieved in some trades, became a goal in many others. But in November 1889 P. J. Brennan moved that the NSW TLC consider the advisability of drawing up a platform and seeking labour candidates for the next election.

By this time rural workers were being organised. So were unskilled urban workers. A great deal of the work available was seasonal (e.g. shearing), casual (e.g. on the wharves or on building sites) or intermittent (e.g. public works like road making or railway building) where labour was required in different places at different times. Organising these seasonal or casual labourers into a union such as the Australian Workers' Union (AWU), to improve their conditions of pay and employment, also proved to be an efficient way of matching the men available to the work to be done. So the appeal of the early unskilled unions was akin to that of a friendly society or a lodge in which membership brought offers of work, preference in employment, and some protection in regard to working conditions and wages. Indeed the Trade Union Act of 1881 required unions to be registered by the Registrar of Friendly Societies. By 1890 there were ninety-five registered unions.³ Employers were not unaware of the usefulness of unions in delivering labour, but before long it became clear that by insisting on preference for their members, the unions could also exercise considerable power over employment. The insistence of unions that their members alone be employed, and only on union terms, in a market where the numbers looking for work were rising daily, lay behind most of the industrial unrest of the early 1890s.

To avoid the high pay rates demanded by the union, the coastal shipping trade hired coloured seamen who were excluded from membership. Anger spread like wildfire through the whole union movement in 1890. In Sydney, the unemployed, accustomed to wait each day near the statue of Queen Victoria for employers to hire them, staged a Great Labour Demonstration on 30 August. A few weeks later it was necessary to read the riot act to a crowd at Circular Quay. The Eight Hours Demonstration on 6 October turned nasty. Further strikes followed.

New South Wales Premier Henry Parkes responded typically by setting up a committee of seventeen experts including six capitalists, nine workers and two academic types under the chairmanship of Andrew Garran, a former editor of the *Sydney Morning Herald* (*SMH*), to inquire into the causes of strikes and suggest possible solutions. They scoured the world for ideas and information and produced a 300-page report, complete with a massive bibliography of the available literature on the subject. The report recommended the establishment of an arbitration system whereby disputes between employers and employees could be handled in a judicial manner. After much trial and error, drawing on Victoria's experience as well, systems were eventually established to regulate wages, working conditions and disputes. Parkes' underlying concern had been that if industrial unrest became endemic, investment would be driven away from labour-intensive areas of the economy, or that there would be even more determined attempts to find docile, and cheaper labour, probably coloured, like the Pacific Islanders employed in the Queensland sugar industry.

Significantly in the light of economic uncertainty and industrial unrest, payment for members of parliament was introduced in New

South Wales in 1890. One of the demands of the English Chartists in 1848, and adopted in Victoria in 1871, it was resisted by NSW MPs until 1890 on the grounds that their independence would be compromised if they were paid. But MPs were regularly compromised when they sought out the paid positions as speaker or as cabinet ministers, or were bankrolled by wealthy friends and supporters. In 1874, in New South Wales a trade union official, Angus Cameron, was elected as a member for West Sydney and paid a weekly retainer by the Trades and Labor Council. Once it became feasible for working men without other sources of income to stand as candidates for election to parliament,[4] their keenness was an attractive alternative to voters. About half the seats won by the Labor candidates in New South Wales in 1891 were outside Sydney, in the major mining centres of Newcastle and Broken Hill, among struggling farmers, railwaymen, semi-employed country town and rural workers and through the spreading influence of the AWU. However, the novelty value of the new party soon faded in its inability to produce quick results and its wrangling over solidarity issues. In country areas too, candidates for the Farmers and Settlers Association, formed in 1873, subsumed into the Country Party by 1922, began to attract the non-unionised rural vote.

As the Labor Party tried to consolidate its initial wins, there were many arguments about both policy and machinery. The movement as a whole was driven by ideas, probably related to the extension of compulsory education since the 1870s. The curious and combative souls who gathered in places like Macnamara's bookshop, and at innumerable meetings, in the Domain, on street corners, in public halls or below hotel balconies spread their 'gospel of discontent' and were always debating and reading. By 1900 the Labor Party had modified its rules to make it a more effective voting force both within parliament and without (devising the pledge, the caucus, and the systematic involvement of party members in constructing the platform through the annual conference). Electors' rights, the precursor of absentee voting, enabled itinerant workers to vote. The party's more radical socialist elements were submerged, and its platform diversified to include policies aimed at attracting white-collar workers and women. Teachers unionised in 1898 and shop assistants in 1902.

To encourage the newly enfranchised wives and daughters of workingmen to make use of their votes, women members of the Labor Party including Mrs Kate Dwyer and her sisters Annie and Belle Golding, formerly active in the suffrage movement, formed a Labor Women's Organizing Committee. Daughters of an Irish Catholic miner from Tambaroora and a Scottish mother, the Golding sisters escaped lives of rural poverty or domestic service by becoming pupil teachers, and active in teachers' associations. Belle, the youngest, in 1899 became the first woman industrial inspector in New South Wales. For a time it was not clear whether women would vote on issues or along party lines. The Women's Liberal League established in 1902 by Hilma Ekenberg, a Swedish nurse, who arrived in Sydney in the 1880s, known after her marriage as Mrs Molyneux Parkes, maintained a prickly relationship with Joseph Carruthers' Liberal Party, though they could agree on issues like temperance.

The collapse of Barings Bank in 1890 in London had sent waves through the Australian colonies, exposing the extent of bank lending for overpriced real estate as well as financial mismanagement during the prosperous years. A sense of apocalypse gripped Victoria as banks and building societies there began to close. In contrast, the threat of bank closures in New South Wales in 1893 was averted by the decisive intervention of premier George Dibbs. In order to avert public panic, Dibbs appeared at the doors of the Savings Bank of New South Wales and wrote in his own hand a proclamation guaranteeing its deposits.

Born in Sydney in 1834, Dibbs was another example of a native-born son, tall with a commanding presence. His father seems to have disappeared while he and his two brothers were still young, leaving his mother to do the best she could for her boys. With his brother, John, Dibbs set up an importing and agency business leading them to think that a branch in Valparaiso would be a good idea. So in 1865, Dibbs and his new wife sailed for South America. The company failed but Dibbs acquired considerable experience of the world beyond New South Wales and the brothers eventually traded themselves out of bankruptcy repaying their creditors. As shipping owners and importers, the Dibbs brothers had plenty of experience of labour relations, especially on the waterfront. Believing that better institutions were needed for labour and capital to work together, he founded a government Labour Bureau in 1892 to supplement private employment agencies that were only interested in the most lucrative work and charged prospective employees exorbitant fees for poor service. But he did not approve of fixed wages, condemned strikes and demonstrations by the unemployed, and as early as 1882 had advocated establishing a court of arbitration for labour disputes. Like many of his contemporaries whose first loyalty was to the land in which they were born, he also came to advocate the protection of local industry and employment by the judicious use of tariffs. His approach to problems was active and courageous rather than cool and disciplined. When his brother's marriage failed, Dibbs chose to go to gaol himself rather than pay a fine, which he thought unfair, for his outspoken comments on a lawyer who was co-respondent in the case and who successfully prosecuted Dibbs for slander. The year in gaol was in fact fairly comfortable and useful for reading and thinking. Nor did it affect the political career on which he had already embarked. The temperament he displayed in his business dealings showed also in politics. He had supported Dalley's despatch of the Sudan contingent and, like Dalley, was, according to fellow politician and lawyer, B. R. Wise, one of the 'younger men of Australian birth, for whom the word "unconstitutional" possessed no terror'.

During the financial crisis, Dibbs may have consulted another brother, Thomas, a long-term employee of the Commercial Banking Company of Sydney, though the brothers were not on good terms and had little in common. Thomas Dibbs (later Sir Thomas for his services to banking) was the soul of careful propriety. More likely, George, the experienced businessman and sometime bankrupt, had already decided that bank notes should be the first charge on the assets of the banks issuing them. He quickly had legislation to this effect in place giving both the banks and the public reassurance to ride out the panic.[5]

Though bank collapses were averted in New South Wales, economic depression was widespread and made worse as the drought showed no signs of easing until about 1902. Businesses and industries faltered during the 1890s and many jobs were lost. Despite the theory of free trade, production of bulky goods in New South Wales was protected by the ready availability of cheap raw materials and the realities of distance rather than artificial tariffs. Bricks and paving tiles, sanitary ware and drainage pipes, corrugated iron and fencing wire were manufactured in conjunction with cheap coal. In Lithgow, potteries associated with the brickworks produced jam jars for Lackersteen and Co., as well as chimneypots, teapots and flowerpots, butter coolers, jugs and shaving mugs, while Sydney factories made cardboard and wooden boxes for packaging.[6]

Tightening economic conditions meant that pressure was placed on workers to produce more for less while at the same time there was a decreased ability in the community to spend. Factories producing food, drink and textiles fared better, but somewhat to the dismay of the authorities, they also tended to employ a higher proportion of women, and were therefore not so well regarded. Women were more easily exploited and less easily organised than men, and health and safety issues were a greater cause for concern. A tendency to neglect safety to raise productivity and rates of pay could have disastrous consequences. In 1887 an explosion at the Bulli Colliery had killed eighty-one miners. Though steps were taken to guard against such explosions, the miners continued to take risks in order to earn more. In 1902 an explosion at Mt Kembla claimed the lives of ninety-six, still the highest number of deaths in a peacetime accident in Australia.

Debates about federation during the 1890s became a welcome distraction from the ailing economy, the drought, and the noisy demands of labour. A draft federal constitution drawn up in 1891 was seen as unfavourable to NSW's economic interests. It appeared that New South Wales could lose control of some of its valuable natural or laboriously constructed resources like coal or railways while at the same time having to support or subsidise the smaller and weaker colonies. The other colonies, Victoria in particular, were keen to create a common market in Australia, especially in the face of the financial crisis and collapsing banks, the increasing cost and competition involved in borrowing money in London, and the sheer stupidity of intercolonial customs barriers. But NSW's resources were huge, their possibilities more varied and therefore less exposed to risk, and their management possibly more hard-headed than in some of the other colonies. Dibbs had dealt decisively with the financial crisis of 1893. His successor, George Reid, was no less realistic. Though Dibbs supported protection and Reid free trade, for both it was the confidence of investors and the efficiency of labour that mattered. However, raising the revenue needed to fund the growing business of government was becoming harder. Traditional sources, the sale and lease of crown lands and government borrowing, were slowing and likely to diminish further. Closer settlement, seen especially by Labor as a solution to unemployment, was also a way of raising additional revenue from land sales and tax.

Reid succeeded Dibbs as premier in 1894, remained in power until 1899, and thus was responsible for guiding New South Wales during the move towards federation. No one could have described Reid as handsome. A *Bulletin* caricature of a capitalist, he was huge, pear-shaped, with a walrus moustache and a great fondness for ice-cream, yet his voice was squeaky, high-pitched, almost comical. More importantly, he was shrewd, skilful, and subtle, incapable of hard feelings or holding grudges against his opponents. Reid enjoyed politics as others enjoyed sport, playing hard for the fun of it. A former public servant without illusions, he embarked on a review of efficiency in government expenditure, setting up a royal commission in 1895 to examine complaints about levels of waste and the patronage system dating from Cowper's time. Fellow public servant T. A. Coghlan helped draft a new Public Service Act establishing a Public Service Board of three full-time members to oversee appointments, promotions, and management practices. Working in conjunction with the treasury, the board accrued power over the years and became, in the words of R. S. Parker, 'long the most powerful and probably effective body of its kind in Australia',[7] until in 1979 in an attempt to impose his own influence on the government of New South Wales, Neville Wran abolished it. Reid brought a new kind of stability to New South Wales by persuading the Labor members who held the balance of power (and were unenthusiastic about the prospect of federation) that he had a more realistic approach to economic management than the Protectionists who were more naturally their allies (but who also supported federation). He also understood that whereas with its exports of wool, coal and other minerals, New South Wales might survive without federation, federation was improbable without New South Wales. So he could afford to drive a hard bargain with the other colonies.

It was also true that economic circumstances were forcing higher levels of protection on New South Wales. Although he continued to maintain free trade in principle, Reid reassessed the tariff schedules so that a new range of goods was added to those on which duties were imposed. By maintaining 'a free breakfast table' – no tariffs on basic foodstuffs – he hoped to retain the support of the Labor members. They, unhappily, were torn between the cheap goods promised by free trade and the employment offered by protection. Additional funding for government came from the imposition in 1895 of the first direct taxes on land and income. In the closing years of the nineteenth century, licence fees, income tax, and stamp duties joined land, customs and excise as major sources of revenue. The loss of customs and excise to the Commonwealth after 1901 placed a greater emphasis on income tax. Such financial arrangements, possible because of the underlying strength of NSW's exports of wool, coal, and other minerals, were not feasible in the less well-endowed colonies.

Among the causes for concern about the terms of federation was the sugar industry in the northern rivers district, flourishing mostly without the use of coloured labour. By demanding an end to Pacific Island labour and a white Australia as a condition for federation, New South Wales hoped to undermine Queensland's potential price advantage through using coloured labour to grow sugar. Another condition for federation was an agreement that if Sydney could not have its historic rights as the first city of Australia acknowledged, a national capital would be established in New South Wales, though at least 100 miles (some 160 km) from Sydney.

Sugar and dairying were flourishing in the northern rivers by the 1890s, where they also escaped the worst effects of the drought. Sugar canes were brought to New South Wales from the Cape of Good Hope in 1788 with the first fleet, grown experimentally at Farm Cove, and from 1821 in the gardens of the convict settlement at Port Macquarie under the superintendence of Commandant Francis Allman. Allman appointed a negro convict from the West Indies named James Williams to take care of sugar cultivation. In 1823, Thomas Alison Scott who had some experience of sugar in Antigua arrived in Port Macquarie and became superintendent of the apparently thriving sugar plantations. Though some sugar of inferior quality was produced for sale in Sydney in the 1820s, the Port Macquarie experiments were discontinued. In part, the problem was frost to which sugar is very susceptible, but technical knowledge and skill in the best ways of extracting sugar from the cane were lacking. It was not until the 1860s that interest in the possibilities of producing sugar on the NSW coast revived and small farms with primitive mills began to appear along the Hastings River. Richard Meares is credited with first manufacturing sugar on a commercial scale from cane grown on the Hastings in 1868, and though there were many growers with a few acres of sugar alongside maize and bananas, milling the cane was both laborious and wasteful.

Once it is cut, sugar cane deteriorates quickly so it is vital to crush it and extract the sugar as soon as possible. Small mills were therefore built on the farms to retain the close connection between harvesting and crushing. However, the technology for producing sugar from the crushed juice is complicated and expensive. The Colonial Sugar Refining Company, formed in Sydney in 1855 to refine imported raw sugar, decided to become involved in sugar production in northern New South Wales by establishing central mills and contracting small growers within a viable radius (about 30 kilometres) to produce cane. Largely as a result of the energy and scientific imagination of the young E. W. Knox, three CSR mills began operation in 1870, at Southgate and Chatsworth on the Clarence, and Darkwater on the Macleay. The Macleay proved too susceptible to frost for continuous sugar production, so Darkwater Mill was relocated to Harwood Island in the Clarence. Southgate was closed after the 1879 crush and its machinery transferred to the Johnstone River in north Queensland, but CSR's Condong Mill on the Tweed began crushing in 1880 and its Broadwater Mill on the Richmond the year after. In 1884 there were eighty-four mills altogether on the banks of the Tweed, Richmond and Clarence, but the smaller mills were closing.[8] By 1887 when Chatsworth was dismantled and its machinery used to extend the operations at Harwood, the CSR with a large mill on each of the three most northerly rivers virtually controlled sugar production in New South Wales.

Knox and the technical staff he employed understood the immense importance of working with the farmers who supplied the mill. If the cane was not properly grown, cut and carried quickly to the

5.1 A contemporary engraving of the sugar industry,
Richmond River, showing the sugar mill at Broadwater, a
barge bringing down the cane, cutting and carrying the cane,
and a vacuum pan to produce crystalline sugar. (Prepared for
Andrew Garran, ed., *Picturesque Atlas of Australasia*,
Picturesque Atlas Publishing Co., Sydney, 1886–88, p. 116)

mill (much of it ferried by barge along the rivers), production suffered in both quantity and quality. So it was important that the
farmers be helped if necessary with credit to buy equipment or to
extend the area they had under cultivation. Along with continual
monitoring to improve the quality and quantity of sugar extracted,
experiments were conducted to improve the quality of the cane,
and seedlings of new higher yielding and disease-resistant varieties
were provided to farmers. Prizes were offered in conjunction with
field trials of new cane varieties. There may have been an unequal,
even an authoritarian relationship between CSR and the farmers,
for without the mills the farmers had no way of disposing of their
cane, but without the farmers, the mills equally had nothing to do.
Through the late nineteenth century, Knox fought to protect the
interests of his farmers, including protection of NSW-grown sugar
against cheap German beet-sugar, despite official free trade policies.
CSR resolutely refused to permit the use of cheap Kanaka labour on
farms supplying its mills. It boasted that its sugar was grown and
harvested by white workers paid proper wages. There were some
Pacific Island labourers in the northern rivers, mostly time-expired
men from Queensland who had chosen to come south rather than
return to their island homes, partly because working in New South
Wales they could demand the same rates as white labour.

This carefully constructed equilibrium in the NSW sugar industry
would probably have been destroyed if exposed to outright competition with the more ruthless and exploitative Queensland industry.
Without sugar, the prosperous farms, sugar mills and shipping facilities of northern New South Wales were likely to revert to their earlier
poverty when maize and cedar, now difficult to find, were the only
products. So New South Wales placed pressure on Queensland to
adopt a system of central mills, and to phase out cheap coloured
labour as conditions of federation.[9]

The dairy industry, begun in the Illawarra and the Shoalhaven by
Irish and Scots immigrants and expanded to the northern rivers in
the late nineteenth century, was also more aware of the value of scientific research and management. Like the sugar mills, co-operative
butter factories effectively supervised and educated farmers to provide higher yielding milk and butterfat. At agricultural shows too,
prizes were subsidised by the Department of Mines and Agriculture

under the influence of the chief inspector of agriculture, W. S. Campbell. Dairy herds were improved by leasing purebred imported bulls to farmers. Especially in areas still too remote to produce fresh milk for the Sydney market, butter production rose impressively. Average consumption in New South Wales reached half a pound of butter per person per week. By 1912 the North Coast Co-operative Company at Byron Bay was the largest dairy co-op in New South Wales, much of its butter going for export.

The co-operative approach to scientific management so effective in the sugar and dairy industries in northern New South Wales came to seem more significant as drought continued. Before the 1890s, record numbers of sheep in far western New South Wales were causing loss of vegetation and soil erosion. The drought exacerbated these problems as did subsequent rabbit plagues. In agricultural areas closer to the coast concern was voiced about the quality of farming methods. In 1888 Campbell, who began as a draftsman in the surveyor general's branch of the Lands Department and rose to become chief inspector of agriculture, had reported, 'the greater part of the farming is carried out in an extremely rough, primitive and slovenly manner without method or the remotest attention to economy'.[10] As early as 1874 the need for an institution to teach better farming methods and to undertake research into ways of improving crops, introducing new varieties, and applying more appropriate forms of land management had been expressed. With the encouragement of his departmental head, H. C. L. Anderson, another early graduate of the University of Sydney who after 1893 brilliantly re-invented himself as state librarian, Campbell located a site, and teaching began in temporary premises in Richmond in 1891. In 1893 Hawkesbury Agricultural College moved into its permanent buildings. A little later chairs of agriculture and veterinary science were established at the University of Sydney.

Elsewhere in New South Wales under Campbell's guidance, two horse studs, six experimental farms, and a model vineyard were established. In 1898 he persuaded his former Lands Department colleague, William Farrer (1845–1906), to join the Agriculture Department on a salary of £350 as wheat experimentalist. With F. B. Guthrie, a chemist in Campbell's department and an expert on wheat flour, Farrer had been conducting experiments on wheat varieties at Lambrigg on the Murrumbidgee. Farrer-bred wheats suitable for different areas and purposes helped multiply by four the area sown with wheat in New South Wales between 1897 and 1915, but it was the variety called 'Federation', released in 1902, that caught the imagination. A 'strong' wheat maturing early and thus avoiding rust, it was also prolific, suited to existing harvesting methods, with good milling and baking qualities.[11] The area under wheat grew from 333,233 acres (nearly 134,900 ha) in 1890 to over 2 million (more than 810,000 ha) by 1915, so there was much emphasis also on clearing new ground and educating new farmers. Experimental plots were established in different parts of the state to work out optimum conditions for cultivation and the varieties best suited to each district. It was found that the soils of the south and west responded more to the application of super-phosphate than those of the north. It was believed that wheat could be grown with barely 20 inches (50.8 cm) of rainfall annually, that is, as far west as Nyngan, if care was taken to plough and conserve rainfall from one year to the next. The major drawback to expansion seemed distance from a railway siding. Farms more than 18 or 20 miles (about 30 km) from transport were not profitable, so there was pressure to extend the railway system as a way of opening more land for wheat. In 1899 a government-sponsored Advances to Settlers Board was established to assist farmers in cases where banks were reluctant to lend – a result of their bitter experience of the land boom a decade earlier. In 1907 the Advances to Settlers Board became the Advances Department of the NSW Government Savings Bank. In 1914 the bank began offering loans for the purchase of small suburban homes as well, thus opening the possibility of home ownership for an even larger number of the NSW population.

In 1884, during an earlier drought, a royal commission on water conservation chaired by Sir William Lyne explored fully the limits to expansion, especially west of the ranges, with existing water supplies. Hugh Griffin McKinney, formerly an engineer attached to the Indian Irrigation Department who had visited New South Wales on furlough in 1876 and who was now in charge of Sydney's water supply, was appointed to the commission sitting from 1885 to 1887. In conjunction with Robert Gibson, a stock and commission agent from Hay, he devised a plan for irrigating land west of Narrandera – country which he thought resembled the irrigated Punjab – from the

Murrumbidgee. On the Darling too, there was talk of the possibility both of regulating the river flow for the benefit of the paddle steamers and also extending natural reservoirs like the Menindee Lakes for irrigation (though a note of alarm was quickly raised in South Australia). One of the more pressing matters discussed in connection with federation became the arterial connection of four colonies through the Murray–Darling river system, with New South Wales the heartland.

By 1906 the passion of Samuel McCaughey, pastoralist, MP, and entrepreneur from Yanco, for irrigation had persuaded Premier Carruthers to act. A dam would be built across the Murrumbidgee at a place known to the Aborigines as 'Boorin-yiak' (precipitous mountain) and translated locally as Barren Jack, with a moveable weir above Narrandera and diversion channels to Gunbar and Hay. Work began in 1907, and the first water became available in 1912. The dam now known as Burrinjuck, designed to store 771,641 acre feet (95,180 hectare metres) of water, and claimed to be the second largest water storage in the world – only Aswan on the Nile was larger – was not completed until 1928, but plans for irrigation settlements at Leeton, Yanco and Mirrool under the direction of L. A. B. Wade the commissioner for water conservation and irrigation (and brother of the then premier Sir Charles Wade) were well underway before the war till his death in 1915 slowed development.[12] A vast, if somewhat naïve, undertaking, the Murrumbidgee Irrigation Area became 'a new province' for public administration, though it was also a 'sink for public money'. Engineering dams, weirs and irrigation canals, however, was simple in comparison to making the settlement work. Pastoral leases were resumed, subdivided into irrigated farms, and made available on perpetual lease. There was government assistance with clearing, fencing, housing, the purchase of seed stock and dairy cattle. Administrative offices, a hospital, and a butter factory were established as the core of a new town called Leeton (after C. A. Lee, the minister for works), and a number of settlers began work, many of them living on their blocks in tents. Architect Walter Burley Griffin was commissioned to draw up plans for Leeton and another irrigation settlement a few miles away, to be called Griffith (after Lee's successor, Arthur Griffith). Thus drought, dreams of closer settlement, and engineering technology came together to change the face of central New South Wales. The

5.2 Burrinjuck Gorge, site of the great Burrinjuck Dam.
(H.M. Maitland, *New South Wales, 1920–1923*, John Sands,
Sydney, 1923, p. 126)

pattern was repeated with the Keepit Dam on the Namoi River in
the 1930s, extended with the Snowy scheme in the 1940s, until a
dam combined with irrigation and hydro-electricity was envisaged
for practically every river in New South Wales.

The inauguration ceremonies for federation on 1 January 1901 were
held in Parkes' Centennial Park. In Muswellbrook, a monument
was raised in the main street, and outside Byron Bay, a small village
renamed itself Federal to mark the event. The NSW turnout for the
first federal election in 1901 was higher than in any of the other
states, and the number of NSW candidates standing for election,
especially for the upper house, was high as well.[13] Many leading
politicians – Barton, Reid, Lyne, Hughes, Watson – were lost to the
federal government, perhaps creating more room in state politics for
the new talent rising through the Labor Party. Since then, state politicians have moved occasionally into the federal parliament, but rarely
with great success. Perhaps experience of the bearpit of Macquarie

Street makes it difficult to adapt at the federal level, or habits learned in New South Wales are not suited to the national scene. Of former premiers who have aspired to national politics – they include Jack Lang and John Fahey – only Reid has succeeded as prime minister.

As an incentive for New South Wales to join the federation, the 1899 Premiers' Conference had proposed that a new federal capital be established in New South Wales, but in its own territory of not less than 100 square miles (259 square kilometres, later enlarged by nine times possibly to provide an adequate water catchment) and at least 100 miles (161 kilometres) from Sydney. At least forty towns offered themselves as possible sites including Bathurst, Orange, Armidale and Albury. Dalgety, Bombala and Tumut were all highly regarded and Dalgety was actually chosen in 1904 but problems arose, according to legend because it was so cold when the Commonwealth commissioners visited during winter. In fact the Commonwealth asked for too much land, and Dalgety was so inaccessible. The people of New South Wales watched anxiously as an ever-lengthening list of government departments and activities was located in Melbourne, and became increasingly impatient (and suspicious) about the delay in choosing a capital site. Not least among the difficulties of NSW politicians was the overnight journey to Melbourne when parliament was sitting. Worse was that while they were in Melbourne at sittings of parliament, NSW politicians were unable to attend to their businesses, their families, or their constituents. Until July 1907 there was no telephone link between Sydney and Melbourne. For lawyers like Barton and Reid, long absences involved a substantial financial sacrifice. The salaries they earned as MPs were small in comparison with what they normally earned from the law. Deakin could stroll from his home to Parliament House in Melbourne and fit in a good day's paid work as well. Discouraged by the difficulties, Barton left federal politics for the High Court; Reid opted for the High Commission in London.

At last in 1908 from a short list including Tumut and Dalgety, a decision was made for Yass–Canberra. The transfer, made on 1 January 1911, included 5 square kilometres at Jervis Bay (increased in 1915 to 72.5 sq km) to provide a federal port. Though machinery was established to design and build the federal capital, progress was

slow and parliament continued to meet in Melbourne. The governor-
general was expected to divide his time between two official residences, one in Melbourne when parliament was sitting, the other
in Sydney where prior to federation, Government House had been
offered in the hope of maintaining a NSW presence. (Robert Towns'
mansion Cranbrook was purchased for the use of the governor of
New South Wales.) But it became increasingly expensive and irritating to maintain Sydney's little-used Government House, and in 1912
after protracted negotiations between the NSW Labor government
and the Commonwealth broke down, the vice-regal Denmans were
effectively evicted. Plans to throw the grounds open to the public and
convert the buildings for cultural uses were stalled by a legal challenge, though the old stables did become home to a conservatorium
of music. In 1915 when the Privy Council found that the NSW government could do whatever it liked with its own government house,
the NSW governor, Sir Gerald Strickland, moved from Cranbrook
back into Government House. Eighty-five years later Labor's 1915
plan to convert Government House into a cultural centre was
carried through by Bob Carr's government, though not without
protests once more from the traditionalists.[14] However, New South
Wales has since gained greatly from the distinguished citizens who
have been more willing to undertake the duties of governor freed
of the constraint of having to live in a rather forbidding official
residence. Lawyer Gordon Samuels and paediatrician Marie Bashir,
with their equally distinguished spouses, have shown by impressive
example the possibilities of a more relaxed, less expensive and
informal style of democracy.

Because the first federal parliament was located in Melbourne
after 1901, the impression of a kind of Victorian imperialism persisted. Certainly the influence of Melbourne in Australian federal
politics lingered well after the move to Canberra in 1927 placed
all politicians on an equally difficult footing regarding access. It is
only in the last few decades that the road between Sydney and Canberra has been improved enough to make the federal capital more
accessible from the north than the south. Now as John Hirst has
noted, Canberra is close to becoming a suburb of Sydney, a possibility made quite plain in 1996 by John Howard's decision to live
in the official prime minister's residence at Kirribilli rather than the
Lodge in Canberra.[15]

5.3 Governor-general's residence, Sydney, in 1907 (*The Cyclopedia of New South Wales Illustrated. Under the Patronage of Vice-Royalty, the Government of New South Wales and the Lord Mayor of Sydney. An Historical and Commercial Review. Descriptive and Biographical, Facts, Figures and Illustrations. An Epitome of Progress*, McCarron, Stewart & Co., Printers, Sydney, 1907, p. 109)

New South Wales not only gave up the land for the Federal Capital Territory. When the federal government assumed responsibility for defence, posts and telegraphs, customs and quarantine, several choice harbour sites became effectively Commonwealth property – Georges Heights, Watsons Bay, Garden Island and the Quarantine Station at North Head. New South Wales also handed responsibility for Norfolk Island and its adjacent islets to the Commonwealth in 1913. A resident administrator was appointed. After 125 years (with the odd gaps), New South Wales was finally free of responsibility for its oldest off-shore settlement. Only Lord Howe Island, discovered by the expedition to found a settlement on Norfolk Island on 17 February 1788, and part of the same volcanic chain, remained a territory of New South Wales. It had an intermittent history of settlement, as a whaling supply station and then in connection with the export of Kentia (howea) palms and their seeds – an industry which thrived during the world-wide craze for indoor palms and ferns lasting from the late nineteenth century until about World War I and one of NSW's more unusual exports. After World War II it became a tourist resort serviced mainly by air.

Luckily for New South Wales, in 1901, Joseph Hector Carruthers (1856–1932) had recently remarried and preferred his new young family in Sydney to federal politics in Melbourne. Nor could he afford to be away from his law practice. In the absence of other talent he was able to liberalise the old free trade party. In a brief term as premier between 1904 and 1907, he completed the reform agenda devised in the 1890s between Reid and the labour movement. Born in Kiama, he was educated at the University of Sydney and trained as a lawyer. As minister responsible for education in 1890 he had time to talk to the young Ethel Turner, future author of *Seven Little Australians*, about an article for her schoolgirl magazine *Parthenon* though he was re-organising technical education and teacher training, and supporting the establishment of a women's college at the university. In 1896, he was a guest at Ethel's wedding to future judge Herbert Curlewis. An enthusiast for closer settlement, as Reid's minister for lands he steered vital legislation for the expansion of agriculture through in 1895. After he became premier in 1904 he encouraged further changes to the education system, reforms to local government, some of which lasted well into the twentieth century, and also the creation of the Government Savings Bank. His vision secured David Scott Mitchell's magnificent collection of Australiana for the state, enabling construction of W. L. Vernon's Mitchell Library building adjacent to Parliament House to commence.

Frequently criticised by conservatives for what appeared to be labour views, he was in fact dedicated to free enterprise. He had been dubious about women's suffrage. Yet because of his interest in education he could not avoid the feminism of the liberal intelligentsia. As socialist ideas had driven the labour movement, feminism lay behind much of the liberal reform of this period.[16] And whereas the socialists gathered in bookshops and on street corners, feminism flourished in elegant drawing rooms where university professors like Mungo MacCallum and Francis Anderson and their wives were active in every kind of social reform from votes for women to sex education, from higher education to free kindergartens. Like many women who came to feminism through the need to earn a respectable living, Maybanke Anderson had been a teacher. When her first marriage ended through her husband's alcoholism, she worked for the adoption of divorce laws rather than temperance. Her children were supported through her teaching – her students were among the first girls to matriculate in New South Wales – while her brother, engineer Norman Selfe, worked with Carruthers on technical education. Maybanke's contribution to the campaign for votes for women, which she believed to be essential if women's concerns were to be taken seriously, was *The Woman's Voice*, a more intellectually ambitious newspaper than Louisa Lawson's *The Dawn*, closer to the liberal feminism of her friend Rose Scott. William Curnow, editor of the *Sydney Morning Herald*, and his wife, Henry Gullett, editor of the *Daily Telegraph*, and his wife, and Edward Dowling who masterminded the campaign for federation for Edmund Barton, were good friends, equally devoted to feminism and liberal reform.

Writing in 1984 about the differences between Victoria and New South Wales, Geoffrey Blainey suggested that a significant difference was the Victorian inheritance of individualism and self-help from the gold rush immigrants and their descendants. Basically protestant, hard-headed and hard-working, it was transmuted into late nineteenth-century colonial liberalism and later into the kind of liberalism which dominated Australian politics for about three-quarters of the twentieth century. Blainey suggested that for a long time one of the strengths of that liberalism was that it actually took cognisance of the power and influence of women. Both the Woman's Christian Temperance Union and the Australian Women's National League 'were powerful in Melbourne's eastern suburbs which were the heart of the Liberal Party'.[17] By comparison he thought New South Wales was profoundly affected both by the shortage of women in the population for at least its first hundred years and also by the aggressive and brash masculine culture and political style this produced.

This is to overlook important alliances shaped by progressive women and men in New South Wales where women were already engaged in the politics of both labour and liberal reform. There may have been an aggressive and brash masculine culture, but it was also for the most part native-born, pragmatic and confident. From this, women were not excluded. NSW liberalism, long overshadowed by its Victorian counterpart, derived something from its free trade origins as well as from the fact that so many of its exponents were second- and third-generation NSW-born. And it was shaped by its interaction with both labour and feminism during the 1890s. These two came together notably in the friendship and political collaboration of Arthur Rae, shearer, unionist and one of the first Labor members of the NSW parliament, and Rose Scott, elegant daughter of an old wealthy Hunter Valley settler family, one of the leaders of the campaign for votes for women in New South Wales. Furthermore, women won the vote in New South Wales before Victoria. Without the strategy devised by Maybanke Anderson for the NSW delegation to the Federal Convention in 1897, women may not have been included as voters under the Australian constitution in 1901 at all. From 1904 on, the knowledge that women would vote had a powerful effect on politics in New South Wales. It helps to explain the interest in social reform and child welfare. It also lay behind the emphasis on temperance and the increasingly shrill sectarianism that made a mockery of the ideals of both Liberals and Labor.

Sometime between 1881 and 1891 the population of New South Wales reached one million, but the rate of growth, steadily increasing since the gold rushes, began to fall after 1891. By 1903 subsidised immigration was seen as desirable. However, with economic conditions improving after the end of the long drought, both the marriage and birth rates rose, the marriage rate reaching its highest level since the prosperous years of the early 1880s. But fewer babies were being born to women once they reached their thirties, and families were becoming smaller. This was not only because of selfishness and love of pleasure as suggested by the royal commission set up in 1903 under the chairmanship of Dr C. K. Mackellar (father of Dorothea, author of 'My Country') to inquire into the declining birthrate.[18] Marriages were postponed or avoided because of the drought and the depressed economic conditions, reducing opportunities for child-bearing and lowering the birthrate. As well, the number of unmarried women in need of paid work had risen. Education and the increasing availability of contraceptive knowledge also made it feasible for a family's size to be limited, thus maximising economic opportunities. From 1903, immediately after the registration of a birth, 'instructional circulars and pamphlets for the guidance of mothers regarding the care and feeding of young children' were sent out. A generation earlier this would have been fairly ineffectual since literacy rates among girls were known to be low, but by the early years of the twentieth century freely available elementary education had reduced the number unable to read to about half a per cent. As well after 1904, 'a trained woman inspector' was authorised to call, especially in the 'thickly populated' parts of Sydney, to observe family circumstances and give advice on infant care.

At the NSW census of 1891 an effort had been made to determine how many Aboriginal people, whether 'full-blood' or 'half-caste', there were. The result was 8,280 (4,559 males, 3,721 females) full bloods and 1,663 male and 1,520 female half castes. After that because of the constraints imposed by the federal constitution, though some statistics were collected, they were partial, especially in relation to Aborigines living 'in the wild'. The drought had a devastating impact on these Aborigines and their food supplies. Yet traditional rations handouts were withheld on the grounds that they could go back to living off the land. At least Aborigines who needed to hunt for their food were exempted from 1903 legislation protecting native animals from slaughter. Tightening union controls in shearing and elsewhere made it harder for them to get casual work as before. Inevitably the population declined. In 1911 there were known to be only 2,021 full blood and 4,512 half caste Aborigines in New South Wales.[19]

The census of 1911 also showed that 45.46 per cent of the population of New South Wales was nominally Church of England. Frederic Barker, Anglican bishop of Sydney (1855–82), had created a moderately evangelical church, adding to its building stock, broadening its membership, and making it feel 'properly Anglican'.[20] He saw the withdrawal of state funding for the churches in 1862 as an incentive for self-reliance and greater involvement through fundraising. His mild evangelicalism during sectarian controversies over education in the 1860s and 1870s had served to distance NSW Anglicans from the English tractarian movement where the conversion of leading Anglicans like John Henry Newman to Roman Catholicism invoked fears among both protestants and Catholics about conversion and kidnapping.

Barker's successors, Alfred Barry (1884–89), William Saumarez Smith (1890–1909) and John Charles Wright (1909–33), found themselves dealing with occasionally hysterical controversies over the introduction of 'ritualism' into the increasingly austere practice of Anglicanism. Moreover Moore College, under the guidance of the Reverend Nathaniel Jones, increasingly trained clergy in the strictest evangelical views, while the harsh conditions of the 1890s were conducive to austerity and suited protestantism in general.[21]

If Presbyterians and Methodists were added to the Anglicans, by 1911, protestants accounted for 73 per cent of the population of New South Wales, a rise of 2 per cent on 1891 figures. Roman Catholics made up 25.54 per cent, half a per cent fewer than at 1901. A mere 2.5 per cent said they had no religion or did not wish to say what it was, but this was the next largest group. Half a per cent said they were Jewish but no other group, Christian or non-Christian, reached even this level. The statistical strength of the protestant churches may partially explain the intensity of the sectarian attack on Catholicism during the first two decades of the twentieth century (and the virulence of the Catholic response during the 1920s), though undoubtedly tighter economic conditions as well as events far from New South Wales played a part.

Along with electoral and constitutional reform, social reform had been part of the platform on which the labour movement had extracted support from the rival political groups of the 1890s. On the liberal side, causes such as the protection of infants and neglected children were promoted to appeal to women voters, while Labor promised maternity allowances and equal pay. With the protestant majority, and especially with women's votes to be won, social reform narrowed to moral reform exhibiting a kind of puritanism – dubbed 'wowserism' by John Norton, owner of the *Truth* newspaper. But Norton was not only hostile to women and satirical about feminism, he was also opposed to moral or social reform.

Despite assertions to the contrary, alcohol consumption in New South Wales was not high in comparison with countries like Germany, France and the United States and had been declining since the 1880s, reaching quite modest levels during the height of the campaign for local option legislation. Those who suffered most from alcohol were probably the Aboriginal people. Even on the Darling where there was still only limited contact, the uses of alcohol were well known. A local option movement had begun in Orange in 1874. It gradually influenced suburban development. At each election after 1904 voters were given the opportunity of choosing whether they wished more or fewer liquor licences granted in their area. In wealthier suburbs, liquor was delivered to the door by the case. Only the workers needed pubs supplying beer by the glass within walking distance. So local option developed a class dimension. A dubious arrangement saw the brewers and hoteliers (many known to be Catholics) providing cars to ferry poorer voters to the polls and helping finance Labor candidates. As cars at that time were a novelty and a luxury, well beyond the reach of working people, they were very popular regardless of class and sectarian implications. Further restrictions from 1906 on gambling strengthened the influence of the wowser element.

Cardinal Moran, leader of the Catholic church in New South Wales from 1885 to his death in 1911, saw the value of temperance and moral reform, but he also understood the importance of the workingman's small pleasures. Like the Anglican Barry, Moran also understood the need to build and maintain his church, its congregations, its schools and its increasing wealth as its adherents became more economically secure. Like Barry, Moran suited New South Wales. Though highly educated and by preference a scholar, he seemed to understand the more ordinary needs and aspirations of his mostly working class flock. He sympathised with trade unionism and sought to exercise a moderating influence on Labor as it grappled with the responsibility of parliamentary representation, urging its leaders to devise a milder practical Australian form of socialism compared with the more revolutionary ideas coming out of Europe.

In response to Moran's leadership, Loyal Orange Lodges (a concept imported from Northern Ireland) and a protestant defence association were formed to oppose every Catholic move. But Moran was aging and losing touch. His private secretary and likely successor, Father O'Haran, was discredited as co-respondent in a dubious divorce case. Finally, in accepting Michael Kelly who was neither clever nor politically astute as O'Haran's replacement,

Moran allowed the leadership of the church in New South Wales to pass into less competent hands, a gift to those who saw Catholics in public life as more threatening than socialists or communists.

In 1901 Francis Anderson, professor of philosophy at the University of Sydney, with his wife Maybanke, prominent in educational circles, attacked the administration of education, unchanged basically since the days of William Wilkins, in a speech to the NSW Teachers' Association. A report with suggestions for improvement, commissioned from G. H. Knibbs, then lecturer in surveying at the university, later NSW statistician, and J. W. Turner, principal at Fort Street Training College, appeared in 1903. Meanwhile, a young school inspector, Peter Board, had taken six months' leave to study education overseas at his own expense. He too produced a short, influential report that led to his appointment in 1905 as director of education. During the next decade or so, Board's ideas as well as the recommendations of the Knibbs–Turner report produced substantial changes enabling an intelligent child to progress from kindergarten to university at virtually no cost to its parents. Where the education was not free, bursaries and scholarships would be available.

In the status-conscious and upwardly mobile society of New South Wales at the time, most parents, especially those who had suffered the disadvantages of illiteracy, were keen for their children to learn to read and write, especially at state expense. Catholic parents were especially torn as they listened to public discussion of educational aims and methods knowing that church schools might be providing invaluable religious training though missing opportunities available in the state system. The fear that Catholic children could be lost to the church if they were educated in state schools was still strong. And since protestants were overrepresented among state schoolteachers, it was likely that a protestant version of respectability was being presented in the classroom.[22] When in 1910 the newly elected McGowen Labor government agreed to let Catholic students compete for, and take up, its newly created bursaries for secondary schooling, but only in state high schools, there was consternation. Only a handful of students were involved but it seemed as if a whole generation of young Catholics was being poached by protestantism.

5.4 'The Minister for Education (Mr Carmichael) explaining to the pupils of a little school in the far west how they may reach the university.' It became government policy in the early years of the twentieth century, through scholarships and bursaries, to create a pathway from primary through secondary school to the university for especially able children. Many of them were destined to return as schoolteachers themselves. (Reproduced from the Department of Public Instruction, *Three Years of Education* (Govt. Printer, Sydney, 1914), in A.R. Crane and W.G. Walker, *Peter Board: His Contribution to the Development of Education in New South Wales*, Australian Council for Educational Research, Melbourne, 1957, facing p. 116)

The worst sectarianism was imported from Ireland. The leader of the extreme protestant faction, W. M. Dill Macky, a pure Orangeman who served briefly as moderator of the Presbyterian Church in New South Wales, had arrived from Northern Ireland in 1886. His opponent, the chief Irish rabble-rouser in New South Wales, Father Maurice O'Reilly, originally from Cork, asserted at a conference on education in 1911, that 'everything that was best and noble in Australia was Irish'.[23] In fact most youthful NSW Catholics thought of themselves as Australian, and were not interested by the old feuds of Britain and Ireland.

In his classic history, *The Making of the English Working Class*, first published in 1963, E. P. Thompson put forward the view that there were many similarities between Methodism and the labour movement. Long before that, the great French commentator, Alexis de Tocqueville, had observed that the tendency of democracy in the United States was to produce a certain kind of levelling conformism as people tried to improve themselves and become more effective members of society. Both could have been describing what had been happening in New South Wales. By the end of the nineteenth century, the efforts of the ordinary working people to better themselves financially and take advantage of opportunities for education were paying off, not only among those who accepted the steady, sober, industrious, god-fearing precepts of Methodism or the other protestant evangelical churches, but also among the majority of the Catholics who were more inclined to steadiness, industriousness, and upward mobility than to the simplicities of piety. They found membership of their union just as beneficial as membership of their church. As the economy began to improve, trade unions, friendly societies, lodges both protestant and Catholic, flourished alongside the churches. By 1912, there were 209 unions in New South Wales with about 200,000 members, 6,455 of whom were women.

Despite the apparent divisions of these decades there was fundamental agreement about a vision of security and respectability, to be achieved through better wages and living standards. Whether inclined to socialism or feminism, all were in search of self-respect and independence through adequate wages for men and access to birth control, higher education and professional employment for women. There was broad agreement, even among freetrading liberals, that the state should intervene to create the conditions necessary for self-realisation whether through employment, arbitration, or local option and temperance.

In every election from 1904, the number of lower house seats held by Labor steadily increased. The number of Catholics among the Labor members also rose. Catholics, both men and women, were being positively encouraged to assert their right to register and vote. Indeed, the Catholic press claimed much of the credit for the election of NSW's first Labor government in 1910 and there was much anticipation of the benefits that must flow as a result, especially state aid to Catholic schools and charities. However, women voters had been seriously courted as well. When they were first able to vote in New South Wales in 1904 66.5 per cent of women did so. The number dropped in 1907 to 60.8 per cent and rose again in 1910 when the first Labor government was elected, to 65.5 per cent. (The figure for men stayed at about 73%.) Labor women believed women had contributed significantly to Labor's success, especially as canvassers and organisers, and had expectations of sympathetic representation and legislation, though they waited many years for the maternity allowance and longer still for equal pay promised in 1904. And while there was considerable interest in the number of Catholics in McGowen's cabinet (there were three, but two of them were far from devoted), there was of course no question of including a woman. Women could vote in New South Wales, but they could not yet nominate for election. One in three of the Labor members was native-born in 1901. By 1910, this figure had risen to one in two.

The electoral success of Labor in 1910 may have been influenced by industrial conditions. Bitter and protracted strikes at Broken Hill (1909–10) and on the Hunter coalfields had once more raised doubts about the cost of strikes to the union movement. Newcastle miners' leader, Peter Bowling, gaoled in 1909 under legislation rushed though parliament while he was on bail for defying the government, featured prominently on posters showing him in prison clothes and leg-irons in the election campaign of 1910. However, the belief that capitalism could be civilised through parliament in the interests of all, men and women, Catholics and protestants, workers and those who provided employment, had also become widespread.

Labor's victory in 1910 was by only one seat. Its legislative programme was hampered from the start by a hostile upper house, and the likelihood of deaths, defections, and by-elections in the lower house. One of the MLAs, J. P. Osborne, a former shop assistant who had been active in bringing his union into the Trades and Labor Council and whose practical skills as a salesman made him one of the best organisers in the party, described the kinds of compromises necessary to get any legislation through at all. 'The power to govern is the essential thing.'[24] Though it was not possible to get ideal legislation in place, much could be achieved by the way that power was administered.

Weary and outclassed, McGowen handed the leadership to his deputy, William Holman, in June 1913. Holman's parents had both been actors, and from his childhood, Holman had been fascinated by the power of words. One of his great strengths was his ability to command an audience. He also understood the need for compromise or diplomacy in government though it is possible that persuasiveness was sometimes substituted for a serious grasp of the problems. At the same time, among the unions there was a clear lack of understanding of the real limitations of government and impatience with the parliamentarians to achieve results. A different kind of sectarianism, the idea of the unions as the only significant force in New South Wales, was emerging.

This, however, was to assume that the people of New South Wales would continue their quiet lives of peaceful co-existence in the modest pursuit of prosperity and security. No one was really calculating on the war about to break out in Europe.

6

1915–1940, division and depression

Since the 1890s, under the management first of William Sandford and then of the Hoskins brothers, the Eskbank Iron Works at Lithgow had been producing steel rails for the NSW government as well as corrugated and galvanised iron for the Australian market. In 1911, Guillaume Delprat, the general manager of Broken Hill Proprietary Co. Ltd (BHP), brought American steel-maker David Baker to Australia to advise on the construction of a new steelworks. Afraid of losing the steelworks to Port Pirie in South Australia, in 1912 McGowen's government agreed that work could begin under Baker's guidance at Waratah near Newcastle on a site hitherto set aside for botanical gardens. When war broke out in Europe in 1914, building was well advanced. The first steel was produced in 1915. The Newcastle steelworks cost about £1.5 million to build. With their ultra-modern design and semi-automated processes they greatly enhanced NSW's reputation for steel-making and were of inestimable industrial significance during the war.[1] David Baker, an admirer of his fellow American efficiency expert, Frederick Winslow Taylor, was keen to produce quality steel of maximum value from minimum labour. As well, the local member, Arthur Griffith, persuaded the government to take advantage of its agreement with BHP to maintain the shipping channel in the river by establishing a state dockyard opposite the steelworks. But the general pursuit of efficiency, typified by BHP, as increasingly the workers of New South Wales were called on not only to volunteer to fight the war but also to produce the wherewithal to sustain the war effort, led to division and bitterness which lasted for a generation.

The war that dominated the years 1914–18 was mostly a matter for the federal government, though in New South Wales, now led by the very able William Holman, there may have been some resentment about the clearly enhanced power of the Commonwealth which for example began to collect taxes for the first time in 1915 (on incomes). Immediate steps were taken to ensure that NSW's less than adequate wheat crop was not sold at profiteering prices. Public service employees who wished to enlist were guaranteed against financial sacrifice and important NSW facilities such as the Randwick Asylum were made available to the federal government for military purposes. Though demands for wholesale dismissal of public servants of German origin were initially resisted, before long legislation was passed disenfranchising all those born in enemy countries. As war conditions began to affect the government's borrowing, the future of its public works programmes became uncertain. Part of the appeal of the Labor government had been its determination to push on with public works ensuring employment on railways, roads and the Murrumbidgee irrigation scheme. Initially there was a fair amount of goodwill and enthusiasm for the war as well.

Recruiting was under the supervision of J. H. Catts, secretary of the Railway and Tramway Union and federal Labor MP for the electorate round the railway workshops at Granville. Catts devised the evocatively named route marches beginning at Gilgandra with the Cooees, but also from Narrabri (Wallabies), Nowra (Waratahs), Wagga (Kangaroos), Delegate (The Men from Snowy River), Coff's Harbour, Parkes and Tooraweenah which brought some 5,000 men to Sydney to enlist.[2] Holman then offered higher pensions. It is difficult to say how many men were recruited in New South Wales altogether because of the way Australia was divided into military districts. The northern rivers were included with Queensland, Broken Hill and the west were counted with South Australia, and the Riverina was incorporated with Victoria. While cynical observers noticed a relationship between levels of unemployment and recruitment, there was also a danger that the wheat harvest could be lost due to a shortage of labour at the crucial time. When the idea of conscription was raised in 1916, there was deep resentment in New South Wales that any government, especially a federal Labor government, would so manipulate the labour market. Catts himself was fiercely opposed and led the anti-conscription campaigns in New South Wales. His argument was that New South Wales was already contributing more men than the federal authorities could handle and that too many men waiting idly in camps for transfer overseas created problems of law and order, as shown by the riots at Liverpool in 1916.

The continuing pressure of the war and especially the two conscription referenda exacerbated existing and potential differences in New South Wales. Holman's insistence on supporting Prime Minister Hughes' call for conscription led to his expulsion along with other pro-conscriptionists from the NSW Labor Party and his formation of a National government for New South Wales in conjunction with George Fuller. Thus Holman confirmed a long-held suspicion that Labor members of parliament could not be trusted with the interests of the people who put them there. Wartime conditions strengthened the industrial unions which preferred direct action anyway, and were not impressed with the limited achievements of the Labor governments already elected in New South Wales.[3] Loyalty was an issue, whether to Australia or Britain, labour or capital. Migrants like Tom Barker (author of the famous Wobbly 'To Arms!!' poster) and the steady flow of ideas from overseas, especially the United States, destabilised the union movement and became a source of suspicion or resentment among deeply nationalistic NSW-born-and-bred union members. (British-born Barker arrived in Sydney in 1914 via Auckland where he had been placed on a bond for sedition. Gaoled for his role in the International Workers of the World (IWW) or Wobblies in 1916, he was deported to Chile in 1918, and in 1959 was Labour mayor of St Pancras, London. His poster which appeared on hoardings all around Sydney in 1915 was addressed to 'Capitalists, Parsons, Politicians, Landlords, Newspaper Editors and other Stay-at-home Patriots. Your country needs you in the trenches!' The workers were advised to 'Follow your masters!!'[4])

Subversive activities advocated by the IWW raised fears that the whole trade union movement had been infected by their 'I won't work' attitudes. Between June and September 1916 at least a dozen shops and factories in Sydney were destroyed or seriously damaged by arson. At the same time a counterfeiting operation was uncovered. The IWW was blamed and twelve of its leaders were gaoled by the Holman government on charges later shown to be dubious, but pursued to discredit the IWW because of the fear that it was a major focus for anti-war sentiment. Employers suspected their workers of deliberate 'go slow' tactics, though the fact that their fittest and most able workers had joined the army was probably the real explanation for loss of productivity. Rejection of conscription (and the vote in New South Wales in 1916 was one of the strongest for 'no') strengthened fears that the ultimate aim of the union movement was the destruction of the social order, church, family, and empire. For their part, the workers suspected employers of selectively sacking men whom they thought should have enlisted, of stockpiling, especially coal, with a view to an eventual lockout, or of using the war as an excuse for profiteering, or to attack the arbitration system and the union movement, or all of the above.

Many of these fears came to a head when men in the Randwick workshops of the Railways and Tramways Department walked off the job on 2 August 1917. Their reason was that job timecards similar to those devised in America by F. W. Taylor to record the time taken by each specific job in the workshop were being introduced at Randwick. Designed to improve efficiency, the cards were seen by the workers as a way of speeding up their work. The strike spread quickly, partly because of a provocative response by Acting Premier George Fuller, and before long all coal handling was declared black, thus affecting a great many industries. The 'great strike' of 1917 eventually involved some 76,000 of the state's workers and lasted eighty-two days. Though it has sometimes been claimed as a general strike, this was not so. Not even the railways where the strike had begun were brought to a total standstill. But more than the defeat of conscription, the 1917 strike in New South Wales was seen as an act of deliberate disloyalty on the part of the NSW working class because ships were prevented from loading supplies essential for the Australian forces fighting in France. It was easy for the government to recruit large numbers of volunteer workers, mostly from country districts (where there was a seasonal shortage of work), to keep things moving. Quartered in camps at the Sydney Cricket Ground (Scabs Camping Ground) and at Taronga Park, and driving a range of commandeered drays and motor lorries, volunteers ferried coal and food supplies.

The original reason for the strike was soon lost in what increasingly became a major confrontation between the government and a recalcitrant working class. Worker solidarity was maintained by defiant daily union processions through the streets of Sydney to meetings, with speeches and family picnics in the Domain. The memory of those daily processions observed from the upper windows of Sydney's establishment clubs, and the experience of organising substitute volunteer labour were to play an important role in the thinking behind both the Old and the New Guard movements more than a decade later when Premier J. T. Lang appeared once more to be inciting revolt among NSW workers.

After weeks and months on strike, the workers began to dribble back to their jobs. The strike may have been an error of judgement by the unions. Certainly it deepened divisions in New South Wales. But behind it lay long-simmering resentment about the way the cost of living had risen during the war while wages had declined. The NSW annual price index had risen by 32.8 per cent since 1914 while the annual real wage index had fallen by 1.75 per cent. That so many workers were willing to join the strike, often on flimsy pretexts, suggests a kind of spontaneous mass protest at what was felt to be the unfair burden they were being forced to carry for a war that apart from its casualty lists was quite remote.[5] And indeed, because of NSW's strong rural exports and significant mining and manufacturing industries, its workers had contributed disproportionately to the war economy. In the aftermath of the 1917 strike, a second vote on conscription was even more substantially rejected in New South Wales.

The employment status of those workers who had been on strike continued as a burning issue well into the 1920s. Labor governments said they should be re-instated; non-Labor governments dismissed them again. One of the leaders of the campaign for re-instatement, an engine driver from Bathurst, name of J. B. Chifley, lost both seniority and pay as a result of the strike. When a High Court decision (in the Engineers' case of 1920) allowed state government employees to be covered by Commonwealth unions, Chifley and his fellow NSW engine drivers seized the opportunity to form and join the Australian Federal Union of Locomotive Enginemen (AFULE) well away from the jurisdiction of New South Wales. Another striking unionist, future NSW premier J. J. Cahill, lost his job at Eveleigh railway workshops in 1917, his file marked 'agitator'. It was 1922 before he was re-instated.

Lingering bitterness produced by the war and the strike helps to explain the ruthless and often punitive nature of NSW's politics during the following decades. Purged of the more moderate and conciliatory Holman supporters, the labour movement became less tolerant, now tinged with a more cynical enmity towards capital. Partly as a result of another long strike at Broken Hill lasting from May 1919 to November 1920, 1919 set a new record for days lost to strikes. For their part, employers influenced perhaps by knowledge of radical and revolutionary movements elsewhere in the world became more ruthless towards their employees.

On 30 October 1920 a small group of men (and three women) gathered at the Australian Socialist Party Hall in Liverpool Street, Sydney. Most were in their thirties. Only about half were Australian-born though all but three were now living in New South Wales. Most had limited formal education though there was a sense of intellectual self-improvement about them. Many had been in trouble with the police and at least half-a-dozen had spent time in gaol. A 'restless, cosmopolitan, resourceful, impatient' group, they were there to form a communist party.[6] Though there had been interest in communism elsewhere in Australia especially since the Russian revolution in 1917, it was probably the effective support provided by Scots-born Jock Garden, a former preacher, now a communist and secretary of the Trades Hall Council, which brought most of these seekers to Sydney. Garden's zealotry and the spectre of Russian communism thereafter added to the edginess of New South Wales. News that Percy Brookfield, a militant unionist and Labor MP for Broken Hill, had died as a result of a shooting spree by a deranged Russian, Koorman Tomayoff, on 22 March 1921 at a railway station somewhere in South Australia suggested an ominous conspiracy.

On May Day 1921, Garden's communist-dominated NSW Trades and Labor Council (TLC) with the sanction of the Storey–Dooley Labor government organised about 400 people to march under the once-banned red flag. The TLC hoped to use a mix of Russian revolutionary ideas and American syndicalist notions to convert New South Wales to 'the socialisation of industry with workers' control',[7] though in fact the existing Labor government was very cautious about communism, and NSW delegates had voted solidly to reject the socialist objective adopted at the Federal Labor Convention in 1921. A battle between the unions and the party branches, the industrial left and the political right, the hard men and the traditional feminists continually threatened the unity of the Labor movement through all these years. The first of many Labor 'machines' set up to maintain solidarity by intimidation came into existence. And though the Communist Party continued to influence union politics in New South Wales, with serious consequences in the 1940s and 1950s, except for those with the need to believe, communism seemed dour, threatening more because it suggested conspiracy than because of the revolution it preached.

The 1917 strike foreshadowed a decline in the power of the railways in New South Wales. For the first time, motor transport was mobilised on a significant scale to substitute for missing freight trains and banned coal. In 1921 there were approximately two motor vehicles (this included cars, lorries and motorcycles) for every hundred people in New South Wales. By 1929 the number had risen to almost ten and motorbuses had begun to supplement trams and trains as public transport in Sydney and Newcastle. The number of motor vehicles declined to eight during the depression but was approaching ten again by 1935. Henceforth, road building and the cost of petrol rather than coal would challenge railway dominance. The condition of country roads, especially, attracted members to the newly formed Country Party. Increasing motor traffic drew attention to the poor quality of what should have been major roads such as that connecting Sydney and Newcastle. Indeed, in 1924 the National Roads and Motorists' Association (NRMA) (founded in 1923 to lobby for

6.1 'Earthworks were a tough physical job for both men and horses during the construction of the Sydney–Newcastle Road' during the 1920s. Bullock teams were used to plough some sections. Spoil was removed by horse-drawn drays, but motor trucks were also used, for example, to spread gravel. (*The Roadmakers: A History of Main Roads in New South Wales*, Department of Main Roads New South Wales, Sydney, 1976, p. 117)

better roads and provide service for members, though there had been an automobile club since 1903) advised members to ship their cars to Newcastle if they wished to drive north. A conference at Gosford on 6 June 1925 attended by Main Roads Board members, representatives of local government, the NRMA, the Post Office, the Tourist Bureau, and the Royal Australian Historical Society, among others, agreed that with a bridge over Sydney Harbour now under construction, it was time to consider the main road to the north. Preparatory work was offered to Hornsby Shire Council as relief for unemployed labourers in the second half of 1925. Eventually about 800 men were given work. They lived in camps in tents about three miles (5 km) apart, working towards each other, using mainly explosives, then picks and shovels, horses and drays. Motor lorries were used to bring in supplies and the water needed both for the men and to mix concrete for the road. Access was a significant problem in rough country. And in summer, bushfires several times destroyed survey pegs marking sections of the route. The road from Hornsby to the Hawkesbury was opened on 2 June 1930 having cost approximately £380,302 or £24,809 per mile (0.609 km). Further north, the section from the river to Gosford was also under construction. Gosford and Newcastle were already connected by a viable road. By 1931 when it was named the Pacific Highway, it was possible, according to the NRMA, to drive from Sydney to Newcastle in $4^{1}/_{4}$ hours maintaining an average of 30 mph (around 50 km per hour) in top gear and allowing time for the ferry crossing the Hawkesbury.[8]

With the war over it emerged that re-integrating thousands of returned servicemen into civil society was a problem of unparalleled dimensions. The returning men were very different from the men who had sailed away to war. They had aged. Because of what they had done and seen, they were more experienced than any of them could have imagined. They also knew they had survived the horrors and privations of war. So many were mature far beyond their years. To self-knowledge was added the discipline learned in the forces and the strength they drew from comrades. Many were impatient to make up for what they felt were the lost years of their youth. They had skills. They had knowledge of the way the world worked, and they were inclined to be severely critical of a society that moved too slowly, systems that were standing in their way. Repatriation was not just a simple matter of returning them to their families and jobs. Of necessity many jobs had disappeared or changed or been taken by others. Women who had moved in as clerical or sales workers were fairly easily ejected because men needed jobs more than women, but it was not so simple to displace other male workers, especially those who though elderly or disabled had filled gaps, who also had wives and children to support. In some cases, competition for jobs was intense. The loyalty of former strikers was impugned, as was the fitness of returning servicemen, physical and psychological.

Obvious cases of physical damage were repaired as well as medicine and the early days of plastic surgery could manage. Various forms of psychological damage were less easily recognised, admitted, or treated. While the burden of providing pensions for disabled ex-servicemen, their dependants, and the widows and children of servicemen who had not returned was assumed by the federal government, New South Wales contributed almost 10 million acres (over 4 million ha) for soldier settlement, mostly in the irrigation areas. Sending ex-servicemen with physical or psychological problems to do battle with the elements that had defeated willing farmers in previous generations was a strange response, though not a surprising one given the belief in farming as a universal panacea. Miners from Broken Hill already dying from dust-induced lung disease were also offered farms in irrigation areas.

There were 65,731 war pensions being paid in New South Wales in 1921, 25,525 to incapacitated servicemen, 26,885 to their dependants, and 13,321 to war widows and orphans. The total value of these pensions was a little over £2 million. By 1932 when the depression was at its worst, the value of war pensions in New South Wales had risen to £2.5 million, a not insignificant sum in people's pockets amid rising unemployment. However, the financial losses incurred as over 9,000 soldier settlers gradually fell away to 6,500 probably more than balanced the repatriation account. Soldier settlers did best when they moved into existing farming areas and where they had some knowledge or experience of farming, as well as support for wives and families. In many ways it was the story of the free selectors all over again. Single men facing tough bush blocks were the most likely to give up and move off. An ex-serviceman chicken farmer struggled gamely at Blacktown in M. Barnard Eldershaw's *Tomorrow and Tomorrow and Tomorrow* till he was beaten by his wife's discontent. And Jill Ker Conway's father lost his life to despair and a faulty pipe in a dam during a drought on Coorain, his block beyond Hillston.[9]

The problems of the soldier settlers came to represent the problems of returned men generally. The war had been the greatest emotional experience of their lives and many missed the rugged masculine environment and the easy camaraderie of life in the services. They sought to retain this comradeship in civilian life, both in ex-service organisations (like the Returned Services League) and in their workplaces. The more ideologically inclined looked for hope and action in the union movement becoming more militant and impatient in the 1920s, or after 1922 they joined the recently formed Communist Party. Others maintained contact with their former commanding officers in informal business or political organisations or joined old comrades in quasi-military organisations such as the Old and New Guards. In Tenterfield, 'the Colonel' Michael Bruxner, DSO mused on his wartime experience of leadership in the Light Horse, and the spirit of mateship and co-operation evident among his men. The hope that these qualities might be sustained and nourished under peacetime conditions led him to a significant role in the Country Party and in New South Wales politics.[10]

After the war there was a tendency to more authoritarianism on both the right and the left. There was also a new sense of protectiveness, of women and children, of personal space and property, and of the values for which men had fought, and for which others had died. Liberty, loyalty to king and country and the right to a better life, though variously interpreted, were frequently invoked. There was a widespread sense of obligation, a duty to respect the sacrifices of fallen comrades and to uphold those things for which they died, but also a pervading sense of sadness which came to be symbolised as Anzac Day became established and as war memorials began to dot the landscape.

In her account of growing up in northern New South Wales, Shirley Walker described the impact of the war through the presence of men like their teacher, an ex-serviceman, thoughtful, gentle, saddened by his experiences.

Reminders of the Great War are everywhere, from the captured German guns in the park in Lismore to the roll of honour in the local hall and the impressively framed illuminated address on the schoolroom wall . . . Our folk-tales are grimmer than Grimm; they concern the Angel of Mons (a deadly apparition which appears above the smoke and flames of the battlefield); the Christmas truce in no-man's land where Australian and German soldiers exchanged gifts in the snow; and the leaning Virgin high on the spire on the cathedral at Albert . . . We stamp around the playground to the marching songs of the AIF, 'Mademoiselle from Armentiers' and 'It's a long way to Tipperary', not realising that the first is about a harlot and the second about a girl who's been left behind by a soldier . . . The Great War has now become a tragic myth, haunting the consciousness of the children.

There are 'ugly rumours, whispered stories', and many mementoes of the dead, diaries, photographs, cigarette cases which have deflected bullets, bullets themselves which have been carefully stored away. Anzac Day is as solemn and affecting as Easter.[11]

Recognising their depressing effect, the minister for education, Tom Mutch, banned war trophies in schools early in the 1920s. But there were the limbless men given jobs as lift drivers or allocated licences for fruit barrows, as well as the drunks, and those who were dependent on the cocaine used extensively as a painkiller in France.

In such an environment, women had no place but as heroic mothers of soldiers and nurses of the sick and wounded. Their hopes for more equal participation in society, nurtured for a generation by their exercise of the vote, were pushed into the background in this new world of masculine need and suffering. Nor was there much sympathy for those men who had not been to the war, especially those who had participated in the 1917 strike. The differential pensions and services available to those who had served overseas and those who had merely served in mines and mills, on railways and wharves, seemed even less fair as unemployment worsened.

To provide immediate postwar employment New South Wales embarked on a new programme of capital works. Long-cherished dreams for bridging Sydney Harbour begun under the management of J. J. C. Bradfield in 1925 came to symbolise re-building the future. At the same time, work was begun on the underground railway in the city, with vast excavations through Hyde Park and the electrification of the city and suburban network. Though the integration of the new bridge with the modernised railway system soon transformed patterns of work, shopping and travel in central Sydney, by 1932 when the bridge was finished, the necessary loans raised in London had become a significant and symbolic burden as well.

NSW voters continued to support the conscriptionist Holman throughout the war though they voted strongly against conscription in the referenda. The probable explanation is that the referenda were seen, in the case of women at least, self-interestedly or compassionately rather than in party terms. Voting figures suggest that demoralisation was high. Women especially were opting out of politics by the latter stages of the war. Just 56 per cent of all registered voters cast a ballot in the 1920 state election, but only 50 per cent of the women. This was the first election in which women were entitled to stand, yet none were preselected by the main parties and only one contested the election, Dr Mary Booth, unsuccessfully, on behalf of her Women's Party, for North Shore. There was considerable subsequent experimentation with the voting system itself. In 1922 in order to encourage participation, electoral enrolment became compulsory. Later a complicated preferential system was introduced. The turnout in 1922 and 1925 was 70 per cent. By 1927 it had risen to 82.5 per cent, but in 1930 after voting was made compulsory, almost 95 per cent of registered electors voted. In 1925 Millicent Preston Stanley became the first woman in the NSW parliament when she was elected as a Nationalist for the Eastern Suburbs electorate. She lost the seat in 1927.

Holman lost the election in April 1920, as well as his own seat and the leadership of the Nationals passed to George Fuller. Labor returned to power with John Storey as premier. This Labor government was more Catholic than before. In 1913, the number of Catholics in the Labor caucus had roughly corresponded with their numbers in the working classes. After the split of 1917 half the caucus was Catholic. When Storey died on 21 October 1921 and was replaced by James Dooley, the Labor government was 61 per cent Catholic. A militant campaign by journalist and political organiser P. S. Cleary, culminating in the formation of a specifically Catholic political party, provoked extreme sectarian reactions once more. Simmering protestant resentment against a 1908 papal decree that no marriage between a Catholic and a non-Catholic was valid unless it was conducted before a Catholic priest now boiled over. According to the 1908 'ne temere' decree, no marriage conducted in a registry office would be recognised by the Catholic church. This effectively banned mixed marriages and meant that children of such a union were illegitimate in the eyes of the church. Pressure on the non-Catholic partner to convert or allow the children to be educated as Catholics was seen as a kind of Catholic poaching of protestant women and children, and vigorously opposed, especially by a lobby known as the Protestant Federation (in response to an older organisation, the Catholic Federation formed mainly to campaign for state aid to Catholic schools). A promise to legislate against the 'ne temere' marriage decree and reclaim NSW's marriage laws from papal interference became part of the highly sectarian 1922 election campaign. In Sydney's eastern suburbs, Dr Cyril Fallon stood as a candidate for the Catholic Federation and was elected. In Newcastle, W. P. J. Skelton, a Methodist unionist, successfully campaigned for the votes of the predominantly Methodist mining population on the slogan, 'Who shall rule Australia – the People or the Priests?'[12]

In this tense environment, the flight of an unhappy nun from Mt Erin Presentation Convent in Wagga in 1921 created a sensation. Sister Ligouri (born Bridget Partridge in Ireland in 1890) had entered the Presentation Sisters' Novitiate in 1909. She was professed in 1911 and taught briefly at Ganmain. However, she was no teacher and was not really suited to the religious life either. After a previous unsuccessful attempt to leave the convent, she fled one night, barefoot and clad only in her nightdress. Strangely she quickly found herself in the care of members of the Loyal Orange Lodge of New South Wales and was taken to stay in the home of a Congregational minister, Rev. William Touchell at Kogarah. The Bishop of Wagga, Joseph Dwyer, sought a warrant for her arrest on grounds of insanity but after an appearance in the Lunacy Court Sister Ligouri was released. She then (with financial support from the Loyal Orange Lodge) sued the bishop for wrongful arrest and mistreatment at Mt Erin. During the two weeks of the subsequent trial in June–July 1921, the people of New South Wales were treated to every thrilling detail of convent life in Wagga, though a judge and jury found in favour of the bishop. That should have been the end of sectarian sensationalism, but on 26 October, Bridget Partridge was 'kidnapped' by a group of men including her brother. When she was recognised and taken to police headquarters for protection she renounced both her brother and the Catholic faith. She returned to live with the Touchells and was still there in 1963 when Mrs Touchell died. (Her husband died in 1954.) Bridget herself died at Mt Rydalmere mental hospital in 1966 and was buried as a Congregationalist.

Labor lost the 1922 election and fell to bitter faction fighting in recrimination. The next Fuller government was both protestant and conservative. Among its ministers was T. J. 'Lemonade' Ley, temperance advocate and protestant extremist. After he was convicted in England in 1947 of murder, it seemed only too likely that he had also been involved in the suspicious disappearance or death of at least three of his political enemies in New South Wales in the 1920s. Education minister 'Briggy' Bruntnell (once a brigadier in the Salvation Army) introduced a Monday morning loyalty ceremony in primary schools with pledges to God, king, and saluting the flag, arguing that this was the best way to impress loyal sentiments on the 'plastic minds' of the children. Teachers were offended by the implication that they were lacking loyalty – their record of war service alone was impressive, oppressive even. High school fees were also re-imposed in the belief that secondary education of an academic or non-technical kind was a private good and that any further expansion of state high schools should be discouraged. The re-imposed fees were extremely unpopular with parents, but approved by Archbishop Kelly because the fewer children in state schools the less chance there was of 'making Australia a pagan nation'.[13]

Fuller's provocative legislation to amend the Marriage Act was watered down by the upper house. Even so he lost the 1925 election (Fallon lost his seat) to Labor, since 1923 led by Jack Lang. A Catholic, though a non-practising one, Lang needed support from wherever he could get it to survive hostility and distrust among his caucus colleagues.

Lang had won the leadership of the Labor Party in 1924 by one vote from mercurial Tom Mutch. Lang was not popular in the parliamentary party when he became leader, but he had support from the unions and the rank and file for his promise to reverse hated legislation from the previous Fuller government – by re-instating the forty-four-hour week first introduced by the Storey–Dooley government but increased to forty-eight hours by Fuller, and restoring the rights of 1917 strikers once granted then withdrawn, also the free secondary education Fuller had abolished. Lang made a calculated bid for the support of women and rural voters.

With Kate Dwyer regularly appearing as a delegate at conferences and in 1914, as party vice-president, NSW women were able to keep their own ideas about reform on the agenda. They had succeeded in persuading Dooley to introduce an equal minimum wage for all teachers, women and men, and in 1921 the first women justices of the peace in New South Wales were appointed. As minister for health and motherhood from 1920 to 1922, J. J. G. (Gregory) McGirr, a devout Catholic, was keen to provide more maternity hospitals but fumbled when it came to financial support for the mothers themselves. In 1925, however, Lang introduced a widow's pension, and in 1927, a motherhood endowment scheme, sought by Labor women for over a decade, was set up. He also took the opportunity of including two women (wives of loyal rural supporters rather than long-term independent party activists) among the new legislative councillors who were supposed to follow ALP policy and vote themselves out of existence.

In contrast to the previous Storey–Dooley government's cautious union focus, Lang had produced policies with broad appeal while at the same time creating a 'machine' to control the branches and the conference. Still he lost the election in 1927. His successor, Thomas Bavin, son of a Methodist minister, himself an Anglican, had no faith in sectarianism as a solution to the very real industrial problems now confronting New South Wales, first among timber workers, and then on the coalfields. Archbishop Kelly, however, remained obsessed with the evil of mixed marriages, encouraging separate institutions for Catholics, beginning in primary school and replicated at all levels of NSW society from sporting clubs to hospitals, to keep Catholics safe from the threat of meeting and marrying protestants. Certain firms were known to be more favourable than others to Catholics. In others (CSR was said to be one) Catholics had little chance of employment and no likelihood of promotion. In their schools, Catholics were taught to be defensive about their religion, but the complaint that they were discriminated against was not entirely convincing. After all, the Governor of New South Wales from 1913 to 1917, Sir Gerald Strickland, was Catholic. Leading Catholic lawyers and professional men like Justice Charles Heydon, R. D. Meagher and Dr Herbert Moran argued that the militant Irishness of the anti-conscription campaigns emanating from Victoria had done a great disservice to the majority of the Catholic population in New South Wales who were loyal citizens with their own proper and very Australian reasons for rejecting conscription. However, the creation of parallel opportunities for Catholics at all levels of society in New South Wales helped to develop an educated and generally experienced Catholic elite which over time, and as religious issues became less important in economic life, seemed able to co-exist with the still dominant protestant majority. It was crossing the boundaries of sectarian institutions that was difficult as John Cramer, a Catholic, found, when he entered the conservative politics of local government on Sydney's lower north shore. The implication was that he had no business in any but Catholic organisations.[14] Similarly, the protestant J. H. Catts was ostracised in the predominantly Catholic Labor Party.

Amid the highly emotional debate about mixed marriages, R. F. Irvine professor of economics at the University of Sydney (who also happened to approve of the advanced ideas of J. M. Keynes) was forced to resign when it became known in 1922 that he had been involved in an adulterous relationship. The next year, students Bert Birtles and Dora Toll (his future wife) were 'sent down', Birtles for 'life' and Dora for two years for their erotic poems in the university magazine *Hermes*. Two years later, poet Christopher Brennan who was associate professor in German and comparative literature was also forced to resign after his adultery was mentioned in the divorce court. The students themselves were a cautious, conservative group. This was possibly because about half of them were at the university on scholarships, bursaries or cadetships linked to future employment, or were part-timers already working as teachers or lawyers' clerks. Though this made for a rather more democratic group of students than at other universities at the time – with a good proportion of Catholics – it also made them both realistic and committed to understanding the problems of society. Across the 1920s university fees rose and student enrolments declined as the economy became more troubled. Influential teachers like the peace activist and historian G. A. Wood committed suicide in 1928, while James Bruce resigned in 1930.[15] Scottish professor of philosophy John Anderson, appointed in 1927, was yet to have any impact.

Against the conservative values of society generally, the sexual rebelliousness of a small group of Sydney writers and artists who thought of themselves as 'bohemians', and drank a great deal, seemed mainly childish. The significant content in their rebellion was their preference for international (mainly European classical) aesthetic models following the tastes of Norman Lindsay who had moved, like many of his followers, from Melbourne or from New Zealand. Not surprisingly, these immigrants found the strength of the traditional NSW bush imagery and nationalist sentiment in Sydney artistic and cultural circles quaintly quixotic, but they were quick to respond to the inherent sensuality of the climate and landscape.[16]

It was easy in the 1920s to pick country people in Sydney simply because of:

the conservative homeliness of their clothes, a relaxed attitude, a leisureli-
ness of movement and speech and, in the case of most males a wide-brimmed
hat, elastic-sided riding boots, and a thoughtful manner of rolling untidy
cigarettes and poking the straggly ends in with a match.[17]

They came for the Royal Easter Show, for the wool sales, the races,
to do business with their brokers and agents, or to visit relatives and
shop, staying at places like the Hotel Metropole, one of the clubs, or
in a seaside flat at Manly or Coogee. Rural discontent with neglect
from Sydney had seen a re-emergence of a new state movement in the
Riverina, and in New England where it was led by various members
of the Page family and carried into federal politics in 1919 when
the youngest, Dr Earle Page, won the seat of Clarence for the new
Country Party. A rail link from Grafton through Murwillumbah
was begun in 1925 with co-operation from Queensland and some
federal funding, to pacify the northern separatists. Though carried
through to Brisbane by 1930, a special ferry, the *Swallow*, was still
needed to carry trains across the wide Clarence River. Discontent
with disproportionate spending on projects like the Harbour Bridge
and the Sydney underground was reinforced in the country by the
difficulties increasingly being experienced by farmers and soldier
settlers alike as prices for rural commodities began to fall, an early
intimation of the coming depression.

The geological distribution of mineral resources in New South
Wales, especially west of the ranges and at Broken Hill, as well as
the strength of the AWU among shearers and other rural labourers,
had given Labor a strong presence and an important insight into
rural New South Wales. After Sydney, Newcastle and Broken Hill
were NSW's largest towns followed by Goulburn (the second wool-
selling centre in New South Wales) and Cessnock (also a mining
town in the Hunter Valley). Railway and post and telegraph workers swelled the population in other rural centres and made for a small
core of potential Labor supporters. However, during the 1920s small
farmers, soldier settlers, and country town business people who had
since the 1890s often sympathised with Labor were moving into
the Country Party formed in 1922 out of the Farmers and Settlers
leagues which had existed since the 1880s. Threatened by the rising influence of the Country Party, Lang campaigned extensively
throughout rural New South Wales. A conference was arranged at

6.2 Group of typical 'Wanganella Estate' rams on Colombo Creek, north-west of Deniliquin. Famous for their large robust frames, superb fleeces and high-yielding capacity, stud sheep like these formed the backbone of the flocks that earned New South Wales massive export incomes from wool for several generations. Stud rams with names like 'Goliath' and 'The General' featured along with details of their value and the numbers of their progeny in tourist guides and advertising material. (H.M. Maitland, *New South Wales 1920–1923*, John Sands, Sydney, 1923, p. 338)

Bathurst in 1926 to pursue non-competitive selling arrangements for primary produce, especially wheat, but also eggs and dairy products.

Country women, too, stood apart from their city sisters not only because their clothes tended to be less adventurous, but also because, in the main, they seemed to be a little more forthright and practical in manner and attitude. In 1922, Grace Munro, a pastoralist's wife from Keera, Bingara, became the first president of the Country Women's Association (CWA) which she had helped to form. Already experienced as a Red Cross worker during the war, she had volunteered to provide services for the strike-breakers at the Sydney showground in 1917, and in 1938 became a member of the advisory council for the university college established at Armidale, to appease the disgruntled people of New England. By 1923 the CWA had

sixty-eight branches, seventeen restrooms in country towns where
women in from outlying farms for the day could feed and change
a baby, put up their feet, or leave their parcels while shopping or
visiting the doctor. There were also two seaside holiday homes and
several maternity centres and it was negotiating for improved facilities on country trains and railway stations for women travelling
with children.

Though country people now represented less than 20 per cent of
the state's population, they still produced well over 50 per cent of
its wealth. New South Wales produced more than half of Australia's
sheep and wool. This made it effectively the largest wool-producing
country in the world. The world came to Sydney for wool. Buyers
and brokers from Britain, France, Belgium, Japan, Italy, Germany,
and the United States worked with agents in Sydney or made regular bookings in Sydney's clubs and hotels. Ironically, the wool trade
which over five or six generations had established the imagery of
western New South Wales as the archetypal Australia also kept the
NSW establishment closely in touch with its British and European
roots. As well, immigration, especially from Britain, since a
subsidised program had been re-introduced before the war, meant
that there were many current family connections to Britain right
through society. Wool prices, still high after the war, began to decline
in the mid-1920s, an early warning of economic problems to come.
Falling prices affected not only the producers. Sydney wool stores,
brokers, auction houses, shipping merchants and wharf labourers
all felt the chill wind.

According to statistics collected in conjunction with the 1933 census there were 1,229 full blood and 8,485 half caste Aborigines
living in New South Wales at that time. Of these, 108 full bloods
and 927 half castes were recorded as in regular employment. New
South Wales spent £54,681, more than any other state that year, on
Aboriginal welfare.[18] Many of the difficulties encountered by NSW
Aborigines during this period are best seen as extreme versions of
the problems faced by rural New South Wales as a whole. Employment was seasonal and mostly unskilled or semi-skilled. Aboriginal
men worked as shearers and fencers, stockmen and labourers, but
unlike poor white settlers with whom they were competing for jobs,
they lacked the security of a small holding where their wives and

6.3 Aboriginal girls 'who have been rescued from neglected conditions and are now living useful lives' as nursemaids and domestic servants. (H.M. Maitland, *New South Wales 1920–1923*, John Sands, Sydney, 1923, p. 181)

children could subsist. Employment for Aboriginal women was usually in domestic service, but this was rarely an attractive job because it was menial work, badly paid, and carried out often in mean conditions in pretentious suburban homes. Domestic service was used as a way of forcing full blood Aboriginal girls who had reached puberty off the reserves, i.e. away from opportunities for becoming pregnant to Aboriginal men. Unlike other country girls who left home in search of paid work in a nearby town or in Sydney, Aboriginal girls had no hope of being accepted to train as nurses or finding jobs as sale assistants or waitresses. Those who came to the city were usually strictly supervised. Not a few homes in the better suburbs solved the servant problem by acquiring a girl through relatives in the country. Other Aboriginal girls were forced to accept placements arranged for them by the missions and church homes to which they had been sent because it was economically impossible for them to do otherwise.

Education remained a chronic problem in the bush, despite innovations like part-time schools, itinerant teachers, correspondence teaching and after 1951, the School of the Air based at Broken Hill. Part of Labor's appeal in the bush had been its plans to extend secondary education and to make it free again. Access to education was most difficult for Aboriginal families. Schools on reserves did not go beyond grade 3 before 1938. Aboriginal parents often experienced rejection when trying to enrol their children in small country schools – it was 1972 before state primary schools were required to accept them – and before 1949 Aboriginal children were simply not admitted to high schools. In part the prejudice Aborigines encountered was couched in simple economic terms. They were desperately poor, badly housed and clothed, and not socialised in the ways acceptable to cautious country people. But there was also a layer of prejudice based on skin colour and levelled simply at difference. Poor Irish settlers had often experienced rejection on similar grounds. But they had the support of the Catholic church through which to claim a measure of respectability. Furthermore, church schools educated their children to a certain level, and in an atmosphere free of daily denigration. Apart from the missions which often seemed a mixed blessing, there was little support for Aboriginal people in the ongoing battle against rural poverty, unemployment, and outright exclusion. The wonder is that they managed, as so many did, to survive with their own sense of dignity and self-respect. Moving quietly, drawing little attention to themselves, and placing great emphasis on the value of family, though often through inter-marriage with the white settler community, and at the cost of suppressing their Aboriginality, they survived. That at least was normal in New South Wales where convict, Catholic, or any kind of foreign or coloured parentage had been traditionally hidden or repressed as one of the surest ways of surviving and becoming acceptable, employable, and ultimately even an upwardly mobile citizen.

Of all the states, New South Wales was most severely affected by the depression, though unemployment was by no means uniform. In 1932, one in three trade unionists in New South Wales was unemployed (the Australian average was one in five).[19] In some areas such as the dairying districts of the north and south coast, there was plenty of chronic poverty, but unemployment itself was relatively low. Inland railway towns, Goulburn, Bathurst, Albury, Dubbo, Cootamundra had a buffer against unemployment. Some of the worst and most persistent unemployment occurred on the troubled Hunter Valley coalfields. When the Rev. Alan Walker made a pioneering sociological study of Cessnock during the early years of World War II, he found unemployment had been a constant since the 1920s. An explosion at the Bellbird colliery in 1923 killed twenty-one, but only fifteen bodies were recovered before the mine was sealed as too dangerous for further rescue work. The spirits of those left behind seemed to haunt the already troubled coalfields. Between 1912 and 1932, exports were falling, coal production was reduced by almost half, and its value declined at much the same rate.[20]

The decline in coal exports and in demand for heavy metal products like galvanised iron and wire led to shut-downs lasting for months at a time. Oil and petrol burning cars and trucks were replacing coal-fired steam trains. Though the wheat farming lobby continued to demand better and cheaper rail transport, at the same time they wanted more and better roads as well. Mine owners tried to force a 12.5 per cent cut in wages, and when miners refused to accept, the mines were closed. But it hardly mattered whether wages were reduced or production ceased for a while, the effect was still to reduce the stockpile. When in December 1929 an impending shortage of coal led Minister for Mines Reg Weaver to attempt to re-open Rothbury mine using non-union labour there was a violent confrontation with police leading to the death of one miner, Norman Brown, and injuries for about fifty others.

More than two-thirds of NSW coal had been produced at the now idle Hunter fields. However, coal continued to come from mines at Lithgow (about 10%) and the Illawarra (about 20%). So did financial support for the unemployed miners in the Hunter. Many jobs were lost in Lithgow when Hoskins steelmills were moved to Port Kembla in 1928 and the small arms factory was scaled back awaiting another war to lift demand for its products. By 1932 perhaps half Lithgow's male workforce was without a job. Other employees such as those in the Lithgow branch of the already insecure Government Savings Bank had been rationed to only three days of work

6.4 The Lithgow branch of the New South Wales State
Government Savings Bank closed in 1931. Its business was
later taken over by the Commonwealth Bank. This building,
one of few State Savings Bank premises still recognisable, is
now used by a doctor and as offices. (Author's collection)

each week. On the other days they took ferrets rabbit trapping to
supplement the dinner table.

The Government Savings Bank itself collapsed in April 1931 and it
was not until December that arrangements were made for the Commonwealth Bank to take over its savings bank business. Its rural
banking department which had provided advances to farmers lan-
guished until the end of 1932 when it was re-constituted as the Rural
Bank of New South Wales. The level of savings in New South Wales
had been dwindling since 1929, so after he was re-elected in late

1930, Lang's defiance of economic orthodoxy, along with the suspension of the Government Savings Bank was bound to cause alarm among those still guarding modest savings accounts. His refusal to cut award wages even though the cost of living had been declining since 1925, to the great advantage of those still in work and at the expense of those who were unemployed, further aggravated concern. The fact that New South Wales was responsible for about half of Australian borrowings in London made Lang's behaviour the more worrying though understandable. New South Wales was in a position to hold the rest of Australia to ransom.

Unemployed workers could no longer afford to pay rent or were evicted from company housing. Despite Lang's introduction of a moratorium on evictions and foreclosures, it was estimated that 2,000 homeless families were camped on wasteland on the fringes of Sydney. Tents and shacks made of salvaged iron and hessian sacks were scattered through low scrub at places like La Perouse, on creek banks on the lower north shore, in caves and hollows in the sand hills along the coast. Sardonically known as 'Happy Valleys', these camps were tolerated, even visited officially by the governor and feature-writing journalists, though the unemployed, camping in more obvious places like the Domain and the Botanic Gardens, were regularly evicted by police. Most country towns, especially in the Hunter Valley, also had their unemployed camps. But there, the role of the police in distributing relief and keeping single unemployed men on the move became a source of resentment and suspicion, exacerbated perhaps by the knowledge that police work was secure employment. (Of 3,590 in the force in 1932, eight were women. In addition, there were 20 black trackers.)

Walker found that in Cessnock with chronic unemployment and low levels of home ownership there was no sense of community. Municipal facilities and local organisations were poor or non-existent. This he attributed partly to the lack of leadership, poor management, too many absentee mine owners, and the fact that Cessnock was close enough to the coast for most of the residents to focus on getting away at weekends. The railway line carrying coal to Newcastle for shipment also took the miners and their families to Nelson Bay or Lake Macquarie where they camped or shared fishing shacks. This was their preferred way of life. Here by the water

6.5 'Off to camp with a sugar bag overcoat' – one of the many children from western New South Wales who were given health-care and a holiday by the sea under a scheme devised by the Reverend Stanley Drummond and his wife in the 1920s. This little girl is in better health than many of the children who required intensive treatment for deformed limbs, cleft palates, or serious respiratory complaints. (Polly Wearn, *The Magic Shoulder*, Far West Children's Health Scheme, Sydney, 1966, facing p. 32)

rather than in Cessnock they made their communities. Recognising the curative effect of the sea, in 1925, Stanley Gillick Drummond, a Methodist minister with his wife Lucy, began bringing children from places like Cobar where he was stationed, to Manly for a holiday including any necessary medical attention, thus creating the Far West Children's Health Scheme. Other organisations and enterprises besides the CWA acquired seaside holiday cottages for the use of members or employees.

In Broken Hill a different mining community had of necessity developed other traditions. In 1923–24 under the leadership of a former shearer and mineworker, now a dunny-cart driver and secretary of the Municipal Employees Union, Paddy O'Neill, the Barrier Industrial and Political Council (later the Barrier Industrial Council) was formed. O'Neill had no time for the kind of militancy which led to strikes but believed in direct bargaining with employers. In part because of its isolation he was able to negotiate living and working conditions with Broken Hill's mine managers quite unlike those prevailing elsewhere at the time. Many of the ideals of the nineteenth-century union movement that had proved unsustainable elsewhere survived in Broken Hill. Only union members (preferably those born on the Hill) were eligible for jobs. O'Neill was a Catholic, morally conservative and old-fashioned in his view of social and economic relations. So there was no employment for married women – their husbands' wages had to be adequate to provide for them. The 1935 mines agreement worked out by O'Neill with a new Mining Managers' Association laid the foundations for long-term material prosperity in Broken Hill. And from 1924 till his death in 1953 O'Neill was its uncrowned king, though until 1950 he continued to drive his dunny-cart.

The impact of the economic collapse spread far beyond those who lost their jobs and homes. For many families the depression, coming so soon after World War I, compounded the loss and suffering they had known for a decade. Marjorie Barnard and Flora Eldershaw's failed soldier settler now unemployed and trying to hawk shoelaces from door to door to keep his family together in *Tomorrow and Tomorrow and Tomorrow* was typical. The war had produced inexpressible sadness: the depression finally destroyed the people's optimism and faith in the future. They lost their confidence that fairness would triumph in the end. Largely because of the way the dole was distributed, they also lost their belief in trying to save and or provide for themselves. Those who had savings or assets were effectively penalised by having to use them up before they could apply for help. So it made no sense to try to be frugal and self-sufficient. There was a marked growth in gambling, mostly in a small way, partly for the distracting thrill, but also for the chance of boosting personal or family finances without affecting eligibility for the dole. Sporting and cultural institutions collapsed as membership fees went unpaid, though the brilliant scoring of a young cricketer from Bowral by the name of Bradman thrilled spectators on the Hill at the Sydney Cricket Ground, creating a much-needed hero for the times. Along with spectator sports, the 'wireless' became a relatively cheap, if passive, source of news and entertainment. SP bookmaking, made easy by race broadcasts, flourished. Though SP bookmaking was illegal, the tendency was to turn a blind eye especially in working class areas. But many small acts of corruption provided fertile ground for occasional large ones, and along with later wartime shortages, the rise of accompanying black markets and racketeering set the scene for massive problems later in policing New South Wales.

The contrast between Jack Lang and Thomas Bavin, who in succession both guided the fortunes of New South Wales in the early years of the depression, could not have been greater. Lang, the former real estate agent, the 'big fella', with a talent for demagoguery, had a salesman's attitude to the problems he encountered – talk big, paper over the cracks, and evade paying the rent because eviction was unlikely without the prospect of other tenants. Bavin, the colourless Chatswood lawyer seemingly in pursuit of personal goals, puzzled both his supporters and opponents. Turramurra solicitor and former World War I artillery officer, Eric Campbell, who subsequently became founder and guiding spirit of the New Guard, described Bavin's government (1927–30) as 'a sorry turnout – inert and dumb'.[21] It was no surprise that Lang won the election in 1930. Though his economic policies were unsustainable, he was at least promising to try to save the working people of New South Wales from being forced, as they felt they had been forced during the war, to bear a disproportionate share of the burden of survival.

Lang became both hero and villain. He was a hero to the unemployed for whom he appeared as a champion against the federal government, a villain to the premiers of the less-affected states, international capitalists, and bankers. He appealed, not only to a strong sense of independence among the working people of New South Wales, but increasingly to the idea of New South Wales embattled against the rest of Australia. But to those who still had savings to lose, who still held, for economic, family or cultural reasons to Anglo-Australian imperial sentiments, Lang's defiance was dangerous. Embryonic pseudo-military organisations which had appeared during the first Lang administration (1925–27) and drew on the experience of subverting the 1917 strike, as well as on the now-great reservoir of genuine military expertise in the community, re-grouped. Separatist movements in the Riverina and in northern New South Wales found a common cause with a group generally known as the 'Old Guard' headed by men who were significant figures in CSR, and Gillespies, the flour millers. Another group from Sydney's north shore and other more prosperous suburbs led by Campbell who regarded themselves as better organised, became known as the 'New Guard'. But apart from staging noisy rallies in the Town Hall, their activities consisted mainly of occasional outbursts of thuggish aggression like beating up communist union leader, Jock Garden, until a plan to prevent Lang from opening the Sydney Harbour Bridge was conceived. So on the morning of 19 March 1932 New Guard member Francis de Groot spurred his horse out of the honour guard to which he had attached himself and slashed the ceremonial ribbon before Lang could do it. It was, according to Eric Campbell's memoir, *The Rallying Point*, 'a grand job' which 'girdled the world with laughter',[22] but at the time it seemed shocking, showing the depth of feeling for both the traditional imperial loyalty of Campbell's New Guard and Lang's aggressive NSW nationalism.

By May 1932 it was possible for Governor Game to dismiss Lang on a legal technicality and, surprisingly, for Lang to accept the installation of a caretaker government led by former public servant and head of treasury, Bertram Stevens. Perhaps Lang was relieved, tired of juggling the disparate groups who kept him in power though he could produce no remedies without betraying most of them. There

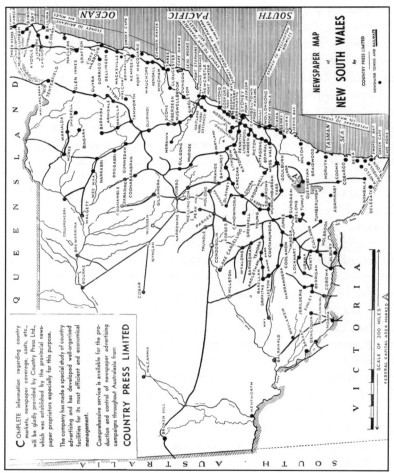

Map 6.1 New South Wales showing railways and towns with newspapers in 1938, when both were probably at their greatest extent. (*The Press Directory of Australia and New Zealand 1938*, Country Press Ltd, Sydney, facing p. 14)

was no prospect of improvement in the economy. While Lang and his supporters (the 'Lang machine') continued to dominate the Labor Party in New South Wales, by the end of the 1930s it had become clear that they would never win government again without wider support and a rapprochement with federal Labor. Rural New South Wales, apart from the mining areas, completely deserted Lang in favour of the Bruxner–Buttenshaw-led Country Party, in its way also a trade union promoting the specific interests of small farmers and the rural community. Lang lost a great many of his moderate suburban supporters, especially women who found his desperate strategies more threatening than the welfare measures with which he had once courted them. Small household savings, women's jobs, and women's welfare provisions were all threatened by his strategy of protecting those who had obvious industrial and union strength.

On election night, 11 June 1932, after it was certain that Lang had lost, Stevens told the radio audience, 'You can go to bed now, for the country is safe.' Stevens saw the defeat of unemployment and the restoration of confidence as his main task. He may have been guilty of some creative accounting, in the way he tackled unemployment, but he also had the advantage of more co-operation from employers, as well as assistance from the federal government in borrowing. Some of the measures adopted for getting people back to work were harsh, most notably the decision to sack married women teachers who had husbands in employment in order to give their jobs to newly qualified, younger, single teachers. Yet schools were hardly over-staffed. In 1933, a survey of class sizes revealed that more than a quarter of primary school classes were over 40. An even larger number averaged between 45 and 60 pupils, and 77 out of 4,429 classes had between 60 and 69 children. There were 11 classes of over 70. Given the results of this survey, the minister for education, David Drummond, ordered that the maximum class size henceforth should be 48.[23]

Requiring people to work building roads and pathways for small payments instead of simply issuing food relief coupons was resented but effective. Employment statistics in 1933–34 showed that New South Wales still had almost twice as many government employees (71,620) as the next most populous state, Victoria (41,675). This included 47,319 railway and tramway workers and 12,597 teachers (5,561 male and 7,036 female.)[24] Meanwhile the pattern of government borrowing was gradually changed; after 1937 more of NSW loans were raised locally than overseas. In any case the economic outlook was brighter. Unlike his anti-Labor predecessors, Stevens did not set out to reverse all decisions made by the previous administration and take revenge on the unions. Some of his colleagues thought he was too inclined to accept a natural bent towards Labor in New South Wales. His deputy Michael Bruxner had no difficulties either about government subsidies or socialistic-seeming government enterprises if he thought they were in the best interests of the farming community or the state's economy as a whole. As minister for transport, Bruxner turned enthusiastically not only to improving country roads, but also to rationalising Sydney's tram and bus services. As a result of urgent separatist enthusiasm led by the local member David Drummond, a teachers' college, the first outside a metropolitan centre was established in Armidale in 1928 as a means of providing jobs and training for young people closer to home. New England University College followed in 1937 with the gift by pastoralist Frederick Robert White of Booloominbah, a fine house built in the 1880s, making it possible for teaching to begin almost immediately.

The sesquicentenary of European settlement in Australia in 1938 was seen as a chance to restore the image of New South Wales nationally and internationally as a safe, respectable place, for investment and tourism especially. When the celebrations were announced, Kenneth Slessor, who was editor of *Smith's Weekly*, responded (4 September 1937), with 'Come to Sydney!'.

> Oh, the scurry and rush of excitement,
>   The scenes of hysterical fun,
> When Sydney goes gay in a devilish way
>   On a diet of biscuit-and-bun!
> There'll be spelling-bees, also eisteddfods –
>   Imagine the hubbub and din! –
> And hectic debates on colonial dates
>   With a lantern-slide lecture chucked in.

. . .
There'll be thousands of tots around maypoles,
    Wherever you happen to look,
And picnics and jaunts to historical haunts,
    With a series of talks about Cook.
So come to the circus in Sydney –
    The programme's a positive gem –
Where bottles go pop till festivities stop
    At 5.57* p.m.!

Smith's (1919–50) was in many ways heir to the *Bulletin* tradition of satire, wit and humour, as well as black and white art. *Smith's* was nationalist, sexist, sympathetic to the plight of the Aborigines but otherwise racist, and in favour of White Australia. It also appealed especially to returned servicemen with various sections devoted to their problems, and became increasingly anti-communist.

The rest of Australia was content to leave most of the celebration to Sydney, especially as Western Australia and Victoria had only recently had their own centenary celebrations, Victoria's graced by the Duke of Gloucester. New South Wales was unable to secure a proper royal personage for 1938 but under the guidance of former bookmaker and sporting identity, J. M. Dunningham, a re-enactment of Phillip's landing was staged, more for dramatic effect than historical accuracy, without convicts, but with a 'troupe' of twenty-six Aborigines conscripted from Brewarrina and Menindee for their surviving knowledge of traditional dancing, and lodged for the duration in the Redfern police barracks. Later they formed a tableau on the first of 120 floats in a procession representing the march to nationhood. The intention of the organisers was to convey an image of peace and prosperity. This meant, after much deliberation, leaving out the convicts. (Despite George Arnold Wood's assertion in 1922 that it was time to get over embarrassment about the convict past, New South Wales was still sensitive on this subject.) No trade unions or labour organisations had been invited to participate either, for fear that reference might be made to bitter labour disputes and levels of unemployment in the recent past. But

* A reference to early closing of hotels, adopted as a wartime form of self-denial and still in force in 1937.

it was leaving Australia's participation in World War I out of the story which caused most disgust.

While Hero Black, Archie Boney, Anzac Williams, Jimmy Wongram and the others were playing themselves in the official ceremonies, about 100 other Aborigines, veterans of a decade of campaigning against the inequities of the Aborigines' Protection Board, had gathered in the Australian Hall in Elizabeth Street to pass a resolution declaring 26 January 'A Day of Mourning and Protest' for them.[25] The Protection Board, set up in the 1870s to shield NSW's remaining full blood Aborigines from exploitation as closer settlement claimed ever more of their land, had clearly failed. The number of full bloods declined to a pitiful level. This was not surprising as levels of nutrition on the board's reserves were often woeful and the withdrawal of rations used frequently as a punishment, while health-care and education were badly administered often by the same under-qualified, overworked and poorly paid manager and his wife. Nevertheless, the board managed to have its powers extended to cover part-Aborigines as well by insisting on its duty to educate part-Aboriginal children excluded from state schools, and to supervise their training as farmhands or domestics. Those Aborigines who were, in fact, struggling for independent economic survival saw the board as a threat to their independence and a barrier to their self-respect. Known by Aboriginal people in the 1930s as the Persecution Board, it represented both charity and the officialdom they desired to avoid, the equivalent of the workhouse detested by the poor in Victorian England.

William Ferguson, the son of a Scots boundary rider and a part-Aboriginal mother, formed the Aboriginal Progressive Association in 1937 in Dubbo to fight the board's increasing intrusion into the lives of part-Aboriginal families. He quickly found supporters among the growing numbers of people of mixed descent like Jack Patten, who had been a boxer, and Pearl Gibbs, who had worked as a domestic servant in the north-west and in Potts Point, whose chances of a decent life as honest hard-working parents and citizens were increasingly threatened by the Protection Board. With the help of Sydney stirrers like P. R. Stephensen and W. B. Miles, as well as good friends in the Labor Party and the union movement, they succeeded in obtaining an inquiry into the role of the Protection Board. Reform came slowly and reluctantly, however, and still failed to reflect the real needs of NSW Aborigines, understood neither by the feared board bureaucrats nor their despised advisors, the anthropologists. Significantly, however, the Aboriginal people had begun to assert themselves in New South Wales.

7

1941–1965, Labor's long haul

The years from 1941 to 1965 returned prosperity, population growth, and steady achievement in living and working conditions to New South Wales with five Labor governments in a row. The population grew from under 3 million in 1941, to over 4 million by 1965. In contrast to their parents, this new generation, the postwar 'baby boomers', grew up without experience of unemployment, depression, or war. They were joined, for the first time since the gold rushes a hundred years earlier, by large numbers of immigrants, mostly from Britain, but also from Italy, Poland, Greece, Holland, Hungary and Yugoslavia. The growth economy made it relatively easy for Labor to continue ensuring jobs. Indeed unemployment rarely fell below 4 per cent and most of the time it was less than 2 per cent.

The mood of postwar reconstruction and social planning suited Labor as well.[1] War-induced shortages excused government initiatives or intervention in all kinds of activities, while high levels of regulation were tolerated for the sake of efficiency and equity. The outcomes may have been mediocre buildings and badly designed products, but the contrast with makeshift or go-without during the previous decades was obvious. Gradually a kind of uniform dreariness overtook New South Wales. By the 1960s, it was beginning to pall. (Perhaps the grand fantasy of an opera house on Bennelong Point can be explained in part as a desperate reaction against this dominant mode.)

To many people life since 1914 had seemed nothing but difficult or disappointing. Stability and a kind of confidence may have returned with Bertram Stevens' careful accountancy, but there was little hope or enthusiasm about the future. Stevens resigned in August 1939 to disappear into penurious obscurity and was succeeded as premier by the colourless Alexander Mair. The war that began in Europe in September 1939 seemed just another burden. A study carried out by sociologist A. P. Elkin in the early months of 1941 found a high degree of hopelessness or apathy about the war in New South Wales. However this was to change with Japan's attack on Pearl Harbor, in December 1941. Darwin was attacked by Japanese fighter bombers in February 1942 and within weeks, New South Wales also had become a target. On the night of 31 May 1942 three Japanese midget submarines entered Sydney Harbour and sank a navy training ship, the *Kuttabul*, killing twenty-one men who were quartered there. Then on 3 June, seaside suburbs in both Sydney and Newcastle were shelled from Japanese ships off-shore. Japanese warships roamed the sea between Sydney and Newcastle from late May to early June with deadly effect.

Industries from Newcastle to Wollongong prepared for attack and invasion. In her Newcastle novel, *Southern Steel* (1953), Dymphna Cusack caught the tension of the time. 'Silver pencils of light' probed the night skies for Japanese fighter planes while BHP's steel-mills worked overtime. Through the 'brown-out' the glare from their furnaces was visible 20 miles (about 30 km) out to sea.[2] Sydney and Newcastle beaches became unsightly and inaccessible with tank traps and barbed-wire entanglements. Parks and suburban back-yards were dug up for air-raid shelters and trenches. Shop windows were boarded up and a blackout prevailed at night. Anxious citizens fled to the Blue Mountains and beyond or sent their children west for safety. The post office clock was taken down. Buildings were com-mandeered for war purposes. Banks, businesses and government institutions moved vital records and other valuables to places like Broken Hill where they could be hidden in old mine shafts. David Jones found themselves facing Christmas in 1942 without the use of one of their city stores, though because of shortages and rationing there was not a lot to sell.

7.1   The author playing in front of the family air-raid shelter
in the backyard in Manly in 1942. (Author's collection)

Though most of the fighting took place off the coast of North
Queensland, Sydney seemed overrun by American servicemen who
began to arrive in 1941 bringing with them new interests and spe-
cial needs, many of which were eloquently described in Dymphna
Cusack's other war novel, *Come in Spinner* (1951), written with
Florence James, and based on the lives of a group of women work-
ing in different capacities in and around a large Sydney hotel.
Major ship building and repair facilities were established in both

Sydney and Newcastle. Unemployment practically disappeared. Women took over jobs hitherto jealously protected for men. Even Aboriginal workers who faced the greatest likelihood of discrimination in employment found good jobs. The railways brought them from remote centres in the north and west and deposited them in Redfern or near the munitions works at St Marys.

The railways and public transport generally received a huge boost from the war. Petrol rationing for private cars ensured steady patronage for trams, trains and buses. The railways actually began to show a profit as they became indispensable for the carriage of troops and munitions as well as rural freight. 'The trains go north with guns', wrote poet Judith Wright at Wallamumbi in New England where she was helping her father on their property. She heard them passing at night with 'a sound like thunder shaking the orchards'. Since 1937 it had been known that the essential Hawkesbury Rail Bridge was in a dangerous condition with cracks in the piers. A new bridge was begun in July 1939 and throughout the war the railways department struggled to complete it with locally available steel and other materials. But until it opened on 1 July 1946, all trains crept across the old structure at 5 miles (8 km) an hour, seriously slowing down heavy and vital north–south traffic.

During or immediately after the war the balance of influence between urban and rural New South Wales began to shift decisively. New South Wales might have been an acronym for Newcastle, Sydney, Wollongong. Manufacturing in these centres had both grown with the war effort and come under enemy threat. Country west of the ranges continued as a relative haven, troubled mainly by labour shortages at harvest or shearing, or by occasional droughts. Wollongong and Shellharbour experienced rapid growth, much of it related to the development and expansion of new steelworks and associated activities in and around Port Kembla. By 1964, the population of Wollongong passed that of Newcastle, though future growth was limited by the escarpment. In Sydney itself, industrial expansion in the inner suburbs, especially between Darling Harbour, Central Station and the airport at Mascot, drove housing south and west towards Blacktown, Bankstown and Sutherland, though Penrith and Campbelltown were the fastest growing suburbs. By 1947, Broken Hill, long the largest city away from the coast, had

7.2 'The new Hawkesbury River Railway Bridge. The old
Bridge is in the background.' Cracks had developed in the
piers of the old bridge by late 1935 and a new bridge was
constructed with difficulty during World War II. As well, a
road bridge to replace the existing car ferry opened for traffic
in 1945. The old bridge spans were removed but the piers are
still standing in the river. This is one of many illustrations in
Peter Hurley's account of his search, mainly by rail, for
history in northern New South Wales in the late 1940s. From
the time he returned from World War I till 1967, Hurley
wrote a gardening column in the *Sydney Morning Herald*, as
'Waratah'. (P.J. Hurley, *Red Cedar: The Story of the North
Coast*, Dymock's Book Arcade, Sydney, 1948, facing p. 22)

been overtaken in size by coal-producing Cessnock and was being
challenged also by the density of settlement in the Blue Mountains.

In the 1950s, a housing boom and a surge of consumer demand
for cars, furnishings, and whitegoods pushed Sydney, especially, a
long way ahead of the rest of New South Wales in sophistication,
comfort, and convenience. While the amount spent on food in 1952
was almost twice as much as on motor vehicles, parts and petrol,
by 1965 the people of New South Wales were spending nearly as
much on their cars as on food. Foodstuffs declined from 31 per cent

to 27 per cent of spending, while motor vehicles rose from 24 per cent to 27 per cent. Spending on clothing, drapery and footwear declined by 3 per cent to 15 per cent of household budgets. And beer, wine and spirits fell from 9 per cent to 7 per cent. The coming of television in 1956 dramatised the gap between Sydney and the rest of New South Wales, though the height of TV masts installed to win reception outside Sydney was an impressive sight on the back roads in the late 1950s. Soon, demand for modern conveniences which could transform the quality of rural life – electricity, telephones, radio, television, and better roads for the growing number of cars and trucks – required an increasing, often disproportionate, allocation of government resources to rural electorates for infrastructure building. Bill McKell's government was elected in 1941 partly because of his promise to extend basic services such as electricity to rural areas. His newly created Housing Commission was authorised to build in country areas, and the government's Rural Bank, whose basic rationale was to support agricultural development, grew stronger as suburban branches were opened to engage in lending for new home building. Water and soil conservation, debt relief for farmers, and orderly marketing of their produce became part of McKell's postwar agenda to keep the Country Party at bay and maintain Labor's share of the rural vote.

Born in 1891, the eldest son of a butcher from Pambula on the south coast, William James McKell left school at thirteen to become a boiler-maker. His father disappeared in 1901 (with a young woman by whom he had fathered another child), and as far as his deserted wife and children in Sydney were concerned, he was dead. McKell's 'caution, frugality, independence and social conscience' were in part a product of the responsibility thrust upon him as a 10-year-old in helping his mother support his brother and sisters. He joined the Labor Party about 1908 and in 1917 defeated former Labor premier James McGowen for preselection in Redfern. When he won the seat later that year he was the youngest member of the parliament. A minister in the Storey government in 1920, not only did McKell remedy his lack of formal education by qualifying as a barrister in 1925, he also became a perpetual student of politics and the public service. By the late 1930s there was probably no one with a better understanding of the history of the NSW Labor Party, its strengths and weaknesses in and out of government, no one who knew better the benefits of being in power, or understood how the public service could be deployed to achieve politically impossible goals. McKell's policies as premier reflected his knowledge of the divisions caused by conscription during World War I and the turbulence engendered by Jack Lang. His understanding of, and care for, rural New South Wales were genuine, based on what he remembered as an idyllic rural childhood, before his father left them, and then, his experience after 1933, on the farm he bought at Frog's Hole, near Goulburn.[3]

Unlike Holman for whom World War I was a disaster, World War II enhanced McKell's reputation. The war was, of course, as close as Sydney Harbour, and the situation, more desperate. And McKell had no ideological battle over conscription. So his firm leadership and co-operative relationship with Curtin's federal Labor government was immensely effective. As well as full employment and federally subsidised services, the war brought five years of surpluses in the treasury (though there was a balancing backlog of public works and services kept on hold for the duration). McKell was also able to dodge union demands for a forty-hour week, using the war as an excuse even after it was over. However, all NSW workers not covered by federal awards did become entitled to two weeks' annual leave on full pay, a major improvement in working conditions which eventually flowed on into awards elsewhere and by 1947, a forty-hour week was implemented in New South Wales.

McKell was the first Labor leader in New South Wales to serve a full parliamentary term and the first to be re-elected for a second, consecutive term. Cautious and restrained in public, he projected an impression of authority, through the war years especially, a little above and apart from party machinations, and ultimately in control of the outcomes. This was possible, in part, because of two very significant allies, Robert Reginald (Reg) Downing, the quiet Catholic union secretary whom McKell promoted to lead his government in the Upper House, a man remarkably skilful at foreseeing and heading off problems within the party, and at the Trades Hall, and Wallace Wurth, chairman of the Public Service Board. Wurth was the ideal public servant, all-seeing, loyal, and discreetly creative with his advice. Bertram Stevens, who had worked with Wurth when they were both in treasury, admired and promoted him, but Wurth's role in the survival of the Labor governments he served with consummate professionalism till his death in 1960 was incalculable, not least because his 'lingering distrust' of Catholics caused him to keep a careful watch on the otherwise heavy Catholic presence in the public service and the Labor government. As well his abstemious personal and professional habits set an effective example at a time when economy was essential. If the government of New South Wales was relatively free of corruption during these years, it was because Wurth gave corruption no air. (Unfortunately his influence did not extend to the then notoriously corrupt Sydney City Council. Nor was he able to forestall increasing complaints about cronyism as, with longevity, an ever larger number of official appointments fell into Labor hands.)

While he could rely on his allies, Downing and Wurth, McKell's hold on his electorate of Redfern was also utterly secure. No one could match his organisational oversight. For most of his time in parliament, McKell's wife, his mother, his sister, and when they were old enough, his daughters, formed part of his electorate support group. From their home in Dowling Street they provided food, clothing, assistance and advice to all who came seeking help. Whatever the needs of the many constituents who came daily to his door, the McKell women were there to provide.

A modest reformer, McKell chose his objects carefully for maximum benefit with minimum political pain, thus setting a precedent for most of his successful successors. Both Neville Wran and Bob Carr acknowledged their admiration. One example could be seen in the relaxation of the liquor laws in 1946 so that some drinking with meals in restaurants, impossible since World War I, was now allowed; restrictions on the transfer of hotel licences were lifted; and 400 new club licences were made available. McKell personally was not keen on the club licences, but they were to transform the way the people of New South Wales spent their leisure time. By the 1960s, NSW clubs, sporting, political or based on ethnic communities, with their poker machines (introduced in 1956), and their low-cost food, drink and entertainment were the envy of visitors from other states. Some like the Workmen's Club at Helensburgh, a mining town near Wollongong were descended from an earlier self-improving

Workmen's Club and Mutual School of Arts. While there was something lost when libraries and reading rooms were replaced by 'pokies', the clubs made New South Wales, Sydney especially, very attractive to musicians and performers from elsewhere in Australia because of the prospect of regular work, and helped foster variety-style entertainment that flowed into Sydney television. The clubs also began to erode the power of the breweries with their tied hotels and eventually to force improvements in drinking conditions in hotel bars. They also took some of the sting out of the anti-drink lobbies. Though a referendum to extend 6 o'clock closing, in force since World War I, was rejected in 1947, by 1955 after another referendum, hotels were allowed to remain open till 10 pm, though they were still expected to close between 6.30 and 7.30 for dinner, a requirement which lingered till 1962. There were token objections from a diminished temperance movement to further deregulation of opening hours in the 1970s but attitudes to alcohol were changing with the availability of an increasing choice of recreational drugs. Drinkers were gradually becoming more sophisticated, moving from beer to wine, increasingly available in the 1960s from bottle shops in inexpensive flagons and from about 1970 in the recently perfected wine cask. Prior to the 1960s wine had been drunk mainly with meals at home or in hotels by the wealthy or the more arty/bohemian types who prided themselves on their cosmopolitan tastes, or, fortified as sherry and port, cheaply by 'winos' in the surviving wine saloons, about to be re-born as wine bars.

McKell took advantage of wartime conditions to reform horse-racing in New South Wales, setting up the Sydney Turf Club to police the sport in conjunction with the Australian Jockey Club. A racing enthusiast, owner and breeder, McKell believed that the many existing 'pony courses' were dishonest, badly patronised and gave NSW punters poor value for their money.[4] The eventual introduction of legal off-course totalisator or TAB betting in 1964 made it easier for the punters. But it was not that long, unfortunately, before ways were found to circumvent McKell's reforming intentions. By the 1960s the racecourses were identified with money laundering and a flourishing SP industry. It is possible that despite McKell's modest changes to the licensing and gambling laws, they remained too

7.3 'Helensburgh Workmen's Club – formerly the
Helensburgh and Lilyvale Workmen's Social and Literary
Club and originally the Workmen's Club and Mutual School
of Arts.' The introduction of liquor licences and then poker
machines saved some institutions like this one on the south
coast near Wollongong from extinction as well as
encouraging new and much grander clubs that changed
drinking habits in New South Wales. (James Hagan and
Henry Lee, eds, *A History of Work and Community in
Wollongong*, Halstead Press in association with the University
of Wollongong, 2001/2, p. 159)

strict, especially in the light of postwar affluence; that a tendency to
interpret regulations loosely or turn a blind eye to minor breaches
led to a fair amount of petty corruption, especially in the police
force. By the 1960s, this too would become a significant problem
as increasingly revenue raised from gambling (mostly a tax on the
poor) became a major fact in government budgeting.

One of the implications of the federal government's control
of income tax introduced during the war and retained thereafter
became the dependence of NSW governments on what came back
to them from Canberra. Beginning with premier Joe Cahill, the 'old

smoothie' of the 1950s, it was usual, indeed necessary, for NSW premiers to blame Canberra for their inability to fund development or welfare. Throughout the years when Menzies was prime minister, elections in New South Wales often involved an anti-Canberra campaign. The fact that there were Liberal governments federally, and with Menzies, Victorian-dominated ones, made such tactics satisfying if not always effective in New South Wales. But there was also a necessary search for extra or alternative forms of revenue, not only from gambling. Excises were placed on alcohol and tobacco. Land tax was re-introduced in 1956 to grow incrementally with Sydney's land booms, as were other taxes on property sales such as stamp duty.

Wartime shortages led to the introduction of orderly marketing arrangements. Deliveries of milk and bread, for example, were regulated to prevent waste and duplication. (Most other deliveries were banned or became impossible because of petrol rationing, but daily deliveries of the basic necessities, milk and bread, could be carried out with a horse and cart, and were zoned.) While there was strict supervision of the quality of bread sold and the correct weight of standard 1-, 2-, and 4-pound loaves, with zoning, consumers had no choice of baker or anything other than white bread or brown. It was 1950 before competition between bakers was again permitted and 1958 before different types of bread, e.g. the rye breads favoured by some European immigrants or loaves in fancy shapes and irregular weights, were permitted by law. Milk vendors whose product was uniform with predictable demand were most reluctant to abandon the order of zoned deliveries. Egg producers also preferred to continue the system regulating production and pricing introduced by the Egg Marketing Board back in 1928. Even wool-growers found they did well out of wartime arrangements whereby wool sales were suspended and the whole clip was purchased by the Australian and British governments for an agreed price. However after wool sales were resumed, the Korean war drove prices to record heights in 1951–52, most satisfactory for NSW's massive wool output. Record wheat harvests in the early 1950s added further to the seemingly endless postwar economic boom.

In 1946 after a lengthy battle with the Dominions Office in London (and support from Prime Minister Chifley) McKell was able to appoint Lieutenant General John Northcott as the first Australian-born state governor. Since Northcott, no governor of New South Wales has been overseas-born. McKell's elevation as governor-general in 1947 was fiercely opposed, but eventually accepted. He was succeeded as premier of New South Wales by James McGirr, young brother of Greg, both Catholics, and once both pharmacists in Parkes. Greg McGirr had been notorious for his slowness as minister for motherhood in the 1920s to introduce the child endowment legislation so earnestly sought by the women of the Labor movement. As premier his young brother did his best to maintain McKell's mix of development and restraint, but he lacked McKell's capacity for maintaining surveillance over the workings of government or making good use of the people available to him.

McGirr was probably not as well equipped as McKell either to manage discontents simmering in the union movement for some time. The war years had by no means been free of industrial disputes. Transport workers were on strike in Sydney and Newcastle in January 1944, followed soon after by coalminers. Christmas 1945 saw half a million workers in NSW steel and coal industries again on strike. Alongside the chronic shortages of everything from beer to building materials and the inability of electricity providers to maintain reliable supplies, strikes often seemed justified. They merely added to the daily difficulties most people faced. But as it emerged that many strikes were led by communists in the unions, some of the general public anger was deflected to the Communist Party itself, seen as un-Australian by returned servicemen who had developed a heightened sense of nationalism, or just foreign, especially among the increasing numbers of British migrants gravitating to the coalfields of the Hunter and the Illawarra.

Despite the introduction of a pension scheme for coalminers in 1941 and the beginning of open-cut coalmining in 1942, conditions in the mines were known still to be harsh and antiquated. In 1946 in co-operation with the NSW government, a coal industry tribunal devoted specifically to dealing with miners' claims had been set up at Prime Minister Chifley's urging. The next year also, after discussions with McKell, a Joint Coal Board was established to regulate conditions in the mines. Rather than attempt the impossible task of nationalising the coalmines, McKell and Chifley sought to regulate them in this way. Neither the extreme nationalisers nor the opponents of any kind of regulation were happy.[5]

Coalminers struck in New South Wales in October 1948 for over four weeks. The next strike which began in June 1949 in New South Wales and spread to mines elsewhere in Australia was ostensibly in support of claims for a thirty-five-hour week and long service leave, but this strike had been carefully planned by union leaders as part of a massive communist offensive in China and elsewhere in south-east Asia. Though the strike became a federal matter with Chifley's decision to freeze union funds and use the army to work open-cut mines in the Hunter, providing coal for basic services during the winter months (it was mid-August before the strike was over), its greatest impact was in New South Wales. Sydney shivered with severely rationed coal and electricity. Trains and trams were badly affected. Industries shut down or put off staff. The extent to which industry in New South Wales relied not only on coal but on electricity became evident.

In order to rationalise the number of suppliers and ensure constant and reliable electricity supplies to both industrial and domestic users, in 1950, McGirr's government established the NSW Electricity Commission bringing together the various power-generating plants operated by different government departments and offering to buy those in private hands. New power stations were planned near Newcastle and Wollongong involving the construction of Warragamba Dam and Lake Burragorang, begun 1948, finished 1960. After an early, but fruitless protest against the destruction of significant Aboriginal, colonial, and natural heritage, work on Warragamba Dam was an important source of jobs.

It is unlikely that the Commonwealth's vast scheme to transfer water from the Snowy River into the Murray and Murrumbidgee for irrigation and to use its fall along the way to generate electricity would have occurred without McKell's enthusiasm and co-operation. For McKell the prospect of adding to the area under irrigation in New South Wales and of increasing water reserves against drought were undoubtedly attractive; however, long-running

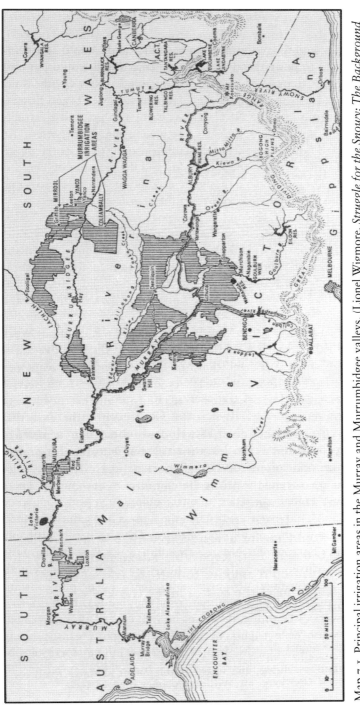

Map 7.1 Principal irrigation areas in the Murray and Murrumbidgee valleys. (Lionel Wigmore, *Struggle for the Snowy: The Background of the Snowy Mountains Scheme*, Oxford University Press, Melbourne, 1968, p. 188)

difficulties with the coalminers made Chifley and McKell both more determined to push ahead with this scheme which would not only increase the amount of electricity available in New South Wales but also lessen the power of the coalminers. Power began flowing from Guthega into the NSW grid as early as 1955 and electricity restrictions normal since the early 1950s were quickly forgotten.[6] An unexpected bonus came from the enthusiasm of some of the multi-national workforce for the snowfields and the creation of Thredbo as a destination for skiers, though it also became necessary to set up Kosciusko National Park to protect the area from over-use.

The strength of the union movement in New South Wales, enhanced by the levels of productivity maintained under difficulties during the war, was used more moderately to win improvements in general working conditions. From 1944 it was usual for most workers in New South Wales to get a two-week paid holiday break. This became three weeks for all those under state awards in 1958 and four weeks for state public servants in 1964. Late 1958 it was also agreed that in New South Wales, equal pay for women doing work of equal value to men would be phased in over the next five years. Women teachers were significant beneficiaries. For many years they were the envy of their sister teachers in other states. Long service leave was granted under state awards in 1951 and extended to all NSW workers in 1955. There was some feeling in the bush that rural workers were not doing as well out of these improvements in working conditions as those in the cities. But in 1953, union membership became compulsory for all workers in New South Wales gathering up more of the isolated labour force in the country. There were some strange misfits as unions acquired members from some unusual jobs, but given the benefits the unions had gained for their members, it was not an unpopular move. The 1950s were probably the height of union influence in New South Wales. The ability of the unions to deliver constantly improving wages and working conditions to their members also helps to explain why, despite constant internal communist-anti-communist sniping that was both destructive and very discrediting, there was no split in the Labor movement in New South Wales such as occurred elsewhere in Australia during the 1950s. But new technology was also beginning to create jobs that seemed less amenable to traditional forms of organisation.

In the immediate postwar years the shortage of housing became a matter of increasing electoral significance. Home building and home ownership were already falling behind requirements as a result of the depression when levels of unemployment and economic insecurity meant that many people could not manage to pay their rent let alone afford the long-term commitment of a mortgage. During the war there was very little building as both labour and materials were needed elsewhere, and in any case many families coped with the absence of husbands, fathers and sons by pooling their living arrangements. After the war, army surplus buildings were redeployed as temporary housing and for a myriad of other purposes. Many eventually accommodated immigrants who began arriving in the late 1940s.[7] Meanwhile, returned servicemen and their families were badly in need of new housing. Whereas a block of farming land had been offered to former soldiers after World War I, in 1945, a war-service home was the preferred option. By 1965, almost 80,000 had been built.

Ted and Phyllis Carr met during the war, married soon after and continued living with her parents in Maroubra. It was 1956 before they were able to buy and move into their own fibro cottage on the sand hills of Matraville (still unsewered in the 1970s). By this time they had three children, the eldest Robert born in 1947, a future premier of New South Wales. For many families like the Carrs it became increasingly irksome for three generations to still be sharing the one house after the war. Buying a block of land on the outskirts of Sydney and camping there at weekends while building your own home became the hobby of thousands of couples in the late 1940s and 1950s. Where to get scarce building supplies became a favourite topic of conversation, with expanding hardware stores a kind of clearing house for information about what was available or tricks of the building trade for self-taught owner-builders. *The Women's Weekly* published simple designs and handy hints on home building. Many of the houses were lightly constructed from fibro and fairly basic by modern standards. Apart from hot and cold running water and an electric stove, the most desired appliance was an electric refrigerator, perhaps a locally constructed Hallstrom Silent Knight.

However, it quickly became apparent that this level of self-help was not overcoming the accumulated housing shortage. Through another joint agreement with the federal government, New South Wales embarked on ambitious public housing plans. In 1941 a Housing Commission had been established to begin work on the housing shortage especially for ex-servicemen, not only in Sydney, but throughout New South Wales. Housing became a priority also for the recently re-formed Aboriginal Welfare Board.

The Housing Commission was itself constrained by the shortage of building supplies, nor was this resolved by re-opening the state brickworks and setting up a state-run tile works. Competition came from other government building projects, especially schools and hospitals now either badly run down from being neglected during the depression and the war, or else no longer located where the people who needed them lived.

The Housing Commission, not surprisingly, became the focus of a struggle between state planners and private developers who saw their profits being extracted from land and housing. McGirr who had been minister for housing under McKell promised in 1947 that if re-elected his government would construct 90,000 new homes within three years. By 1950 it seemed as if McGirr could think of nothing but housing and the main aim of his government according to its election propaganda became the provision of 'a home of your own', also money to buy it in the form of a low-interest loan, and protection against exploitation by maintaining rent controls. It became something of a joke that the government's response to every criticism was to announce another building project and hastily arrange to lay the foundation stone, though that was probably as far as it went.

As well as building new homes, a programme of slum clearance and re-housing people from some of the older, more densely crowded parts of Sydney was established. Some inner-city residents were to be re-housed in new blocks of medium-density and high-rise high-density flats on old sites such as in Redfern. Others were moved to new housing estates like Green Valley near Liverpool where the population grew from about a thousand in 1960 to over 20,000 by 1965. Among the early arrivals in Green Valley were Don Latham, who worked at the Redfern Mail Exchange, and his wife Lorraine. Their baby son, Mark, born 28 February 1961, served briefly as federal Labor leader in 2004. The Lathams were typical of the

7.4 Some of the last of the solid new houses built in the outer suburbs before World War II. Shortages of labour and materials caused by the war resulted in significant housing shortages and more flimsy construction. (Author's collection)

families re-housed in Green Valley but by no means among the most disadvantaged. At least Don had a job, though his daily journey to work in Redfern may have shortened his life.

Poor families, fatherless families and young families in over-crowded or otherwise unsatisfactory housing were given priority in the new estates. To them later were added Aboriginal families like that of Ruby Langford. But new housing was not the solution it seemed. The problems of disadvantaged families moved with them and were often exacerbated by distance and isolation. Employment was hard to find or reach locally. Many residents had to rely on public phones (frequently vandalised), and depended on poorly co-ordinated public transport to maintain contact with work, family, friends, and all the other services needed so badly. By the early 1970s, the name Green Valley, whether fairly or not, had become synonymous with unemployment and various forms of juvenile delinquency.[8]

Other nineteenth-century inner suburbs slated as slums for demolition and redevelopment were taken over temporarily by European immigrants and thus luckily preserved for restoration and gentrification a couple of decades later. Some flats and apartment blocks had been built in the city and the eastern suburbs as far back as the 1920s (such as the Astor on Macquarie Street), mostly for rent or on company titles. In 1961, however, the Strata Title Act saw the first block of 'home units' built on a site belonging to the Catholic church overlooking Middle Harbour. Quickly this form of high-density housing came to make up a significant number of the new homes built. With the changed regulations about the height of CBD buildings in the 1960s and tall blocks of apartments like Blues Point Tower rising on vantage points overlooking the harbour and the coastline, Sydney ceased to be 'a seven storey city of trams and verandah-posts'.[9]

The need for more accommodation, the dramatic changes brought by increasing use of motor vehicles, the inability of planners to manage or control the extent and the urgency for development had some unattractive consequences, not least of which was the demolition of a great many solid, handsome old buildings either for new roads or because of the good-sized parcels of land they released for redevelopment. The demolition of historical buildings especially Burdekin House, Macquarie Street, in 1934, the Commissariat Stores at West Circular Quay in 1939, and the continuing threat to others in the rising tide of development outraged Annie Wyatt, one of the founders of the Ku-ring-gai Tree Lovers' Civic League and a grand-daughter of Archibald Forsyth, the rope maker who in the nineteenth century had founded the Society for the Prevention of Cruelty to Animals in NSW. In 1945 with her Ku-ring-gai tree-loving ally, W. Cresswell O'Reilly as president, she became secretary of Australia's first National Trust based on the British National Trust. Though John Tate, chairman of the Cumberland County Council, gave support, the National Trust itself could only do so much, debating whether to try to deal with problems as they arose or to try to pre-empt them by creating a register of endangered buildings. Soon it was caught up in the fight to preserve the natural environment as well, in the cause of Montague Island and its fairy penguins.

On 30 November 1945 the Cumberland County Council made up of representatives of all local government authorities in the Sydney region first came together to devise an overall plan for future development. Its ambitious scheme to regulate urban development in the city and on the outskirts of Sydney so that housing bore a rational relationship to the provision of work, schools, hospitals, shopping centres and other services while maintaining adequate open space became law in 1951. A royal commission into the improvement of Sydney and its suburbs in 1909 had emphasised the importance of railways as the dominant form of transport, even recommending the overhead road and railway, eventually opened in 1962 at Circular Quay as part of the Cahill Expressway. The suburban rail system was generally neglected in the 1940s and 1950s, and trams were phased out by 1961 in favour of more flexible buses servicing new outlying suburbs. Trams were said to take up too much space, but buses cost less. Cars seemed more desirable still as they privatised transport and were paid for then mainly by the middle classes. As well the NRMA and the oil companies were hard to resist as advocates. But this begged the question of road building, long a burning subject throughout rural New South Wales. By the 1950s it was clear that modest road widening and straightening as had occurred on William and Oxford streets after 1909 was not the solution to the growing number of cars now choking Sydney streets. The Cumberland Plan's green belt around Sydney was destroyed by developers and their land-hungry clients, but the general pattern of freeways marked out in the plan survived. A great many of them are now reality on the map of Sydney and environs. Writing in 1956, town planner Denis Winston thought that the possibility of dredging Botany Bay so that shipping could be moved from Sydney Harbour would have to be considered more seriously. Almost fifty years later this has come to pass. He also pointed to the spectacular rise in the number of aircraft movements (then 500 a day) at Kingsford Smith Airport, suggesting that land for a second airport should have been set aside in the plan, and that a landscaped freeway connecting the airport with the city was desirable.[10] Though the site of a second airport remains in the 'too hard' basket, the freeway, part landscaped, part tunnel, has been built and is now supplemented by an airport rail link.

With so much government-sponsored development, there was no repeat of the kind of unemployment following World War I. Indeed, New South Wales was able to find work for an impressive number of immigrants as well as returning servicemen. Aborigines in rural New South Wales were the first to feel a shortage of jobs

7.5   'The Green Belt near Ryde: Epping Highway is on the
right, Lane Cove in the distance. Great quantities of fresh
fruit, milk, eggs and vegetables for Sydney are still produced
in the county: the nearness of the big city market, the
availability of piped water for irrigation, good education and
health services and good roads are all added advantages for
the farmer.' (Denis Winston, *Sydney's Great Experiment. The
Progress of the Cumberland County Plan*, Angus &
Robertson, Sydney, 1957, p. 51)

after the war. It had been estimated that employment levels among Aboriginal men reached 96 per cent during the war years. By the mid-1950s, however, the wool boom was fading, opportunities for employment on pastoral properties which included accommodation and the chance to gather 'bush tucker' were declining. Aboriginal people were forced, partly because the policies of the Aboriginal Welfare Board closed former reserves, relocating their inhabitants in towns like Walgett, to search for both jobs and housing in the towns.[11] Council work, or work on the roads or railways was still available, though no longer with housing attached, and in many towns, especially in the north and west, there was considerable resistance to the construction of new houses for Aboriginal families, and to the policy of integration in general. The Aborigines had no choice but to camp in places avoided by whites like flood-prone riverbanks or a tip on the outskirts of a town, thus adding to their insecurity because they had no right to be there. They were likely to find their camps demolished if they left them for any time in search of the seasonal and itinerant work that was their livelihood.

Itinerant rural labour brought people from traditionally quite different groups together but it spread the message of resentment and resistance. The 1943 amendment of the Aboriginal Protection Act which allowed individual Aboriginal people to apply for exemptions permitting them to live away from the reserves and control their own lives had already created a division in the community between those who welcomed the opportunity to better themselves and those who resented the patronising controls implied in what they called the 'dog licence' or the 'beer ticket' act. The loss of historic reserves such as the beachfront at Fingal in northern New South Wales, the object of development in 1969, partly fuelled the movement for land rights in New South Wales.[12] The loss or closure of old reserves was devastating. Much as they resented the separatism the reserves implied, the reserves had come to represent land which Aborigines felt was theirs, land given to them 'by Queen Victoria' in compensation for all they had lost. On them an Aboriginal identity was being preserved or re-created from remnants of the old culture mixed with a folklore of persecution by white authorities and a tradition of resistance to rules and oppressive laws. Closure of old reserves threatened that culture.

Despite these difficulties, however, the Aboriginal population was growing, from a low of 953 full bloods and 10,607 half castes in 1947 to over 40,000 people who in 1976 identified themselves as of Aboriginal or Torres Strait Islander origin. Ruby Langford's story, *Don't take your love to town*, gives some idea of the reasons why.[13] Despite the harsh conditions in which she lived, moving frequently between bush camps and overcrowded housing in Sydney, still she had access to her child endowment money, charitable agencies, and health-care so she could feed and otherwise care for her children. Unlike most white women by that time, she seems to have made no attempt to limit the size of her family, and all nine of her babies survived to adulthood. Diseases like tuberculosis and trachoma that had ravaged Aboriginal populations in the past were largely products of malnutrition, poverty and bad housing. (So was dependence on alcohol and other drugs.) As Aboriginal people belatedly gained their rights to federally funded child endowment and invalid and old age pensions in the 1940s, and with even small improvements in Aboriginal access to country hospitals and maternity services – Ruby was lucky to have several of her babies in Coonabarabran where she said both the hospital and the doctor treated her decently – the improvement in their health meant survival.

Increasing numbers of Aborigines were arriving in Sydney not only from rural New South Wales, but elsewhere in Australia looking for both work and the anonymous tolerance only a big city can provide. They found them at the Eveleigh railway workshops and in cheap, run-down housing in old working class suburbs like Glebe and Redfern. Among the arrivals in 1961 were Charles Perkins and his German-Australian wife Eileen from Adelaide, Charles to play soccer for the Greek club, Pan-Hellenic. Perkins said it was easier to captain a multi-racial soccer team than to be accepted among the Sydney Aborigines.[14] However, with the encouragement of Rev. Ted Noffs whose Methodist Wayside Chapel in Kings Cross ministered to the social outcasts of the city, Perkins embarked on a degree at the University of Sydney in 1963, and became manager of the Foundation for Aboriginal Affairs, an organisation inspired by Noffs to provide assistance with housing, employment, education, health, legal and other problems for Sydney Aborigines. Perkins' involvement with a small group of students, influenced by their knowledge of civil rights politics in the United States to stage a 'freedom ride' in New South Wales and the subsequent 'integration' of a swimming pool and a picture theatre in Moree, brought him (and the conditions of Aboriginal people in rural New South Wales) international attention. As in the United States, the images generated for the television news were far more impressive than anything lasting that could be achieved by the 'freedom riders'. But the possible uses of the media, television especially, for political purposes were still being invented.

During the 1960s, old established institutions like the churches and the university still dominated debate about the nature and future directions of society in New South Wales. One familiar voice in Sydney was the light Scots burr of John Anderson. In many ways, Anderson continued a significant Scots influence over education in New South Wales, going back at least as far as J. D. Lang's involvement with the founding of the University of Sydney, continued through George Robertson's influence as a publisher of school texts as well as major local authors, the work of Peter Board as director-general of education from the early twentieth century and of David Drummond as minister for education in the 1930s. (Both Board and Drummond were born in New South Wales though their parents were of Scottish origin and placed great store on the value of education.) When Glasgow-educated John Anderson (1893–1962) was appointed to the Challis Chair of Philosophy at the University of Sydney in 1927, he sympathised with the ideas of Karl Marx and the still youthful communist movement which also had significant Scots overtones in New South Wales with members like Jock Garden, J. B. Miles and Christian Jollie Smith. Anderson's rejection of war memorials as fetishes preventing critical thought about war and society led to an early clash with Sydney conservatives. During the 1930s, driven no doubt by his own complicated marital arrangements, he became fascinated by Freud, and obsessed with James Joyce's ultra-modern novel *Ulysses*. The fact that it was on the long list of books banned in New South Wales under the influence of the churches, both Catholic and evangelical protestant, stoked his campaign against censorship. By the 1940s, however, he had grown extremely critical of Marxism, and by the 1950s was complaining that there was too much interest in sex.

The influence Anderson exerted over both the University of Sydney and several generations of students was remarkable. In part it came from widespread acceptance of his constantly reiterated argument that 'the measure of freedom in any community is the extent of opposition to the ruling order, of criticism of the ruling ideas'[15] and his willingness to engage in debate both inside the university and in the community beyond, insisting that all questions be examined thoroughly from every point of view. In this he often appeared to be attacking prevailing hypocrisy or old shibboleths thus delighting the young. They naturally were only too willing to experiment with the idea of sexual freedom and other forms of liberation. Under Anderson's influence, students at the University of Sydney gained a reputation for sexual sophistication and worldliness. His atheism and his opposition to censorship brought him often into conflict with the churches. And his frequent statements on the nature or function of the university kept him at the front of all educational debates. But over the years his influence on the university was conservative. At a time when Marxist ideas were driving new areas of research in sociology and economics for example, Anderson's lack of interest in such ideas meant that there was little demand for knowledge about them from his students, and even less from Anderson's genuinely conservative colleagues who did not mind that they were not required to modernise. Through the Freethought Society over which Anderson presided from the 1930s for a decade or more, much of the intellectual energy of his followers was diverted to an increasingly arid criticism of any kind of commitment to ideas or expertise, or frittered away in hedonism. His influence on the study of philosophy and politics produced what appeared to be a critical edge (developed by his students such as P. H. Partridge and J. A. Passmore as Australian realism), but by the 1960s it had become both uncreative and soul destroying.

Anderson's legacy, a habit of criticism espoused by the NSW educated elite, lasted into the 1970s, even beyond. It was suited to the critical views of the new left, and adapted easily to postmodernist thinking. But it had a stultifying effect on intellectual life in

New South Wales and was only slowly dispersed by the can-do money-makers and the ideas they brought in their train, mainly from American think-tanks and degrees in business administration. In a rather depressing way Andersonianism suited the old pragmatic tendencies of Sydney and New South Wales. It was clever but super-ficial, superior but remote, and it did little to infuse a sense of seriousness or imaginativeness badly needed to balance the tendency of the market merely to copy whatever seemed to work. Rather than suggesting ways in which New South Wales might build on its past, it reinforced the idea of the past as a trap from which there was no escape apart from hedonism, drifting easily to enjoyment of sun, surf and the racetrack.[16]

Anderson died in 1962, but his spirit lived on as his students took up university teaching positions in philosophy, political science and history, mainly in universities in New South Wales and at the Australian National University. Many of his ideas were simplified or corrupted by the inheritors of the Freethought Society, the Sydney Libertarians, and later, the Push. But attitudes and values which under his influence had become part of the intellectual climate of the University of Sydney permeated the whole of New South Wales through several generations of graduates, teachers especially. The impeccably conservative Peter Coleman documented Anderson's obsession in *Obscenity, Blasphemy, and Sedition: Censorship in Australia* (1962), while Donald Horne's *The Lucky Country* (1964) could only have been written by someone trained to oppose the ruling ideas and the ruling order. The Freethought Soci-ety evolved into the Push, ritually gathering at the approved pub and adopting a bohemian lifestyle. The Push subverted and blighted the careers of a number of talented people with its cult of anarchy, its denial of the social usefulness of paid work, especially work in the service of the state, then gradually found it was becoming fash-ionable. With the changing mood of the times, the market turned increasingly to sex, sensuality, and libertarian ideas to sell more to increasingly younger and less discerning consumers. The values of the Push meshed easily with the 'swinging sixties'. It became a rite of passage at the University of Sydney and also at the relatively new University of New South Wales, where Richard Carleton and Wendy

Bacon inherited Anderson's campaign against censorship, for intellectually ambitious students like Les Murray and Germaine Greer
to spend a period lounging about with the Push.

In his study of a man sunbaking on Culburra Beach, photogra-
pher Max Dupain caught something of the contentment of Horne's
lucky country. A benign climate and almost a thousand miles of
Pacific coastline made 'going to the beach' one of the most popular forms of recreation in New South Wales, far more popular than
any intellectual, cultural or educational activities. By 1910 several
surf-lifesaving clubs had been formed to protect body surfers against
dangerous conditions. Regular competitions and carnivals produced
iconographic images of blue skies, golden beaches and bronzed male
bodies. Surfboard riding was introduced from Hawaii, also in the
first decade of the twentieth century, but surfing as a youth culture
really began to flourish on NSW beaches with the introduction of
lightweight surfboards in the late 1950s and the names of surfing
champions like Bernard 'Midget' Farrelly and Robert 'Nat' Young
became well known. In many ways modern, youthful adaptations of
some of the old masculine rituals of mateship, the scenes described
by Gabrielle Carey and Kathy Lette in *Puberty Blues* (1979) were
played out in kombi vans near beaches up and down the coast. The
surfing culture's instrumental view of women and of sexuality was
not unlike that of the bohemians of the 1920s, or the freethinkers
and Push members of the 1950s and 1960s. In writing of woman
as 'the female eunuch' (1970) Germaine Greer drew upon her experiences in Sydney and spelled out some of the consequences of the
good life as interpreted by NSW's men for their women.

After 1954 when federal Labor leader H. V. Evatt's denunciation
of the industrial groups brought about splits in the ALP in Victoria and Queensland, Labor in New South Wales not only survived,
but under Joe Cahill's leadership went on to win elections in 1956,
1959, and with Heffron as leader, again in 1962, aided by anti-
Canberra discontent arising from Menzies' credit squeeze. A common criticism of Labor in New South Wales now was that its leaders
were all old men. However, the old men remembered how close to
destruction the movement had come during the faction fights of the
Lang days. They were determined to avoid that kind of divisiveness
again.

Part of the explanation also probably lay in the shared experiences of Cahill and Cardinal Norman Gilroy, Catholic Archbishop of Sydney. Cahill was born in 1891, of Irish-born parents in Redfern. His father was a labourer and Cahill as a boy was apprenticed as a fitter at Eveleigh railway workshops. Like Chifley, he lost his job in 1917 in the great strike and was not re-employed until 1922. Gilroy was born nearby in Glebe in 1896. Unlike Melbourne's Catholic Archbishop Mannix with his Irish preoccupations, Norman Gilroy who succeeded Michael Kelly as Catholic Archbishop of Sydney in 1940 was thoroughly Australian. Though his parents were of Irish extraction, both were Australian-born. When Mannix was inciting pro-Irish resistance against the war in 1915, Gilroy was serving as a wireless officer on a ship off Gallipoli. In 1917 a way was found for him to begin training for the priesthood without depriving his parents of his much-needed financial support, and he progressed rapidly in the church. He identified strongly with moves to expand and strengthen the Australian-born priesthood being trained at St Patrick's Seminary at Manly established by Moran in 1889 and modelled on Maynooth in Ireland.

Gilroy was neither an intellectual nor a theologian and St Patrick's had its limitations, both intellectual and emotional according to novelist Thomas Keneally who studied there for the priesthood. A Catholic university such as was being discussed in 1949 under the influence of Gilroy's assistant, historian Eris O'Brien, might have introduced desirable new elements into the church. But Gilroy had a shrewd understanding of men and the ways of the world. His sympathies were naturally with the Irish-Australian working class from which he had come, and he cultivated good relations with the NSW Labor Party. The needs of his church as he saw them after 1945 were more churches and schools to follow the building boom into the suburbs and to cater for the Catholic immigrant population. More than Mannix he understood the aspirations of working class people and knew well the long-standing hostility of the Labor movement in New South Wales to communism. He believed that Labor in government was good for his church. So he resisted the influence of B. A. Santamaria's anticommunist 'Catholic Social Movement', and with the help of auxiliary bishops Eris O'Brien, then James Carroll, played down its activities in New South Wales. Carroll also had strong links into the Catholic working class of New South Wales, understood the importance of their relationship with the ALP and continually counselled moderation.

Elsewhere in Australia the ALP, driven by the zeal of Western Australian Joe Chamberlain, tried to exorcise Santamaria's movement and the allied anti-communist Industrial Groups from the unions by driving them into the DLP. In New South Wales, under the leadership of Laurie Short who was staunchly anti-communist though not Catholic, many of the Catholic Groupers remained in the ALP. However, it was a NSW Grouper, Jack Kane, who coined the name, Democratic Labor Party (DLP), and won enough votes to hold a DLP senate seat for many years. Even so, the DLP was never the force in New South Wales that it became elsewhere. Instead the persistence of Catholics in the NSW ALP in the face of suspicion elsewhere about their conservatism and loyalty to the church rather than to the party gave rise to a sectarian right–left division in the NSW ALP. By the late 1970s infighting between the NSW Right, pragmatic, preoccupied with power, and dominated by hereditary Catholics, and the Left, made up of idealistic former communists and impractical new left socialists, had become compulsive, violent, and once more potentially destructive.

An unusual addition to the Labor government's traditional policy of public works to ensure continuing employment was Cahill's decision after his overseas trip in 1953 that what Sydney needed was an opera house. Eugene Goossens had been agitating about the inadequacy of the Sydney Town Hall as a performance venue for the Sydney Symphony Orchestra of which he was musical director. Established jointly by the Sydney City Council and the NSW government in 1946, it was the first permanent orchestra in Australia to work with the Australian Broadcasting Commission. It seems as if Goossens may have envisaged something like the War Memorial Opera House used by the San Francisco Symphony Orchestra as a concert hall as well as for opera seasons.

By late 1954 Cahill was convinced and set up a committee to select a site. An international competition was held and in 1957 the inspired sketches of the young Danish architect Jorn Utzon were chosen for Bennelong Point. Cahill was keen to press ahead while there was still enthusiasm for the project. A public appeal for funds was launched in August 1957 and by the end of the year £900,000 had been collected. As this was nothing like enough, even for the £3.5 million the opera house was estimated to cost, the next year, the first of the Opera House lotteries with 100,000 tickets at £10 each (later reduced to £6) and a prize of £100,000 was launched. Since 1931, New South Wales had been raising funds for consolidated revenue from state-run lotteries, ordinary, special and mammoth with tickets at 5s 6d, 10s and £1. About half the cost of any ticket went into state revenue. The rest paid for prizes (there were enough small prizes for dozens of winners every week) and administration. The special opera house lotteries were earmarked for the opera house appeal and eventually contributed $101 million to the spiralling costs of construction, said to total $102 million.[17] Initially quite fashionable, even among people who were not regular lottery-ticket buyers, it became notorious after eight-year-old Graeme Thorne, son of a winner in 1960, was kidnapped, offered for ransom, then murdered.

Neither Cahill nor Goossens survived to see the Opera House finished. Cahill died in 1959 soon after a mighty campaign to win another term for his government, fractured but still functioning after the Split and the premiership passed to Heffron. Goossens was forced to resign from the orchestra and flee Sydney in 1956 after assiduous customs officials seized 'indecent' books, films and photographs from his luggage at Sydney airport. He died a broken man in England six years later.

The Opera House, planned to open on 26 January 1963 to mark the 175th anniversary of white settlement, became a media scandal too as technical problems were reported to be insoluble, completion seemed as far off as ever, and costs escalated. It probably contributed to the end of the record run of Labor governments in 1965 when part of Robin Askin's election platform came to be cleaning up the mess. Utzon resigned in 1966 having realised that he could no longer work with the new Country Party minister for public works, Davis Hughes. So a new team of architects was brought in to complete work too advanced to be abandoned. In the time between its conception and completion, ideas and priorities had changed. The Opera House eventually opened by Her Majesty the Queen in 1973 was in many ways a different building from either its original specifications or its imagined realisation. However, as a long-term investment for the people of New South Wales and especially Sydney, its value has been incalculable, both as an instantly recognisable symbol and as a magnet for tourists and performers from all over the world. International stars like Joan Sutherland, originally from Waverley, and June Bronhill, whose stage name came from her birthplace, Broken Hill, have returned to its stages.

As the postwar babies began to grow up, so there was need first for primary schools, then secondary schools, and eventually more university places to educate them. The minister for education from 1944 to 1960 was Robert Heffron, born in New Zealand in 1890 and named James and brought up as a Catholic. He left his Catholicism behind to become a 'proselytising rationalist', and added Robert to his name about 1920 when he was a socialist union organiser and, like future premiers Robin Askin and Robert Carr, came to be known as Bob. Though Heffron was responsive to the baby-boomer growth in the school age population, class sizes were enormous. Filmmaker and Labor Party speech writer Bob Ellis claimed his school, Lismore High, was the 'biggest secondary school in Australia' when he was there (1954–58) with first-year classes running from A to P and never fewer than forty-two in a class.[18] An inquiry into education by Harold Wyndham set up in 1953 reported in 1957, with legislation to be implemented in 1962, recommended the most extensive overhaul of the system since the days of Peter Board, significantly with the addition of an extra year of secondary education. This would give NSW children the same time in school as in Victoria where it was noted that university students and young workers were more mature because of that extra year.

After his experience of manpower planning during the war, Wallace Wurth knew that steps must be taken to train more engineers, chemists, and technologists for the postwar world. He had little trouble persuading Heffron of this, and a new university was established fairly quickly by transforming the old technical college in Ultimo dating from the 1880s into a 'university of technology' in 1948. It became the University of New South Wales in 1958 despite protracted opposition from the University of Sydney where, under Anderson's influence, vocational training was considered unworthy of a university. The University of NSW took responsibility for vocationally oriented university colleges at Newcastle and Wollongong as well as the School of Mines at Broken Hill. There was nothing backward looking or romantic about these new institutions, modelled as they were on American institutes of technology, and it was not easy to staff them. Early administrators were conjured out of the public service. Wurth who became chancellor of the UNSW in 1955 had no interest in the humanities or in education for its own sake. It was competent technicians he wanted. So buildings and working conditions were utilitarian even self-defeating. (Army surplus huts were still in use at UNSW in the 1980s.) By the early 1960s as well a search had begun for a site for yet another university in Sydney's north, leading to the construction of Macquarie University on a former orchard at North Ryde in 1964 with classes beginning in 1967. Like the University of New England, its main function was the training of teachers for the baby boom still working its way through the population.

Due partly to a higher birthrate among Catholic women and also because of immigration, the proportion of Catholics in New South Wales was growing. Whereas in 1961 Anglicans made up 44 per cent of the population and Catholics only 29 per cent, by 1966 these figures were 42 per cent and 30.5 per cent. A decade later Anglican numbers had declined to 36 per cent and further still to 31 per cent by 1986, a smaller proportion than the Catholics (31.5%). At the same time the proportion claiming no religion grew from 0.86 per cent to 11 per cent, possibly accounting for a fair number of earlier nominal Anglicans.[19] There was added pressure on Catholic schools, probably contributing to the brutal discipline portrayed so eloquently in Ron Blair's play *The Christian Brothers* (1975) based on his education at Lewisham Christian Brothers in the 1950s. The gasp of recognition Blair's play produced in audiences suggested that there were many who according to Edmund Campion had learnt 'obedience, deference and the recognition of authority'.[20] While some reacted strongly and became outspoken critics of authority, others practised evasion or were often troubled by guilt. At the same time, Vatican 2 was sweeping away the remnants of Irishism and sentimentality in the NSW Catholic church, and Catholic migrants from Europe were bringing a different kind of Catholic culture as well as their own expectations of the church and its school system. The old religion that demanded obedience was softened, but 'the peculiar moral casuistry which made up much of popular Catholicism' remained a habit among many who had learnt it as children. When allied to an equally powerful penchant for nit-picking legalism that seemed to grow out of the peculiarities of Sydney Anglicanism, there was little escape for hypocrisy in public life in New South Wales.

Once again the demand for education raised the spectre of state aid. In New South Wales it had become Labor government policy, while not permitting outright state subsidies for Catholic schools, to assist them in all kinds of other ways, e.g. they were permitted to purchase school equipment and textbooks from the factories and repositories established to supply the state system and at similar rates. Within the Labor Party long experience had taught the importance of moderating sectarianism for the greater good of solidarity. At the same time, the importance of a sound basic education as a foundation for survival and upward mobility was nowhere better appreciated than by working class people. There were many Catholic families for whom a freely provided state education was preferable to no education. 'Choice', the new slogan of economists and advertisers, was for those who could afford it.

In July 1962, soon after NSW Labor narrowly won an election by foreshadowing further assistance to Catholic schools that did not eventuate, all the Goulburn Catholic schools went on strike, vividly demonstrating the role they played in the education system as a whole. The federal executive of the ALP then countermanded policies introduced by Heffron's government to placate the Catholics of Goulburn. With Menzies' 1963 offer to fund science blocks in non-government as well as government schools, the question of state aid moved into federal politics, long-standing covert arrangements between NSW Labor and the Catholic church in New South Wales were upset, and the way opened for the Liberal leader Robin Askin to begin courting middle class Catholic voters by offering more state aid in New South Wales. The process of breaking the link between the Catholic vote and the Labor Party, forged in the sectarian struggles of the first two decades of the twentieth century, which had so far survived even the Split and the rise of the DLP, had begun.

Most other issues canvassed in the 1965 election were linked to generational change. The Labor cabinet was old and tired, and though Heffron retired at seventy-three in 1964 so that his deputy Jack Renshaw who was slightly younger than Askin could take over, its ideas were still old-fashioned and backward looking. Typically, at a time when consumption had become the reward of affluence, and women were returning to work to earn extra spending money, the government bowed to union demands for further restriction of trading hours. So when families had leisure time for shopping, the shops were closed. It was even suggested that laundromats should not be permitted to open in the evenings or at weekends. The Liberal Party (with a lot of financial help from Frank Packer) ran a sharp modern election campaign based around the slogan 'With Askin you'll get action' (devised by Donald Horne at the Jackson Wain advertising agency) and spread over many small issues where there was some generational difference.[21] Still it was a close election. Eighteen electorates were decided on preferences. It took ten days for the results to be finalised and the Liberal–Country Party coalition to be declared the new government.

8

1966–1987, everyone's doing it

The late 1960s and early 1970s have been seen as a time of hope, a time of change in Australia. In New South Wales the twenty-four-year succession of Labor governments came to an end in 1965 and a Liberal–Country Party coalition led by Robin Askin and Charles Cutler came to power, keen to release the market forces which many felt had been repressed for too long.

If there had been constraints on enterprise during the Labor years, they had not affected the growth of population in New South Wales and Sydney in particular. This was partly the result of immigration – immigrants arriving in these years came mostly through Sydney – and partly a product of the postwar baby boom. The mix of frustrated free enterprise and youthful idealism proved volatile. As the baby boomers became an ever larger proportion of the population and found their own aspirations frustrated by structures and systems they saw as self-serving or obstructive, there were many explosions.

Sydney had begun to reassert her position as the first city in Australia. Since the gold rushes of the 1850s, Melbourne had been the financial capital. BHP's head office remained in Collins Street. Melbourne's Stock Exchange was older than Sydney's and its organisation better suited to handling large underwriting projects. Melbourne stock-broking firms were also older, more experienced and used to operating on a large scale. Most of the company formation and investment activity associated with the growth of Broken Hill, important though it was for Sydney as Broken Hill became the third largest city in New South Wales, was managed through Melbourne.

However, the fact that the headquarters of the Commonwealth Bank were established in Sydney in 1912 and remained there when the Reserve Bank was hived off in 1959 helped keep Sydney's financial credibility alive. Had Denison Miller, first governor of the Commonwealth Bank who was born at Fairy Meadow and grew up at Deniliquin, not built a home, Cliffbrook, overlooking the sea near Coogee, the story might have been different. At the time of its foundation, no one could envisage how the Commonwealth Bank would become both banker and financial manager for the Commonwealth government during two world wars. With major financial institutions like the Bank of New South Wales (later Westpac) and the Australian Mutual Provident Society, Sydney's significance to Australia's financial market eventually led J. B. Were and Sons, one of Melbourne's oldest and most influential brokers, to establish a northern branch. Encouraged by Were's partner Staniforth Ricketson, the Sydney money market began to modernise. Ricketson's influence on the Liberal Party and as a personal friend of Menzies has probably not been fully appreciated, nor his significance in maintaining Melbourne for so long as the financial centre of Australia. After his death in 1967, Melbourne's financial influence was diminished. Subsequently, John Valder, chairman of the Sydney Stock Exchange 1973–76, played a leading role in integrating the Sydney and Melbourne stock exchanges on terms not unfavourable to Sydney. He also became finance director and president of the NSW Liberal Party in the 1980s, raising its morale, paving the way for Nick Greiner's election in 1988, and promising a return to the grand days before New South Wales became a Labor stronghold.

With the mining boom of the 1960s, international capital became interested in Australia and Sydney attracted more than its share of head offices. Finance companies established to facilitate hire purchase of cars and household equipment in the postwar boom also began to attract overseas capital, much of it from foreign banks who were not yet permitted to open branches in Australia. Finance companies and accounting services gravitated to Sydney for its proximity to Asia and thanks to the proximity to the International Date Line, its early opening stock market. By 1976 Sydney had become ninth among international investment centres, with Melbourne twenty-ninth.[1] When the federal government deregulated banking in 1985, ten out of seventeen foreign banks licensed to begin full banking business in Australia located their head offices in Sydney.

From the late 1930s the Australian Broadcasting Commission (later Corporation) had located its head office in Sydney. As television became more confident and the technology allowed more networking, Sydney's creative influence through the ABC became more apparent through its training of young talent. With lively and innovative programmes like *This Day Tonight*, a Sydney slant permeated public affairs reporting. The new economic service industries and the new media and communications were more volatile than the old mining and manufacturing industries which had been the backbone of the NSW economy for nearly 200 years. And their relationship with politics was different. Advertising and the media especially were capable of political influence quite different from anything the big end of town had ever exerted.

Other factors were hastening the move to Sydney as well. In the 1960s immigrants who had formerly made the sea voyage from Europe with Melbourne as their main port of arrival began arriving in Sydney by jumbo-jet. Sydney was closer to the United States and Asia and the Pacific by air than Melbourne, which because of the shipping routes had formerly had better links with Europe. And until Melbourne's Tullamarine airport was opened in 1970 Sydney had better international facilities anyway.

By the late 1960s, there was a mad scramble for office space in the Sydney CBD, especially with harbour views. Projects like Harry Seidler's Australia Square, and Centrepoint with its landmark tower, were welcomed by the Askin government. During the 1960s and early 1970s there was a mad rush to buy and consolidate city blocks to build new office space. Small old sandstone offices that had housed a single firm gave way to multi-storeyed office blocks built to accommodate the most up-to-date air-conditioning for office machines and communications systems. They were leased floor by floor to numerous tenants. On the northern side of the harbour, old working class communities and once sleepy suburbs of red brick villas with harbour glimpses were destroyed to finish the Manly-Warringah Expressway and create a satellite city in

North Sydney. By the mid-1970s the oversupply of office space had become legendary and property investors began to look at retail centres and home units instead. Then in the 1980s they began thinking about hotels in anticipation of tourism on the back of the 1988 bicentenary.

Robin Askin's government (elected 1965) was sympathetic to private developers. Publicly owned land was made available for development or redevelopment. Zoning was changed, planning controls were overridden, and the price of land and housing soared. In 1966, the cost of a block of land was 30.8 per cent of the cost of a new home in Sydney. By 1974 it was 60 per cent.[2] The Manly-Warringah freeway was pushed through to completion, as were extensions to the freeway system now linking Sydney with Newcastle, Wollongong and Parramatta. Sometimes, local campaigns to halt the building of freeways or to retain or restore sites as open or public space were successful. Plans to demolish Paddington (designated a slum) or the elegant nineteenth-century houses in Jersey Road, Woollahra for a freeway, or to turn Kelly's Bush at Hunters Hill over to a private developer for home units were defeated after sustained campaigns by local residents and in the case of Kelly's Bush, the Builders Labourers' Federation (BLF). Plans for a huge new sporting complex in Centennial Park announced in 1970 brought together conservationists, writers and local residents including Vincent Serventy, Judith Wright, and Patrick White, as well as Jack Mundey of the BLF again to defeat them. The Rocks redevelopment collapsed after persistent resident action, BLF green-bans, and a growing stench of corruption about its management. The disappearance and probable murder in 1975 of Juanita Nielsen, a local newspaper editor and persistent opponent of plans to redevelop Woolloomooloo and Victoria Street, Kings Cross, highlighted both the dismissive attitudes of the developers and the incompetence of local police, ensuring a sinister notoriety for that scheme. It too foundered and much of the area razed for high-rise office buildings was turned over to low-rise public housing.

There were conservation failures too. For example, there had been some sand-mining on the NSW coast since the 1950s but in 1968 a government inquiry set up in response to protests that beloved holiday places were being ruined suggested that of 640 kilometres of coastline, only 96 should be set apart as national parks and of these, only 19 need be exempt from mining. Despite a persistent campaign, only part of the Myall Lakes system was saved from mining.[3] Askin's reluctance to co-operate in proposals for renewal put forward by the federal Labor government after 1972 may have won approval from the anti-Whitlam forces, but they cost real opportunities for New South Wales to renew aging and expensive railway infrastructure, for example.

Elsewhere in New South Wales, the growth of Sydney threatened the provision of resources and began to distort local government. Small country towns were dying, though larger centres had begun to acquire more sophisticated functions. A study commissioned by the City of Tamworth in 1969, for example, showed that Tamworth exerted a dominant influence for a radius of 30 to 40 miles (about 48–64 km) and a strong but more specialised and administrative influence for about 70 to 100 miles (112–161 km) around it. People from surrounding centres came to Tamworth fairly regularly for medical treatment, to visit the hospital, and to shop, purchasing staples like flour, sugar, jam and tomato sauce in large quantities and large containers. They came less often, and from more distant centres as well, to buy motor vehicles and agricultural supplies, and to take part in sporting and social activities.

In the interests of decentralisation, growth areas were proclaimed in the Bathurst–Orange and Albury–Wodonga areas and the delivery of government services was redistributed to some country centres. However, it proved difficult to move whole government departments out of Sydney as envisaged, and the perceived failure of rural New South Wales to participate in decisions on service delivery eventually became an electoral liability for Askin.

Twenty-four continuous years in power had enabled Labor in New South Wales to establish its hold on the future through many sympathetic appointments to key positions and in major institutions. Even the Legislative Council had ceased to be a hostile force. Complacency about the right of members of the ALP to the jobs available through patronage and power at all levels of government, especially in the public service, had become entrenched. Labor's long term had also created a substantial full-time party organisation and within it the possibility of a salaried career leading eventually to a seat in parliament. This was an inviting prospect as an alternative to the existing routes through the union movement or as a result of hard work in the branches or in local government, especially for the sons (and to a lesser extent, daughters) of Labor stalwarts now benefiting from access to universities through Menzies' Commonwealth scholarships.

The development of career paths through the ALP, however, was a mixed blessing. At best it opened the party to quick and clever minds and new ideas on a scale not seen since the heady 1890s. At worst it produced desperate careerism with scheming, conniving and corruption as individuals sought to shore up their positions or hang on to advantages in a game of winner take all. The battles within the party, right against left, pragmatists against idealists, became more intense and bloody than any battles fought against electoral opponents. Perhaps these internal struggles, disguised by a veneer of solidarity at election time, greatly sharpened the political wits of the party and kept it several steps ahead of its more gentlemanly rivals in electoral cunning. And where New South Wales led, other state Labor organisations followed, adopting, for example, the dubious expedient of taxpayer funding for election campaigns introduced in 1981 at the urging of a party organisation already hooked on very expensive television advertising as a way of appealing to voters.

However, this period also saw the beginning of a decline in the traditional industrial power base of the NSW ALP with the rise of new industries based on real estate, electronics, entertainment and service provision. The largest and most powerful union in New South Wales by the 1970s was no longer associated with coalmining or the railways. It was the Teachers' Federation, still resisting affiliation with the ALP. There was an associated shift in the role of government as the stimulus to the development and exploitation of natural resources, to the guardian of the 'quality of life' of working people. Rather than fighting for improved pay and working conditions, it was often necessary to try to preserve what had already been won. The worth of resource development, opening new coalmines, logging remaining forests, building factories, dams or houses on unspoiled land, was questioned and sometimes rejected. Job creation ceased to depend simply on exploiting natural resources and began to be measured against costs to the environment and living conditions.

By contrast, the non-Labor parties in New South Wales had been on the defensive ever since the defeat of the Stevens–Bruxner alliance in 1941. A branch of the federally reconstructed Liberal Party was formed in New South Wales in 1945, but its emphasis was determinedly on Canberra. Unlike Labor it seemed amateur, a part-time organisation, drawing mainly on business for its leaders, and as after World War I, on ex-servicemen who retained an affection for organised action, men who were used to command, and had little interest in the arts of persuasion.

There was something of an old-style Labor machine man about Robin Askin, leader of the NSW Liberals from 1959. Indeed as a former executive of the Rural Bank Officers' Association he could claim to be a trade unionist. A hearty gregariousness may explain why despite increasing disgust with his behaviour and his methods among traditional conservatives, he managed to keep winning elections. Not a little of his support came from traditional working class voters who saw him as a battler like themselves, a man who shared their fondness for a drink, and a bet, and who was kind to animals. His background was poverty-stricken, in Glebe. At fifteen he joined the Government Savings Bank and was kept on after its reconstruction as the Rural Bank in the 1930s, becoming president of the staff officers' association. Service in the army during World War II led him like many other ex-servicemen into politics, mainly on the non-Labor side. Askin followed his former commanding officer, Murray Robson, into the leadership of the NSW Liberal Party. Christened Robin, he changed his name by deed poll to Robert in 1972 when he made himself 'Sir Robert', but he was commonly known as Bob. Probably best remembered for his advice reported as 'ride [drive?] over the bastards' when the car in which he was travelling with the American president L. B. Johnson in 1966 encountered demonstrators lying in the roadway in Liverpool Street, Sydney, he increasingly became identified with corruption in the administration especially of illegal nightclubs and gambling venues. During scuffles between protestors and police as demonstrations against the war in Vietnam became more insistent, the fact that police removed their identifying badges, and that Askin as police minister seemed to approve, suggested that the police were being politicised. The emphasis on law and order was satirised in a cartoon character, 'Laura Norder'.

A swimmer and footballer in his youth, Askin was also a bridge and poker player, and a regular punter on and off the racecourse. He had been an SP bookie on the side while he worked in the Rural Bank and when he was in the army. In 1962 he campaigned to legalise off-course betting, but was upstaged by Heffron's decision to open the first TAB agency in December 1964. A royal commission into off-course betting in 1962 had revealed there were 6,000 illegal bookmakers in New South Wales with an annual turnover of £275 million and a clientele comprising 28.7 per cent of the state's adult population. The proceeds of this betting were supposed to be siphoned into the treasury through the state-owned TAB. But Askin was not interested in suppressing SP bookmaking. Indeed he made it clear that he would prefer licensed private enterprise SP bookies to any form of state-organised gambling. While he was premier, Parliament House had its own (illegal) SP agency. There was clearly no serious intention to enforce the law, and with such hypocrisy, all law enforcement suffered. Askin may have used his contacts in the SP network to assist his election campaigns. Subsequently he encouraged and probably profited from a well-organised police protection business including illegal casinos and abortion clinics. SP bookies became a significant source of funds for organised crime, and the racetrack more than ever the place where the profits from illegal activities could disappear without trace. What had been fairly informal and randomly condoned small-time but widespread gambling, part of the folk culture, gradually became well organised and highly profitable to both Askin and the police.[4]

Corruption, already a problem in the police force before 1965, flourished during Askin's administration. Between 1962 and 1979 every NSW Police Commissioner retired under a cloud. Police caught engaging in criminal activities were quietly retired as medically unfit. Often, as in the case of the notorious Fred Krahe, they then set themselves as private inquiry agents or as security agents, without official objection, and went to work for developers or the proprietors of shady businesses such as illegal casinos, brothels or abortion clinics.[5] Philip Arantz who in 1971 exposed problems in the collection of crime statistics and refused medical retirement was dishonourably discharged after vilification in the parliament by Askin himself in his capacity as police minister. New South Wales was not unique in its policing problem, however. In both Queensland and South Australia, the police force was politicised and police commissioners were forced to resign during these years. But the scale of the problem seemed greater in New South Wales and was undoubtedly linked to the growth of civil unrest and the drug traffic as discussed below. There was a feeling that changing moral values were no longer reflected in the existing laws. The reform of the Summary Offences Act in 1978 recognised modern reality and lessened the penalties in matters like soliciting and drunkenness, but despite changes of government, and attempts at reform by several ministers and commissioners, corruption in the police force seemed endemic.

In addition to the Summary Offences Act there were other laws now apparently out of touch with the normal behaviour of the younger generation. Rising numbers of fines for parking and speeding, as well as minor offences under the tenancy laws, were bringing otherwise law-abiding citizens into contact with the courts of petty sessions. From 1954 a system of dealing with fines for minor traffic offences by post had been introduced, and though there were benefits to both the treasury and the court system in this, the effect was also somewhat to devalue the legal system. Impecunious young men boldly allowed their parking and speeding fines to accumulate then paid them off by spending a weekend in gaol. The number of arrests made as a result of mass demonstrations organised first against the Vietnam war and later against the Springbok rugby tour, Anzac Day marches, and various unwanted developments, both urban and rural, gave many of the educated middle classes contact with the law in a way they had never had before. The magistracy itself was at the same time in the process of being transformed from a fairly lowly branch of the public service into a qualified profession. Academic lawyers, civil libertarians, and a clientele that was increasingly better educated than either magistrates or police drew attention to the many defects of the justice system.[6] At the same time intensive police surveillance for drugs, peddled increasingly in conjunction with the arrival of American servicemen on leave from Vietnam, uncovered some murky connections between the criminal world, politics, and the justice system. In the 1980s a series of charges relating to alleged political interference in drug-related cases saw former Chief Magistrate Murray Farquhar, an old style magistrate with a reputation for a lenient and innovative approach towards the treatment of chronic minor offenders, sentenced to four years in gaol for perverting the course of justice.

The use of Sydney as a rest and recreation centre for American troops from Vietnam from 4 October 1967 had a huge social impact. It made the war seem very close, especially to young people who came in contact with the servicemen in bars and nightclubs around Kings Cross or were involved in opposing conscription. And it gave a great boost to the organisers of sex- and drug-related industries. American servicemen in New South Wales during World War II had placed enormous pressure on existing leisure-time facilities, then modest as might be expected in a community still dominated by evangelical religious beliefs. Nightclubs and gambling clubs where baccarat, roulette, craps, blackjack were played sprang up and police were instructed to go easy on them because they were a source of entertainment for the Americans; likewise prostitution was often linked to the clubs. With Americans from Vietnam in Sydney, however, the Askin government actually intensified prosecution for prostitution and drunkenness to the extent that the daily parade in the court of petty sessions became a farce, adding considerably to the potential for police corruption. But whereas in the 1940s, the supply of alcohol had been considered a problem, in the late 1960s it was other drugs.

Before the 1960s there was little heroin (or marijuana for that matter) on the streets of Sydney. The troops brought drugs with them and set up a demand for more. At Griffith in the Murrumbidgee Irrigation Area, Robert Trimbole organised production and distribution of marijuana in conjunction with fruit and vegetable growers Tony Sergei and Tony Barbaro. A lucrative traffic in drugs was carried on under the cover of the Sydney fruit and vegetable market netting Frank Nugan's trucking business a fortune. Nugan was then able to set up a 'Swiss style' confidential merchant bank in conjunction with Michael Hand, an American ex-serviceman. Their turnover was in the vicinity of $1,000 million in seven years, some from financing the purchase of poker machines from the Bally

Corporation of Las Vegas and the importation of drugs through the Mr Asia syndicate. From the early 1970s, Griffith shopkeeper and parliamentary candidate Don Mackay waged a campaign against the local 'grass' growers, provoking police raids on marijuana plantations at nearby Coleambally in 1975 and again in 1977. On 15 July 1977, Mackay disappeared. He was presumed murdered. Charges were laid eventually in 1984 against James Bazley and George and Gianfranco Tizzone. No body was ever found but Robert Trimbole was said to have ordered the killing. In January 1980, Frank Nugan's body was found in his car on a back road near Lithgow, apparently a suicide. Not six months later Hand disappeared in suspicious circumstances. There were rumours that the American CIA was implicated. The Nugan-Hand bank had a $20 million deficit. Yet another inquiry uncovered more of the detail, but the problem of drugs and crime seemed insoluble.

Along with sex, drugs and American servicemen came the gay restaurants, nightclubs and bathhouses set up in the mid-1960s by Roger Claude Teyssedre and Dawn O'Donnell with financial input from Abe Saffron, owner of the all-male revue at Les Girls and strip clubs in Kings Cross. Though male homosexual sex acts were illegal in New South Wales, Sydney beaches had long offered the attraction of male bodies on display. Discreet meeting places in hotel bars, private clubs, and more dangerously, in public lavatories, were tolerated often in conjunction with protection paid to the police. Despite some notorious episodes of entrapment, they flourished and with them, Sydney's reputation as a place with a congenial gay culture. Their illegality, however, meant that they too contributed to the turnover of illegal drugs as well as the extent of organised crime and corruption. Hypocrisy about sex of any kind was as traditional in all churches in New South Wales as opposition to gambling and alcohol, and policing the laws relating to prostitution and homosexuality was random, and open to blackmail. A gay liberation movement, largely influenced by American experience, sprang up in Sydney, and in 1971 a lobby group CAMP (Campaign Against Moral Persecution) was formed, though changing the law seemed a hopeless idea. On a warm February night in 1978 about 1,000 people set off on a march down Oxford Street to mark International Gay Solidarity Day. Though they had a permit, the police revoked it. There were angry encounters and about fifty arrests were made.

The next year another march, more defiant, took place, and was allowed to proceed peacefully. Such was the beginning of the Gay and Lesbian Mardi Gras, soon an important and lucrative event in the NSW tourist calendar. Now claimed as the largest night-time outdoor parade in the world, it has attracted large numbers of visitors from overseas and interstate, and helped create a substantial gay residential and business precinct in south Sydney. As well, by 1984 the threat to public health of AIDS helped lessen the resistance of religious groups in the parliament, both Catholic and extreme protestant, and decriminalising legislation was passed.

There had been criticism of the state of the NSW prison system for some time, both from those who worked inside as warders and from prisoners' action groups and lawyers. By the 1970s action became inevitable. On Sunday 3 February 1974 prisoners at Bathurst rioted and burned the gaol down. Eighteen months later there was a riot at Maitland Gaol and buildings were again set on fire. The answer was not a new high security gaol, Katingal, completed in 1975. It was closed two years later because its conditions were deemed so harsh as to contravene the human rights of prisoners. In April 1976 Mr Justice J. F. Nagle was appointed by Askin's successor, Eric Willis, to head the first royal commission on the prison system since an 1878–79 inquiry into the management of Berrima Gaol. As head of the Corrective Services Commission (1979–81) Tony Vinson attempted to reform the system along lines suggested by Nagle's 1978 report, but the problems seemed intractable. Like the police force, the prison system had become a world of its own, generally remote from the knowledge or experience of the ordinary citizen. The legal profession too remained deeply conservative, sometimes seeming closer to its nineteenth-century origins than to modern life.

The Age of Aquarius dawned in New South Wales at the Metro Theatre in Kings Cross in 1970, when the rock-musical *Hair*, imported from California by impresario Harry M. Miller, opened. The paying public came from far beyond Sydney for its nudity and penetrating beat. Sex shops and hippie heavens proliferated in nearby streets. Following the tracks of the surfies, at Nimbin on the north coast, an anti-war, anti-authority student-organised festival of free love with hash cookies, transformed itself into a site of permanent protest, pioneering the alternative lifestyle, new age therapies, tree-hugging, sea-changing and eventually other tourist attractions.

8.1 An early demonstration outside the Sydney headquarters of the Liberal Party seeking homosexual law reform (c. 1970). Tom Hughes was federal attorney-general at the time. The Campaign Against Moral Persecution (CAMP) established in 1971 in Sydney to pursue law reform was later overshadowed by the more flamboyant Gay Liberation and the Gay and Lesbian Mardi Gras. (Author's collection)

8.2 Uki butter factory in the Tweed Valley with Mt Warning in the background. No longer simply dairying country, these beautiful north coast river valleys were 'discovered' by hippies in the 1960s and are now sought after by tourists, conservationists, and sea-changers. (Maurice Ryan, *Norco 100: A Centenary History of Norco, 1895–1995*, Norco Co-op Ltd, Lismore, 1995, p. 178)

Students, hippies, flower children of the postwar baby boom began joining the ALP in increasing numbers, especially in old branches in gentrifying suburbs like Balmain and Paddington. Most had not seen a federal Labor government in office and few remembered New South Wales before Askin. The idea of Labor seemed an exciting possibility. In their idealism, however, they quickly clashed with the traditional practices and the cynicism of the old Labor machines. Membership records were falsified. Branch meetings became violent. Thugs were hired to protect the interests of developers who thought they had secured rights over old-fashioned ALP branches and aldermen.

During the early 1970s the median age of the population dropped to twenty-seven. Baby boomers, already politicised by conscription and the Vietnam war, almost swamped the electoral rolls after the age of consent was dropped in 1971 from twenty-one to eighteen, i.e. to the age of conscription. Between 1950 and 1973 there were nine elections and seven redistributions. Askin regarded an electoral redistribution as a natural preliminary to calling an election. That his government survived so long can be partly explained by the loyalty, experience, and ability of the public service under the Public Service Board chairman, John Goodsell (1960–71), who had worked his way up from his appointment aged fifteen as a junior clerk in the Department of Public Works. Askin was returned again in 1973, though he was already disliked. But he had succeeded in securing the votes of increasing numbers of Catholics, partly because of his cynical support for Catholic schools. And, like Henry Bolte in Victoria, he actively supported the DLP, especially in electorates where this had a significant impact on Labor. Askin was able to divide the Catholic vote in a way that the Split had not in New South Wales.

There was a widening rift between the older generation, many of them like Askin, ex-servicemen from World War II, who were ruthless and realistic about survival, and this younger generation, veterans already, but of the campaign against the war in Vietnam and conscription. Theirs was the more intense moral position. Having grown up in prosperity with educational opportunities and employment prospects unimagined by their parents or grandparents, they were afraid neither of unemployment nor authority, political, religious or otherwise. They could afford to be idealistic about social reform and deeply concerned about such issues as censorship and equal rights for women, Aborigines and homosexuals. To them, Askin's behaviour seemed crude, his morals objectionable. His death in 1981 conveniently coincided with David Marr's publication in *The National Times* of ferocious accusations of corruption against him.

Stories of the bribes Askin was paid for the protection of illegal casinos or in order to purchase knighthoods (said to cost from $20,000 to $60,000) could not be proved because his personal finances were so confused by his gambling and by the many deals he made. Askin's sixty-odd knights included men who had been politically useful, among them public servant John Goodsell, Vernon Treatt, former leader of the opposition and chair of the three-man City Commission set by Askin to govern Sydney after he had sacked the council in 1967, former lord mayor, Emmet McDermott, and Asher Joel, advertising executive and chief organiser of the 1970 celebration of Captain Cook's landing at Botany Bay, as well as the Pope's visit in the same year. Businessmen, and racing and cultural identities like road haulage company boss Peter Abeles, Woolworths executive Theo Kelly, developer Paul Strasser, artist William Dobell, AJC chairman Brian Crowley and Clyde Kennedy of the Sydney Turf Club were knighted. So was Cardinal Norman Gilroy. When Askin retired he moved into a 'palatial' home in Manly, provided for him at a nominal rent by the Catholic church in recognition of his support.[7] And when he died, he left almost $2 million, mostly to his widow, Mollie, along with a life tenancy of the house. She left almost $4 million when she died three years later. The Taxation Department tried without much success to establish what proportion of this money came from 'race winnings'.[8] A subsequent attempt by his former press secretary, Geoffrey Reading, to dismiss the allegations only succeeded in confirming what was already known. Askin represented a hard-drinking, gambling, whoring hypocritical masculine culture that was surely passing away.[9]

A sign of changing attitudes everywhere was the election in 1974 of ALP stalwart Joy(ce) Cumming as Lord Mayor of Newcastle – quite an achievement in the once tough mining city, though possibly also a sign of Newcastle's changing fortunes. An alderman since 1968 when, like many women entering politics in the wake of a husband or other male relative, she followed her father onto the council, she was the first woman in Australia to be elected lord mayor, though in New South Wales since 1929 when Lilian Fowler became the first woman in local government, ten women had served as mayor and a total of 362 women had been elected as aldermen or shire councillors.

By 1975, the ALP had decisively retired its old men, begun to play down its Catholic connections, and proclaimed Neville Kenneth Wran as leader. Wran's accession was swift, cunningly engineered and controversial, but he certainly presented a real choice to the younger electorate. The best thing about Balmain and the working class where he was born in 1926, he said, was being able to get out of it. As the youngest son of an easy-going often out-of-work father, he had the support of a strong and capable mother as well as older brothers and sisters. With the depression over, the family moved to Five Dock and Wran was able to follow the traditional path for a clever boy through articles in a solicitor's office to a degree in law, part-time. Good-looking, with a theatrical talent, he might have done well in the Liberal Party. However, working in industrial law, he joined the Labor Party in 1954. By the late 1960s he had cast himself as a more desirable leader than cautious, long-serving Catholic Pat Hills. As the youngest ever Lord Mayor of Sydney in 1954 Hills welcomed the even younger Queen Elizabeth to the city, but as Labor leader he seemed dutiful rather than dynamic.

Wran looked and sounded modern; he was clever, educated, not tied to the Catholic clique. He had a real skill in using the media, especially television, and he needed it, not only to speak directly to the electorate but so that he could use his popularity to repress opposition within the caucus and the party. From the beginning he adopted a presidential approach to the leadership and, after he scraped into government in 1976 on fewer than a hundred votes after a count lasting ten days, to the premiership. According to Graham Freudenberg, Wran took over much of the agenda Whitlam had developed for the ALP federally – 'the environment, the national estate, funding for the arts, aboriginal land rights, child care, the status of women and anti-discrimination laws'.[10] Legislation introduced in New South Wales in 1976 proposed to prevent discrimination based on 'race, colour, sex, marital status, age, religious or political conviction, physical handicap or condition, mental disability and homosexuality', but because of difficulties in having so many grounds accepted, the 1977 Anti-discrimination Act was limited to race, sex and marital status.[11] As part of a new focus on policy development, the Women's Advisory Council, the Women's Coordination unit, the Ethnic Affairs Commission were established and an Anti-Discrimination Board was set up to hear and resolve complaints about discrimination and human rights. Yet Wran took care to distance himself from Whitlam, seeming, especially in his first term, to do very little very slowly. Though the 1978 election was dubbed a 'Wranslide' because it gave him a majority of 27 seats, Wran continued to cultivate the media, even irritating old-fashioned Labor supporters by his closeness to conservative talk-back host, John Laws, and his attempts to buy support from media owners Rupert Murdoch and Kerry Packer through the rights to run Lotto and World Series Cricket.

Kerry Packer's World Series Cricket was launched in May 1977. At first the trustees of the Sydney Cricket Ground were opposed to providing access but almost immediately, the sports minister, Ken Booth, announced that the government would change the law so that new trustees more sympathetic to the World Series games could be appointed. Then, lights to permit day/night games were installed by the new trustees who agreed to pay two-thirds of the cost, the rest to come from the taxpayers of New South Wales. Cricket had been a traditional and rather exclusive game with New South Wales often dominating the interstate competition. It became fast-paced entertainment for the masses, whether in brightly coloured clothes under the lights or on Packer's Channel 9. Wran's government took credit for opening this stuffy establishment game for the enjoyment of the people. However, cricket hooliganism quickly came to disfigure the games played on the still traditional turf of the SCG. Though Wran may have hoped to win Packer's goodwill, the winner was undoubtedly Packer. By 1979 cricket had become mass entertainment and televising it belonged virtually to Channel 9. The new cricket crowd was young, partisan, and irreverent. But cricket was remarkably cheap television for the ratings it achieved, and in a sense it had been Australianised because at Lord's and elsewhere, cricket administrators were forced to accept changes Packer and television had introduced to the game.

The NSW bureaucracy had become large, complex, and exceedingly difficult to oversee. Through its oversight over appointments and the economy, the Public Service Board had come to have enormous influence on government in New South Wales. Wallace Wurth's successor, John Goodsell, aimed for efficiency rather than the economy espoused by Wurth. Goodsell believed that public servants should be treated more like their equivalents in the private sector. He was sympathetic about travel and entertainment allowances, better office accommodation – the State Office Block on the corner of Macquarie and Bent streets, now demolished, was his initiative. He also began computerising the state's record-keeping revealing substantial gaps, errors and inconsistencies in management systems devised in an ad hoc fashion over almost 200 years. In the police department, for example, computerisation exposed massive problems, including forms of corruption that had grown up over a long period. However, Goodsell was unable to change the prevailing system of seniority in public administration. Indeed, he may have accentuated its status consciousness. Lingering sectarianism led to deference and evasiveness. There were cases of wasteful demarcation, duplication, and outright obstructionism, while feather-bedding had become an art form. The problems generated by this culture were apparent in the inefficiencies of the transport system, and contributed to constantly low expectations of local government.

When he took over the government in 1975, Wran feared that he might suffer the kind of public service obstruction he believed had hampered Whitlam's reforms federally, so he commissioned a study of the NSW public service from Peter Wilenski, Whitlam's former private secretary who had worked on a review of the federal bureaucracy with 'Nugget' Coombs. At the same time Wran recruited Gerry Gleeson, a former teacher and Public Service Board inspector, one of many who had systematically inspected government departments to determine how efficiently and economically they were carrying out their functions, to run the Premier's Office as the main engine of government, asserting itself over the long-held powers of both the Public Service Board and the Treasury.

Wilenski's Interim Report in 1977 sought greater equity, social responsibility and political accountability in the public service as well as reforms already being pursued by Goodsell. Departmental status and efficiency had come to be judged according to the ability to capture and hold an ever-increasing share of the budget, and the purposes of administration and broader notions of effective policy delivery had been lost. Though often in disagreement about their aims and methods, Wilenski, the unorthodox and impatient intellectual, and Gleeson, the canny Catholic public servant, succeeded in reshaping public administration in New South Wales. Wran responded intuitively to Wilenski's urgency, but he also relied instinctively on Gleeson's unfailingly accurate perceptions from his Catholic perspective.

The new Public Service Act of 1979 effectively destroyed the old Public Service Board, and began moving public administration towards greater economic efficiency and accountability. Many existing practices were exposed, but bringing about change in the prevailing culture was sometimes a painful process. Wilenski had noted that intellectual skills as opposed to program skills were undervalued, that there was too much scrabbling for a share of the budget, and too little cost–benefit analysis of the outcomes.[12] Most of the public service had been recruited at the base level from among school leavers, and had developed a dowdy image. Women rarely achieved the seniority necessary for promotion and were discouraged by the expectation that they would retire after marriage. Recruiting graduates at levels higher than base grade gradually added talent and ideas. It was soon possible to see the effect of contemporary university teaching in economics, politics and public administration coming into the public service. By 1988, the economically rational ideas Nick Greiner wished to introduce to the government of New South Wales were in fact already in place and being implemented in small ways.

In the substitution of 'merit' for seniority in promotion, however, the meaning of 'merit' was frequently contested, especially when 'merit' had to be understood in a female form. As Wran himself observed, intellectual ability was not given to men alone. To compete, New South Wales needed the skills and abilities of its clever and competent women. The most visible changes in the service were forced by second wave feminism. Old expectations and hierarchies were shaken out in the name of much resisted 'equal opportunity'. As director of Equal Opportunity in Employment, Alison Ziller agitated and offended many people who thought their jobs and power were a natural right. But she also had a moral advantage not only in addressing women's rights to jobs hitherto denied simply because they were women, but also in applying similar reasoning to men kept out of jobs because of their ethnic or religious background. Equal opportunity turned tribalism and sectarianism upside down and made some hitherto cosy workplaces rather uncomfortable.

In other legislative reform, a state ombudsman was appointed in 1975. And after more than a century of debate and agitation, in 1978 the people of New South Wales were able to vote for the election of the Legislative Council. The variety of candidates and causes offered for the statewide electorate thus created came to show the extent of voter frustration or disgust with the constraints now imposed by the party system. In subsequent elections, tree lovers, shooters, marijuana smokers and Aboriginal groups among others fielded candidates. The spirits of George Ardill and Dill Macky a century earlier reappeared in the form of husband and wife Fred and Elaine Nile elected by the evangelical Christian Call to Australia Party. Huge ballot papers, occasionally containing a hundred names or more, were derided as 'tablecloths'. However, optional preferential voting was introduced for all state elections with the choice of voting either 'above the line' for a party and its stated preferences or 'below the line' for individual candidates in Legislative Council elections. Since the average voter was well trained by filling in TAB forms and Lotto coupons, how to vote in Council elections presented merely a different set of options and voters made calculated use of them. With the statewide constituency for the Council more women and representatives of ethnic communities like Italian-born Franca Arena, Helen Sham-Ho whose background was Chinese and Lebanese businessman, Eddie Obeid, entered the parliament. The long-standing arrangement whereby country electorates had much smaller populations than city ones came to an end with the institution of an automatic one vote, one value system. In 1984, the maximum term of a government in New South Wales was extended from three to four years.

In 1971, 23,101 people in New South Wales (11,682 male and 11,419 female) answered Aboriginal to the census question on racial origin now designed to encourage pride instead of evasion or suppression. In the census of 1954, only 12,213 Aborigines had been counted in New South Wales and in 1966, the figure was 14,219. Though these figures were regarded as unsatisfactory and certainly an underestimate of the likely Aboriginal population, the number by 1971 was an indication of acceptance demonstrated already in the historic federal referendum of 1967. At the same time, rising pressure for development, especially along the coastal strip of New South Wales, was beginning to force Aboriginal people from the places where they had hitherto survived in obscurity. On the far north coast, land hitherto reserved for Aboriginal use attracted developers who saw it as potential holiday homes and tourist villages. South of Wollongong, likewise, the holiday homes advanced on the beaches, and Aboriginal communities that had survived largely unnoticed except when they were useful as casual labour found themselves being pressed by development.

In 1983 New South Wales adopted an Aboriginal Land Rights Act under which Aboriginal land councils were permitted to claim remaining crown land not needed for other public purposes. Twenty years later 122 different land councils had claimed 79,000 hectares. The legislation had weaknesses, however. Land was given as freehold to the land councils whereas it probably should have been inalienable. Land councils then found themselves like families inheriting property, under pressure to sell to meet the multifarious needs of their members, and land meant to provide security and some economic resources still found its way into the hands of developers. And unlike the heritage legislation to protect historic buildings, there was no allowance made for the protection of Aboriginal sacred sites on land already alienated and therefore not available for a native title claim.

But there were other provisions to assist Aboriginal self-improvement. By 1980 guidelines for the employment of Aborigines in the public service were established, an Aboriginal training scheme was set up and an Aboriginal advisory officer appointed.[13] In 1981, Attorney General Frank Walker became the first NSW minister for Aboriginal affairs and in November that year, Patricia O'Shane became head of the NSW Department of Aboriginal Affairs, the first Aboriginal woman to hold such a senior position in the public service. In 2003 one of her successors, a Wiradjuri woman, Linda Burney, was elected member for Canterbury and so became the first Aboriginal person in the NSW parliament. Rising awareness of Aboriginal issues compounded by rural unemployment and a new kind of sometimes aggressive self-consciousness especially among young men led to increased racial tension in north-west towns like Walgett.

Traditionally, the Labor Party had made jobs and employment conditions their top priority in government, borrowing if necessary to fund public works. By the 1970s and 1980s chasing economic growth through investment and trade had become more important for the premier and his ministers. Though employment in the Hunter was shored up with new electricity and aluminium smelters, New South Wales could no longer support its people merely by exploiting coal and other natural resources. The rampant development of Sydney during the 1960s and early 1970s showed the need for urban planning. It seemed that quality of life could not be entrusted to private enterprise or delivered by the market. Wran saw the possibility of job creation (and votes) in environmental protection. Some regulation was necessary.

The environment movement in New South Wales dated back to at least 1895 when the Warragamba Walking Club was formed. Milo Dunphy's Mountain Trails Club in 1914 marked the emergence of modern bushwalking in New South Wales, and the dream of a national park in the Blue Mountains. Threats to the blue gum forest in the Grose Valley were beaten back in the 1930s and, in 1967–71, to Colong Caves and the Kanangra-Boyd wilderness. Vindication came, in 1994, with the discovery in a remote gorge of the Wollemi National Park of a type of pine thought to be 150 million years old and hastened acceptance of the Blue Mountains as a world heritage area.

The destruction of beloved coastlines by sand-mining at Myall Lakes or a coal loader at Clutha on the Illawarra escarpment brought out protest groups. New South Wales was also discovering that its history went back a long way beyond the beginnings of European settlement. In 1980 the government nominated the Willandra Lakes system – 3,700 square kilometres in south-west New South Wales where in 1969 at Lake Mungo an anthropologist, Jim Bowler, had uncovered remains, subsequently known as 'Mungo woman', said to be 26,000 years old – for inclusion on the world heritage list. Registered in 1981, it was soon recognised as one of the most important archaeological sites in the world containing some of the earliest evidence of human burial practices.

Another NSW world heritage site was declared in 1986. After years of intense campaigning by conservation groups including the dramatic blockade against logging at Terania Creek by conservationists along with large numbers of 'hippies' from nearby Nimbin, some 203,088 hectares of subtropical rainforest in sixteen national parks stretching from the northern Border Ranges to Barrington Tops were listed. What had once been seen merely as scrub to be cleared and burnt after the valuable red cedar had been extracted, then used for dairying or sugar, was now to become part of the international heritage and tourist business.

In the south of the state, violent confrontations between conservationists and timber workers in the forests of Eden produced a divided community. Since the nineteenth century these forests had been providing timber selectively for use mainly as railway sleepers. Former dairy farms were now producing more valuable beans and peas for trucking overnight to the Sydney markets and the local Aboriginal communities had added bean picking to timber getting and fishing as forms of employment. In the 1960s, however, the Japanese pulpwood manufacturer Harris Daishowa came to an arrangement with the NSW government to clear large areas for woodchips. After protests in which the local Aboriginal community was joined by conservation groups and the by now familiar 'greenies', and during which more than a thousand arrests were made, in early 1988 another 80,000 hectares of forest were added to the national estate in the Tantawangalo and Coolungubra national parks. Even so this failed to translate into 'green' votes for Barrie Unsworth in the ensuing election.

The need to drown more river valleys for irrigation or town water supplies began to be questioned. In 1979 for example, the NSW Water Resources Commission proposed a dam at Paynes Crossing to inundate the Wollombi Valley. Besides being the area where the Awabukal of Lake Macquarie, the Kamilaroi of New England and the Darkinung of the Hawkesbury converged, and therefore rich in Aboriginal records, it was also the route of the convict-built Great North Road. Many examples of the incredible building feats exacted from the chain gangs were awaiting recovery and restoration. Furthermore, the historic villages of Wollombi and Laguna survived. Time had passed them by. It seemed too much once more to pay the kind of price extracted for Lake Burragorang. So after a sustained public campaign, Paynes Crossing dam was abandoned.

The ALP in New South Wales had begun as a party of small farmers, settlers and bush workers. Of its twenty-five seats in the lower house in 1904, only six were in Sydney, though the mining towns were important Labor strongholds. Successful Labor governments had always been mindful of their rural constituents. But Sydney was inexorably eating into its surrounding countryside, and railway workers and shearers along with miners no longer formed the hard core of rural Labor voters. Wran too was careful to pay attention to the needs of the provincial towns and rural voters, making some impression even in the north-east which had long been Country Party territory. Nearer to Sydney where land prices had driven prospective home-buyers as far as Gosford and the Blue Mountains, transport services had become utterly inadequate. Wran's dramatic appearance on morning commuter trains from Gosford, and then Katoomba was a preliminary to appointing former radical economics tutor and subsequent ministerial adviser David Hill to modernise management of the railways. Bitter industrial action followed, but as the outer urban areas were recognised as part of the metropolitan network it became possible to get a seat at peak hour instead of standing all the way from Woy Woy to Hornsby. New electric trains were added to make country services more attractive, but much of the track was now old and slow regardless of the quality of the rolling stock and it proved almost impossible to eradicate outmoded railway work practices.

With the approach of the bicentenary of the arrival of the first fleet in 1988, Sydney again became the focus of attention at the expense of the rest of New South Wales. Under pressure to ensure the availability of new hotels and other tourist facilities, once more it was deemed necessary to dismiss the elected Council of the City of Sydney. In 1967 it had been argued that an elected Labor council had been holding up essential redevelopment in the CBD and adjacent areas like the Rocks and Woolloomooloo. Now it was said that the independent members of the council were putting the needs of a relatively small number of residents ahead of jobs that could be created by an expansion of tourism. As part of a vision to promote Sydney in 1988, plans for the redevelopment of redundant railway yards and wharves at Darling Harbour were devised and carried out with increasing ruthlessness under the personal supervision of Gerry Gleeson. By then Gleeson had accumulated immense power through his position at the centre of government and his considerable personal skills. He was feared and resented, while charges of corruption against the Wran government were souring the reform agenda.

As early as 1923 V. G. Childe had suggested that the structure of the labour movement made timidity and corruption inevitable.[14] Wran inherited a kind of corruption from the Askin years which was in part a reflection of the changing relationship between government and the economy as the whole western world moved away from the Keynesian ideas which had guided at least two generations. Corruption or mismanagement became a common phenomenon in Australian state politics elsewhere during the 1980s – Bjelke-Petersen in Queensland, Brian Burke in Western Australia, the collapse of state banks in Victoria and South Australia. In New South Wales, controls exerted by the long-lived postwar Labor dominance eventually created an atmosphere desperate for change. Mounting criticism of the role of the state in the lives of individuals discouraged significant numbers of capable graduates from entering the public service. The sense of moral vacuum was evident too at the Sussex Street headquarters of the labour movement where former Catholic tribalism was reduced to the pursuit of power either for its own sake or for the spoils it would deliver.

Wran's instinct for camera angles and a presidential style may have established him as the face of government in New South Wales but it did not overcome the fact that he was actually leader of the Labor Party and carried its baggage too. He may have distracted public attention from the increasingly unattractive activities of the Labor machine in Sussex Street with its thoroughly modern manager, Graham Richardson; however, Wran could not avoid all the filth that had been accumulating about the wheels for years. Something of the traditional Catholic tendency to close ranks, to avoid speaking about difficult or potentially divisive matters, had become the Labor way. Wran's ability to tailor the needs of government so that they appeared to be what the people wanted, his skill at juggling problems so that they were never actually confronted began to exacerbate the atmosphere of urgency and secrecy Sussex Street created and maintained.

Much as 'Nifty Nev' may have wished to ignore these facts, eventually he too fell victim to Sussex Street's grubby backroom operations. In a *Four Corners* programme on ABC TV on 30 April 1983 it was claimed that Wran had asked Chief Magistrate Murray Far-quhar to drop charges of misappropriating funds against former secretary-manager of the Balmain Leagues Club, Kevin Humphries. A simple denial was not enough. In the wake of revelations of corruption in Askin's government, there was no way that allegations being made about the use of Wran's name to pervert the cause of justice could be tested except by bringing them into the open, as they were in a royal commission chaired by the chief justice of New South Wales, Sir Laurence Street. Wran was replaced as premier for three months by his loyal deputy, Jack Ferguson, claiming that a campaign was being waged by the ABC and the Fairfax press to 'get' him for his failure or inability to cultivate them as he had done with Murdoch and Packer. Street's commission fully exonerated him, but Wran continued to attack those in the media whom he blamed. And there was more to come. Rex Jackson, Wran's minister for justice, was found to be taking money to arrange for the early release of prisoners, and lying about it in parliament. He went to gaol. So did Murray Farquhar. Yet the smell of corruption lingered through the pursuit and destruction of Wran's old friend, Lionel Murphy, now a High Court judge, for attempts to interfere in the administration of the law. In June 1986 Wran retired as dramatically as he had arrived as leader, leaving serious problems about a successor. Those who knew him said that he had lost his enthusiasm for politics. But perhaps he knew he could no longer use the media as he once had. Like Faust he had made his bargain with the devil and lost.

The vitality of the 1970s and 1980s inspired young actors and playwrights graduating from the drama school founded at the UNSW in 1958, its associated Old Tote and Jane Street theatres, and the Nimrod Theatre created by actors John Bell and Anna Volska and their lawyer friends from student days at the University of Sydney, Ken and Lilian Horler, and built roughly inside old stables on the edge of Kings Cross in the early 1970s. Audiences thrilled to social comment as in Alex Buzo's assault on racism in *Norm and Ahmed*, or irreverent versions of Australian history like *The Legend of King O'Malley*. Ron Blair savaged his Catholic education, while in *A Hard God*, Peter Kenna wrote eloquently of repressed homosexuality in a Catholic family. There were plays written about and from inside the prison system, memorably by Aboriginal author Kevin

Gilbert. Established writers like Dorothy Hewett, Thomas Keneally and Patrick White rediscovered play scripts satirising society's comfortable values. After 1979 they were joined by Melbourne's David Williamson who travelled north and began dramatising his own adventures in Sydney with *Sons of Cain* (1985), a very contemporary account of corruption in New South Wales, and *Emerald City* (1987) exploring why money, creativity and the film industry were now so attracted to Sydney.[15] 'No-one in Sydney ever wastes time debating the meaning of life – it's getting yourself a water frontage', Elaine, the tough theatrical agent in *Emerald City*, tells a playwright newly arrived from Melbourne.

> People devote a lifetime to the quest. You've come to a city that knows what it's about, so be warned. The only ethic is that there are no ethics, loyalties rearrange themselves daily, treachery is called acumen and honest men are called fools.[16]

The city and suburbs with their 'colourful identities', many known to police, featured vividly in the adventures of Peter Corris' very Sydney private eye Cliff Hardy, installed in suitably run-down premises in East Sydney and Glebe. Some things in Sydney had changed little since the 1850s.

One of Askin's new knights in 1968 had been Philip Charley, president of the Royal Agricultural Society, still then a semi-rural route to respectability. But the Metropole Hotel, once a haven for country folk in the city, was demolished in 1970 and at the Australian Club nearby, a lucrative property deal saw remnants of the old building installed inside a modern multi-storey office block. Askin's rise coincided with the declining influence of the old landed families in Sydney society. The wharves and mighty stores that had once housed their wool clip before its shipment overseas were about to be transformed into luxury harbour-side apartments with berths for the pleasure craft of the new rich, celebrities from advertising, radio and television. The kind of wealth that had once come from the land and flowed into traditional institutions, the church, the law, and the education system, gave way to the new media and its new money. Creative accounting, asset stripping and tax-effective takeovers were producing a new class of celebrity lawyers, show-off businessmen and finance experts. It was proving much easier to conjure wealth out of the air than to extract it from the soil. Discreet society faded away to be replaced by an 'A list' of 'socialites', advertising, public relations and the radio and television 'personalities' who were deemed essential to every promotion bolstered by business and retailing executives, corporate lawyers and financial sector cowboys. Traditional charity functions were elbowed aside by new showy, self-promoting methods of raising money that paid their way in useable publicity. Larrikin behaviour was expected from media-heir Kerry Packer, advertiser John Singleton, showman Harry M. Miller. Talk-back radio hosts John Laws and Alan Jones were courted by all who had something to sell, even or especially if it was only themselves. At this level it was often hard to see the difference between salesmanship and blackmail, a clever deal and a confidence trick. Politicians at both state and federal level were caught up in the wheeling and dealing and the frequent recourse to litigation. It is no wonder that the message that eventually found its way to the listeners, readers, and viewers was strange to decipher, smelling as it did of wealth, glamour and tales untold. The sexual adventures, the wild parties, were widely reported. So too were the innuendoes of gambling on a huge scale, involvement with drugs, and occasional underworld figures. Kerry Packer's name was linked to the Costigan Royal Commission, John Singleton narrowly avoided assault charges, Harry M. Miller did time in gaol for fraud.

In most periods of its history New South Wales has had a handful or more of colourful characters in public life, the wild men of Sydney in the 1890s including newspaper owners John Norton and Robert Murdoch as well as parliamentary rogues like Paddy Crick. In the 1970s and 1980s, the likes of John Singleton and Paul Hogan re-created the larrikin as the authentic Australian male in public life, the 'ocker'. Though not necessarily working class they seemed to convey a kind of male egalitarianism. In part, it was a rejection of a cultural cringe; in another way it was a response to feminism. Comparable perhaps with the ex-servicemen of earlier wars, and even with the native-born currency lads and larrikins of the 1890s pushes, by the 1970s these modern larrikins were necessarily dissociated from army experience and naturalised on television.

Deteriorating economic conditions during the 1980s culminated in a dramatic stock market fall in 1987. Historic NSW institutions collapsed, were taken over, or destroyed – Grace Bros, David Jones, Arnotts Biscuits. Angus & Robertson, having survived the vagaries of publishing for 100 years with its stable of authentic Australians including author Ion Idriess and children's classics like *The Magic Pudding* and *Blinky Bill*, in May 1989 became part of the international HarperCollins. Even the *Sydney Morning Herald*, founded in 1831 as the *Sydney Herald* and since then the generally conservative voice of New South Wales, was subject to a disastrous privatisation by young Warwick Fairfax, the result of a family feud inflamed by money market madness. Hated equally by Askin and Wran during the 1970s and the 1980s for its relentless pursuit of corruption in NSW politics, by 1990, the Fairfax family company was in receivership, and the paper was taken over by Canadian Conrad Black, owner of the London *Daily Telegraph*.

Worsening employment figures in New South Wales brought about a change in the focus of government. After a period of electoral reform and experiment with new social and environmental approaches, a return to a more traditional Labor emphasis on jobs and equity seemed desirable. Only now job creation in the form of a tunnel under the harbour, and an overhead monorail to connect the redevelopment of Darling Harbour to the city proper became controversial, the tunnel because it seemed as if with less haste and better bargaining, the government might have made better financial arrangements, the monorail because it was and remained ugly above the narrow streets, and Darling Harbour because it seemed and was a dubious investment for taxpayers' money. Attempts to improve equity by moving people with mental disabilities from institutions to community care (as recommended by David Richmond in 1983) and relocating hospital beds from the centre and east to the west of Sydney where the weight of population was now to be found, caused other difficulties. The loss of traditional institutions was resented, while professional staff were as reluctant to move to the western suburbs as to remote rural areas.

9

1988–2005, the event-led economy

After 200 years of European occupation New South Wales was a vastly different place from what it had once been. During the nineteenth century a small relatively homogeneous society ruthlessly exploited the natural resources with which the land was so well endowed. It was able to afford education for its people, provide them with the basics of good health and a high standard of living and, because of its homogeneity, create an impressive form of democracy. By 1988, however, it was no longer a small society. The population of New South Wales had topped 5.5 million, with 3.5 million of them now living in Sydney. It was also far from homogeneous. Many of the resources underpinning the high living standards of earlier times were now in short supply or were no longer considered so valuable, while expectations of living standards had risen exactingly. Sydney no longer took its fresh air or a plentiful supply of clean water for granted. No longer could grass simply be converted into export income as wool, timber cut, or coal loaded into ships' holds and furnaces. The systems and structures needed to manage the economy had become immensely complex, requiring great skill and much organisation. So too had the ways of maintaining standards and order in a society which was now comprised of many competing communities. No longer could basic literacy be assumed. Once official forms had only ever been written in English and were widely understood. By 2000 half-a-dozen languages had become standard. Never was it more important for the good of all that society worked as a community, but never had it been harder to maintain the infrastructure. Amazingly, though, most of the time it worked, more or less. And the response to breakdowns and disasters was often inspired, an indication of huge reserves of skill, intelligence and sheer good sense throughout the population. So too was the quality of leadership which often emerged only when circumstances required it.

Sydney was naturally the focus for celebrations of the bicentenary of European settlement in Australia in January 1988, now also described as the invasion. In an attempt to create an Australia-wide celebration, the bicentenary was largely managed by the federal government, though with a sizeable input from New South Wales. Whereas there had been public controversy in 1938 about the version of history portrayed, the 1988 celebrations avoided history, merely re-enacting the arrival of the first fleet. No convicts came ashore to encounter the Aborigines and nothing happened thereafter. It was as if the version of Australian history taught in years gone by at the University of Sydney, ending ludicrously and prematurely with the arrival of the first fleet, had become universally accepted. Arguments about the ownership of Australian history were now orchestrated from Canberra and Melbourne. New South Wales no longer mattered. But as in 1938, Aboriginal people came to Sydney for the event, this time in busloads from all over Australia, and were billeted, not in the police barracks, but at La Perouse or with friends already living in Sydney. The only procession on Australia Day 1988 was their protest march from Redfern Oval to Hyde Park.

The runaway international best-selling version of Australian history for 1988 was yet another re-telling of the convict story, *The Fatal Shore* (by expatriate art historian Robert Hughes), focused on fashionable preoccupations – violence, repression, and sexuality – followed soon after by Mollie Gillen's *The Founders of Australia*, a biographical dictionary of the first fleet with the author arguing that Australians need not be ashamed of their convict origins, that the emphasis of blame should be laid on the brutality of the British government which established the system and thus set in train the 'tragic destruction of Aboriginal society'.[1]

Though the ghosts of the convicts absent in 1938 were thus appeased and the guilt assigned elsewhere, neither view reflected the reality of New South Wales 200 years after its foundation.

9.1 A re-enactment of Governor Phillip's visit to Broken Bay
in March 1788, one of many events staged around New
South Wales in 1988 to mark the bicentenary. (Gloria Zucker)

Tasmania's convict heritage has decayed into stunningly atmos-
pheric ruins, but in New South Wales convicts are a vanishing
memory. Most of the significant sites have been buried, built over,
destroyed or diminished by the relentless growth of Sydney and its
environs. In the multi-cultural climate of the 1990s, descendants of
the first fleet in the Fellowship of the First Fleeters referred to each
other quaintly but democratically as FF followed by the name of
their ancestor, whether convict or free.

January 26th 1988 became a great party for hundreds of thousands cramming the foreshores of 'the chief amphitheatre of
Australian life'.[2] Sydney's beauty was as stunning ever, but much
had changed since 1938. Instead of progress and development, the
talk now was of pollution, land and river degradation, sustainable
industries, and overpopulation. While the bicentenary encouraged
temporary employment for many, produced some worthwhile heritage restoration and a short-term boost to tourism, the long-term
hope was once more that business and tourists would be attracted
to Sydney, if not the rest of New South Wales. Indeed, even before

the bicentenary was over, much of the expertise it had assembled was looking ahead to the Sydney Olympic Games for 2000.

New South Wales continued as the largest and most diverse economy among the Australian states. With about a third of the total output, it was also about a third larger than its main rival, Victoria. The economy of New South Wales was larger than that of New Zealand, Singapore or Malaysia. Thanks to its convenient location within the time zones and the strength of its financial services, its links with the Asia Pacific had overtaken those with the United Kingdom or the United States. Over half of its manufactured goods and services were exported compared with only 45 per cent from the rest of Australia. Wool is no longer the great export it once was, and by 2000 was fourth behind coal, aluminium, and 'medicaments, including veterinary medicaments'.[3] Manufacturing is still viable, though it may have been shored up by decline in the 'rust-buckets' of Victoria and South Australia. But even in New South Wales there were signs of decline during the 1980s such as the closure of the shipyards at Newcastle. Rising unemployment in former industrial areas was reflected in the ALP's loss of some of these electorates for the first time since early in the twentieth century. Like Victoria and South Australia, New South Wales began to look seriously at newer and alternative forms of employment in an economy more attuned to the services sector, especially in finance and in tourism. But changing an education system dedicated to enterprise, and predicated for a hundred years on the needs of industry to one geared to the provision of services has been bewildering. Media, creative, and entertainment skills have been recognised since the early days of the clubs and television, but hospitality and the services required by tourism have needed re-invention in an egalitarian spirit. The cost of highly specialised skills that take many years to acquire is resented, and fast-tracked 'training' through TAFE colleges has replaced most time-consuming apprenticeships, so important old-fashioned skills are in danger of being lost. By 2001 telecommunications equipment, automatic data-processing machines, motor vehicles and aircraft, parts and accessories for all of these, and oil and petroleum headed the list of imports to New South Wales.

From the early nineteenth century, New South Wales attracted tourists, at first those curious about the strange settlement itself with

9.2 'Teams leaving the farm with wheat.' This photograph is
typical of many publicity shots in the early twentieth century
illustrating the beauty and potential of New South Wales.
They appeared in travel books like this account of his journey
in a horse and cart through New South Wales by writer and
publicist Edwin Brady, also in guidebooks and 'encyclopedias'
aimed at potential immigrants, tourists and investors.
Enlarged and framed, they were also used to decorate railway
carriages in order to tempt travellers further afield. (E.J.
Brady, *The King's Caravan*, Edward Arnold, London, 1911,
facing p. 66)

its convict underpinnings, or wishing to see unusual flora and fauna
and strange landscapes. As early as 1866, concern about damage
being caused by careless visitors to the Jenolan Caves led to protection of the area and the employment of Jeremiah Wilson as the first
warden. Premier J. H. Carruthers decided in 1905 that New South
Wales should emulate Tasmania by advertising itself and established
an Intelligence Department. Soon its main focus became encouraging immigrants, but it also managed a Tourist Bureau closely
linked to the promotion of railway travel in New South Wales where
the carriages were decorated with handsome framed photographs

of interesting places and things to see, from mountain gullies, waterfalls, dense forests, idyllic beaches and majestic headlands to the man-made marvels of dams, irrigation canals, orchards, canneries, wheat silos, and woolsheds.[4]

Mass international air travel and the knock-on effect of postwar immigration intensified the flow of tourists to New South Wales, probably more interested in Sydney, especially after the opening of the Opera House in 1973, than in the rural landscapes of earlier times. The golden Georgian sandstone buildings became precious as tourist attractions, Gothic remnants like St Mary's Cathedral especially so. When he was prime minister, Sydney Catholic Paul Keating saw that its spires, unfinished since the 1860s, were paid for at last and lifted into place by helicopter. But many historic buildings have since been disfigured by towers, converted into hotels.

Something special, like Colleen McCullough's novel *The Thornbirds* (1977), could create interest in specific outback locations. For a while the convict era, elaborately re-created in a theme park at Old Sydney Town near Gosford, provided work and entertainment till it became unfashionable and was closed. With the approach of the bicentenary of white settlement in 1988, much effort was invested in rediscovering any history that could be directed at encouraging tourists, both local and international. The government's Heritage Office and Historic Houses Trust joined the National Trust to protect, restore and promote New South Wales' material past. Great efforts were made to discover and incorporate Aboriginal heritage, especially into local histories, while in western New South Wales, Aboriginal tourism produced new jobs.

The affluent young flocked to public spaces for pop and rock concerts, and big days out to indulge their craving for entertainment, take part in festivals, music, literary, ethnic, or just to have fun by the harbour as on New Year's Eve. Venues old and new, out doors and in, found new uses – the Sydney Entertainment Centre, the Hordern Pavilion, the Domain, the Botanic Gardens, Centennial Park, the showground, the cricket ground, the football stadium, the old wharves of Walsh Bay. Hyde Park is pressed into service with marquees. The Domain is cluttered with temporary facilities for frequent outdoor events. The steps to the Opera House become seats in an amphitheatre for pop concerts. No space is safe from temporary enclosure to charge admission. Though the NSW government has not been as aggressive as some in attracting major events, it has quietly supported a variety of conferences and conventions attracted to Sydney by its tourist potential. The flow-on in tourism from events like the Olympic Games and the Rugby World Cup three years later were worth billions of dollars.

In 1998 the Royal Easter Show was moved to a bigger space at Homebush Bay, and its old Moore Park site, leased from the government since 1881 by the Royal Agricultural Society, handed over to Fox Studios (with heritage controls over certain buildings) to be converted into a film production lot. Associated commercial areas filled with the familiar mix of cinemas, video and music stores, fashionable youth clothing, sporting and homewares stores and overpriced bars and eating places were built on the site. Quaint old structures with obvious 'heritage' appeal such as old public lavatories became restaurants. Some like the Walter Burley Griffin incinerator at Naremburn or the unique mortuary station at Central from whence special funeral trains carrying both coffins and mourners once left for Rockwood Necropolis, proved intractable to developers. Old churches, schools, warehouses, wool stores, factories, breweries now conveniently close to public transport or the CBD, became up-market apartments with loft conversions. Old industrial sites were recycled greedily or badly as in the case of Darling Harbour where every modern commercial cliché – the museums, a casino, hotels, bars and restaurants, a fun park, cinemas, shopping precinct, linked by 'gardens' composed mostly of water and stone – was crammed in around the foreshores of what had once been Sydney's busiest harbour and railway marshalling yard. The old railway workshops at Eveleigh eventually acquired new uses – part museum but mostly translated into spaces for the use of new technology: a 'research park', computing, and associated activities. Redfern was threatened with the kind of 'redevelopment' inflicted on North Sydney, Pyrmont, Ultimo, and the Haymarket.

The denizens of the inner city, both those who came daily to work and the increasing numbers who were returning to high-rise flats or converted warehouses to live, could be justified in feeling that inch by inch their sunlight and open space were being eaten up by paving, glassed atriums and new freeways. In order to fit increasing numbers of people and purposes into ever more crowded spaces, there was a great deal of neatening, work for designers and landscape gardeners. The little wild places, remnants of bush, vacant lots, became as endangered as the native plants and animals they once hid. It is hard to believe that once Christmas bush grew wild in Darling Point. Despite the introduction in the 1940s of legislation to protect wildflowers like waratahs, Christmas bells, and Christmas bush they have become hard to find even in the bush. It is true that native planting has been used increasingly along the verges of freeways, but only certain species can survive in such regimented and busy spaces. The hint of naturalness was gone.

By the 1990s Sydney could be portrayed successfully in films like *The Matrix* as the archetypal anonymous international modern city. 'Sydney is the only Australian city with the potential to be a truly global city', says Allan Gyngell, executive director of a new Sydney think-tank, the Lowy Institute (founded with $30 million from shopping centre magnate Frank Lowy). But according to Gyngell its weakness is its 'fragile intellectual backbone'.[5] Back in 1886 J. A. Froude had complained of the lack of intellectual activity in Sydney, and an emphasis instead on whatever kept life bright and pleasant.[6]

Integral to the growth of service industries and tourism has been the development and redevelopment of Sydney, with ever higher towers, while North Sydney then Chatswood and Bondi Junction have grown skywards to compete with the CBD on the horizon. High-rise living has become fashionable, creating urban densities unimaginable fifty years ago. The buying and selling of houses and properties, a preoccupation in Sydney for 200 years, has become a huge industry involving property developers, freeway construction companies, builders and real estate agents as well as the promoters of TV 'reality' programmes, not to mention the value of taxes on land sales and property-owning to the government. Overseas investors acquired property in Sydney as the preferred headquarters of both international and national firms. The prices at which important harbour-side mansions changed hands and office towers were rented became a measure of prosperity (and the despair of the increasing numbers who can no longer afford to live anywhere near their place of work).

Between 1993 and 2003 the size of a new house in New South Wales almost doubled. The Sydney housing market was, according to *Sydney Morning Herald* journalist, Dugald Jellie, about 'the soft focus of make-believe and illusion: a trade in talking up dreams, prices and capital gains in a bubble of feel-good fantasy'.[7] And while long-term immigrants, short-stay visitors, and young people moving from the country or interstate to search for work in Sydney's throbbing economy continued to place pressure on housing in the city, the old, the retired, and those no longer needing the pace have moved north or south along the coast. Some relocated to Queensland, but the Hunter, the Illawarra, far south coast and northern rivers all attracted retirees expecting to establish comfortable new lives on the proceeds of their Sydney property. A natural consequence of this movement has been the need for new infrastructure like water supply and sewerage as well as health services outside Sydney. At the end of the twentieth century about a quarter of state government spending went on health, another quarter on education, 10 per cent law and order, and the same on social and community services, on transport, and on general public services. The remaining 10 per cent was divided between environment and agriculture, economic services, and recreation and culture.[8] Though some habits leading to health problems such as smoking and drinking too much alcohol had declined a little since the indulgent 1980s, about a quarter of the population (more men than women) smoked, and 17 per cent of men aged 45–65 were still drinking too much. At the beginning of the twentieth century, a well-fed population had been a source of pride and overweight gentlemen, a sign of success. By 2001 the health of nearly half of the adult population was compromised by overweight and 35 per cent did not get enough exercise.

In many ways, Newcastle rather than Sydney remained the quintessential NSW city. Market researchers have long been aware of Newcastle as a typical modern postindustrial working class mass-consumer society, a favourite place for testing new products and ideas. After its long history of uncertain employment dependent on the mines and their allied industries, and incipient poverty, the post-war boom and the Labor-managed economy delivered economic security to Newcastle, and with it, the modern consumer society.

However, by the 1980s, postwar prosperity began to falter. Coal production in the Hunter Valley and industry in and around Newcastle had been declining since the 1970s. Ship building in Newcastle fell away and the state dockyard ceased functioning as a public enterprise after 1988. Negotiations to privatise part of the power-generating industry fell foul of the unions and were suspect among voters. Plans to develop aluminium smelters using cheap power generated from coal in the valley came into conflict with a prospering wine industry, its vineyards and their potential for tourism and exports. Still aluminium became the major export from 'Wran's Ruhr', as the valley was dubbed. In 1982, John Patterson, head of the Hunter Water Board and one of the new econocrats fostered by Wran, began introducing commercial pricing for water in the Hunter Valley. This was not entirely perverse. Despite the cost of storing and delivering clean safe water, its cost to the user has been negligible at least since the late nineteenth century when plentiful cheap water was deemed essential in the fight against water-borne disease. Now with the likely increase in water consumption by new industries such as aluminium smelters, commercial pricing made economic sense. The residents of Newcastle and the rest of the valley paid more for their water than anyone in New South Wales. Their displeasure became evident and was yet another reason for the defection from Labor in 1988, but by 1992 the Hunter Water Board had been fully corporatised.

An earthquake that shook Newcastle on 20 December 1989 and demolished the Workers' Club, killing twelve, seemed the symbolic last straw. But to some the earthquake was an opportunity, heaven sent, to demolish and redevelop a significant part of the city and there was some over-enthusiastic bulldozing. In *Aftershock*, Peter Corris, a faithful chronicler of Sydney's seamy side since 1980, sent his private eye Cliff Hardy to Newcastle soon after the earthquake to uncover more than a little crime and corruption. However, the earthquake also re-awakened a strong sense of local pride and with the help of the National Trust, historical parts of the city were not only saved from the demolishers, but restored with disaster money. Despite the closing of BHP's steelworks on 30 September 1999, Newcastle has been re-inventing itself as an education city, proud of its civilised heritage buildings, parks, and historic, artistic and cultural precincts, with its own postindustrial sound in the all-male tap-dancing Tap Dogs and the pop group, silverchair.

Historian James Docherty has argued that Newcastle and its people have contributed rather more to New South Wales and Australia than they have been given credit for and that they deserve a better deal.[9] And as Newcastle has been to New South Wales, so it might be said that New South Wales has been to the rest of Australia, underwriting prosperity and subsidising development in the less well-endowed states. Ever since 'Yes-No' Reid pointed out the obligations and dangers of federation, New South Wales has been both constrained and exploited for the national good. Jack Lang came closest to a revolt, but as the economy tightens, unfairness seems unavoidable. Good ideas come out of New South Wales, but selling them to the rest of the country has often been difficult, fraught with suspicion.

There has been consolidation of other major towns in New South Wales, some following the lead set in Armidale with teachers' colleges and universities anchoring centres large enough to sustain other services for the surrounding communities. Retirees with pensions or their super seeking cheaper housing or cooler climates bring steady incomes and create a demand for more services. So do leisure industries and tourism. Most country towns have a heritage of public buildings now old enough to be exploited along with other attractions like a food festival in Orange, an annual motor-race in Bathurst, or Tamworth's country music festival. It has become one of the responsibilities of local government to try to create attractions such as the Byron Bay Writers Festival or to work in conjunction with tourism promoters.

Where Sydney has developed a trans-Pacific lifestyle, a more traditional way of life has continued in the bush. Sydney has always been separate. In part this is physical, because of the Hawkesbury to the north, the Illawarra escarpment to the south, the Blue Mountains to the west. On days when the Sydney sky is thick with smoke or fog, over the range at Katoomba, the air is clear and sharp. But it is more than that. Travelling along the Darling in 1908–11 C. E. W. Bean found a great curiosity about what it was like in Sydney. Radio, television, the internet may have brought the city closer to the bush, but Sydney has always been about ten years ahead. The more remote parts of the north, west, and south of the state have become harder to reach than in the early twentieth century as rail connections close and local residents become dependent on access to private motor vehicles or expensive airlines. In towns like Bourke and Brewarrina, where Aboriginal populations are large and constant, grilles and roller doors on shopfronts indicate a still-violent frontier.

The huge harbour-side party on 26 January 1988 marked the end of the Wran years. Labor lost the election held on 19 March as dramatically as when Lang was dismissed by the governor and rejected by the people in 1932, and when Askin defeated Renshaw in 1965. Wran's unexpected replacement as premier, former boiler-maker and unionist, the well-meaning, cardigan-wearing Barrie Unsworth had never seemed 'with it' for the late 1980s, but the underlying issues were the endless stories of corruption and the associated fears about law and order. For every person who believed that 'greed is good' there was someone who knew someone who had profited unfairly from the new morality in business and in politics. Unsworth fought the election on the slogan 'back to basics' but the people were thoroughly disillusioned with the continuing cuts to services. Unsworth underestimated anxiety about loss of jobs and overestimated enthusiasm for stricter gun controls implemented in the wake of mass shootings in New South Wales and elsewhere.

Eighty-two independent candidates contested the election in 1988 (compared with thirty-six in 1981) and won seven seats. Balmain, the former working class suburb which claimed to be the birthplace of the NSW Labor Party, but was now gentrified by 'basket weavers' in Paul Keating's memorably dismissive phrase, returned an independent, former Olympic swimming champion and local hotelier, Dawn Fraser. And Bligh, the inner-city electorate encompassing the 'gay ghetto' of Oxford Street and Surry Hills, voted for Clover Moore, an old girl from Loreto Convent and one of the Sydney city councillors dismissed in 1987. The new premier, Nick Greiner, was, however, more inclined to executive action and 'king hits' than to the messy politics of consultation with independents.

Elected leader of the Liberal Party in 1983, the eighth in as many years, Hungarian-born Nicholas Frank (Hugo) Greiner was educated at the prestigious Catholic boys college at Riverview, had an economics degree from the University of Sydney and an MBA from Harvard. He married wisely. His wife, Kathryn, a trained social worker, was the daughter of Bede Callaghan, a former governor of the Commonwealth Bank, and said by some to be more canny about politics than her husband. Greiner enthusiastically took up the challenge of making New South Wales more efficient and profitable according to the latest economic theories – a process begun, as we have seen in the early 1980s (with John Patterson and the Hunter Water Board). Greiner believed in the superiority of market forces over both government and politics for regulating society. He cheerfully saw himself not as premier but as a 'managing director' who had to 'obtain better returns for the shareholders of New South Wales Inc'.[10]

Wran's government had supported its economic habits by raiding 'hollow logs', assets David Hill found hidden in government departments and statutory authorities. As soon as he became premier, Greiner set up an audit commission, the first since 1900, headed by finance industry executive Charles Curran, then used its report ruthlessly to pursue his vision for New South Wales. Terms such as 'deregulation', 'corporatisation', 'privatisation', vaguely familiar from Ronald Reagan's America and Margaret Thatcher's Britain, became everyday currency in New South Wales. In the private sector ruthless executives like Al 'Chainsaw' Dunlap piled up bonuses as they cut jobs. With his chief advisor Gary Sturgess, Greiner was determined that a more business-like culture would be developed in the public sector, less bureaucratic and more responsive to the customer or consumer, no longer a mere voter or taxpayer. The public service was 'downsized'. Senior executives were placed on performance contracts and issued with corporate credit cards. Accrual accounting was introduced. Gary Sturgess devised the concept of corporatising government agencies, moving them off budget or converting them to business units, requiring them to manage their own finances and if possible, return a dividend to government. Theoretically, this made them more efficient and competitive. It also meant that in cases where similar services were available in the private sector, government agencies could no longer hide their costs or provide unfair competition, creating the legendary 'level playing field'. They could be privatised, disbanded or sold. The government printing office was an early target. All government printing and bookbinding was contracted to the private sector. Former bookbinding employees quickly formed a company to tender for their old work because it was highly specialised and only they had the skills and expertise. They were not cheap. Rail services to remote areas were cut; rural courthouses and police stations were closed, mirroring cuts by banks and other businesses in country towns. Public transport fares were raised. After seventy years even egg production was deregulated, at the cost of $60 million in compensation.

It was not so easy to turn welfare, health, education or policing into profit-making businesses. The result was generally cheaper or more austere services. It became harder to attract professionals like doctors and teachers to jobs seen as more difficult and less rewarding under the new conditions, especially in remote areas. Before long problems attributed to starved management showed up. The Sydney water supply, corporatised in late 1994, was found to be contaminated and unfit for drinking in July 1998, due probably to a lack of maintenance at Prospect Reservoir. It became necessary for the government to resume control of the water supply at least until public confidence was restored.[11]

Interestingly, most of the Greiner reforms were welcomed at senior levels in the public service. Recruitment policies had been bringing a new generation of university-educated economists to the public service, and they, like Greiner, were fully aware of the latest economic and management theories. However, corporatising or privatising threatened a serious loss of revenue to New South Wales. The new enterprises were taxable under federal company law. Suddenly and unusually, there was a high degree of co-operation between Canberra and Macquarie Street. Under the influence of treasury bureaucrats, the federal Labor government had become similarly engaged in down-sizing and cost-cutting, exacerbating unhappiness and insecurity. Both Greiner and Keating paid politically for their economic rationalism.

Greiner had declared that corruption 'had been happening in NSW since the First Fleet' but that he would fix it.[12] To this end in 1988 he established an Independent Commission against Corruption (ICAC) with the powers of a royal commission. A former director of public prosecutions, Ian Temby, was appointed for a five-year term as commissioner. It was assumed that ICAC would be pursuing weaknesses already revealed in the previous ALP government. Temby, however, chose to concentrate on issues that would define acceptable standards of public behaviour, such as local government relations with developers, pursuing cases involving councils in Waverley and on the north coast. Then in 1992, Greiner himself, two other MPs, and two senior public servants came under scrutiny for the way in which a convenient top public service post had been arranged as an exit from politics for Greiner's troublesome former education minister, Terry Metherell.

Metherell had generated immense hostility for his persistence in pursuing a hugely unpopular restructuring of the education system. There was an almost gleeful public response when he was charged with an offence under federal tax law and forced to resign his ministry. Clumsy attempts by old friends to find him a comfortable job in the public service came before ICAC. Though Greiner was judged not personally responsible, he was forced to resign as premier and left politics. ICAC's existence, reassuring though it was to the electorate, became a potentially explosive device to all in government, to be defused if possible.

So when new allegations of corruption in the police force were raised in 1994, instead of referring them to ICAC, another royal commission was established under the chairmanship of Justice James Wood. For the next three years the people of New South Wales watched the often bewildering and always discrediting procession of witnesses, 640 in all, before the Wood Commission. Though supposedly concerned with a long-standing impact of corruption on the police force, the commission was side-tracked by accusations of paedophilia in high places. Though the Mardi Gras was apparently accepted and at last, in 2003, the age of consent for males standardised at sixteen, there was still a considerable amount of community anxiety about homosexuality, manifesting itself in the early 1990s in a kind of hysteria about child sexual abuse and paedophilia, a preoccupation permeating western society in the 1990s. Senior figures in politics and the law in New South Wales were named as paedophiles leading to libel suits, a murder, several suicides and the virtual end of their political careers for Deirdre Grusovin and

Franca Arena, who had made their accusations under parliamentary privilege.

Following the Wood Commission, police commissioner Tony Lauer resigned, exhausted. He was replaced by Peter Ryan, an Englishman whose chief virtue, besides his undoubted experience, was that he was a 'cleanskin'. But Ryan was also resented as an outsider, and because of the hint of colonialism his appointment brought. Though he failed to overcome corruption in Cabramatta that had defeated Lauer, he tackled the re-organisation of the police force effectively enough to make him unpopular with the police union, and ensured that security never became a problem during the Olympic Games. When it emerged that he had become Australia's most highly paid public servant, earning more than twice as much as the premier, and almost double the prime minister's salary, his reputation as an arrogant whingeing Pom seemed justified.[13]

The 1996 census showed that almost a quarter (23%) of the people in New South Wales had been born overseas, predominantly in the UK, NZ, Italy, China, Vietnam, Lebanon and the Philippines. Changes to federal immigration policy from the 1970s meant increasing numbers of Asian immigrants, with a disproportionate number arriving and choosing to stay in or near Sydney. For example over a third of the Vietnamese refugees between 1975 and 1980 (approximately 13,900) settled in New South Wales.[14] Whereas Melbourne had become the centre of Greek and Italian migration in the postwar years, Sydney and New South Wales now had Australia's most Asian population. A great many entered the service industries. By the 1990s country towns, which had once had stores run by the nineteenth-century gold rush Chinese, again had a Vietnamese baker, a new Chinese restaurant, a Filipino wives group, while to visit some Sydney suburbs like Fairfield or Cabramatta was almost like a trip overseas. Enclaves of Indians and Fijians yielded the exotic ingredients for their home cooking, while a small but wealthy Japanese community and the large numbers of Japanese tourists produced impressive numbers of shops and services catering to Japanese speakers. The contrast with an older New South Wales where the Irish had been the most significant non-English group was striking. Now an Irish background had become part of the natural inheritance of New South Wales.

On 5 September 1994 on his return from a local ALP branch meeting, the state member for Cabramatta, John Newman, was assassinated in the driveway of his home in front of his fiancée Lucy Wang. There had been earlier attempted political assassinations in New South Wales, none successful. In 1868 a deranged Fenian Henry James O'Farrell had shot and wounded the Duke of Edinburgh during a picnic on the beach at Clontarf. And at Mosman Town Hall in 1966, an unhappy young man, Peter Kocan, fired desperate shots at federal opposition leader Arthur Calwell. After Newman's death, it was some time before Phuong Ngo, an aspiring local Vietnamese ALP rival, was gaoled for his murder and an embarrassed silence descended. Assassination seemed somehow un-Australian, and indeed there was something alien in all these cases, but especially in the ethnic melting pot of Cabramatta. Newman himself was of Yugoslav origins, having simplified his name from Naumenko. His relationship with a young Chinese woman was unusual, and his past was complicated by links to ASIO and martial arts. However, Newman's murder and continuing problems in Sydney's west could also be seen in the context of factional wars that have disfigured the NSW ALP since at least the sectarian times of Jack Lang. In 1980, in Marrickville, an ALP member, Peter Baldwin, was savagely beaten and lucky to escape with his life. It was assumed that factional opponents were responsible, but no charges were ever laid. There had been branch stacking and manipulation of the local upwardly mobile Lebanese community, partly in relation to local government elections, property development applications, and influence over immigration matters. In Cabramatta, factional wars became open confrontations between competing ethnic groups, including the Vietnamese, exacerbating problems with law and order, policing, and dealing in drugs.

The event-led economy reached new heights with Greiner's successor, John Fahey, who saw the role of government as securing investment and image-building projects for New South Wales, often at considerable cost and of dubious long-term benefit to taxpayers. His triumphant response to the announcement in Monte Carlo in 1993 that the 2000 Olympic Games had been awarded to 'Sy-de-ney' pushed other projects such as the stalled restoration of Luna Park and the misguided expense of the Eastern Creek Speedway

9.3 Bob Carr as Minister for the Environment in conversation with local resident Phillip Westlake at the dedication of a reserve in memory of his predecessor Paul Landa at Pearl Beach, November 1991. (Gloria Zucker)

into the background. Even so, winning the games did not secure the next election for Fahey. Amazingly, the reluctant Carr government, which acquired responsibility for the games by winning office in 1995, were able to carry them off thanks to some ruthless work by the minister responsible, Michael Knight, and senior public servants, Sandy Hollway and David Richmond.

Fahey, like Nick Greiner, Peter Collins and John Hannaford, was one of the upwardly mobile boys from Catholic private schools who had begun to reshape the NSW Liberal Party. While the labour movement has a republican tradition dating back to the 1890s, the Catholics now joining the NSW Liberal Party in increasing numbers brought their Irish inheritance to bear on the monarchism of John Howard and the federal Liberals. Peter Collins, perhaps the most 'working class' and progressive, was an outspoken republican, an advocate for the creative role of the arts in the economy, and far from committed to the federal Liberal hard-line on economic 'reform'. Probably because he was an unlikely Liberal, his time as

opposition leader was brief. But his memoir, *The Bear Pit*, canvassed
interesting questions about New South Wales politics.

'When Bob Carr became Labor leader we couldn't believe our
luck', Collins wrote.

Carr had only really held one portfolio, Planning and Environment, and
everyone knew that he didn't want to be in state politics anyway. He wanted
to be Minister for Foreign Affairs. The idea of Labor being led by someone who didn't want to be in Macquarie Street was too good to be true.
Collectively, Carr was underestimated from the outset. He even looked the
underdog. His own party had barred his exit to Canberra and given the
federal seat he coveted, Kingsford Smith, to his rival Laurie Brereton. Carr
was seen as detached, academic and impractical. He didn't even drive a car.
He would have about the same appeal as a university lecturer from some
obscure faculty. He wore shorts on bushwalking expeditions and looked
dorky. But Bob Carr proved everyone wrong.[15]

Carr went on to win three four-year terms and surpass Wran's
record as the longest serving premier of New South Wales. Part of
his success was that although his government funded popular spec-
tacles with all their implications for tourism and the entertainment
economy, he personally maintained a lively intellectual engagement
with many of the more thoughtful people in the community, writers and historians especially, though he was not averse to offering
his views on any interesting subject. In this way he gained not only
a degree of intellectual support but also some wide-ranging input
and unsolicited advice from the thinking classes. A former journalist
and arguably the most literate premier since Sir Henry Parkes, he
published essays, memoirs and a selection from his political diaries
and was capable of quoting from Irish poet, W. B. Yeats, Roman
philosopher, Marcus Aurelius, or his American hero, Abraham Lin-
coln, in parliament. Wran's use of the media was legendary (and
ultimately disastrous). Carr's skill at reading and responding to the
media was more reminiscent of the old-time political habit of taking
a stroll down Martin Place, meeting the people, listening to their
views, saying the right words, both leading and following public
opinion by floating ideas and assessing the response. Contemporary
comment, mainly by journalists, was both admiring and critical of
his skill. However, unlike many journalists, Carr did not underestimate the intelligence of his audience. He was criticised in the early

days for talking above the heads of the people, being too remote, too much a professor. But he proved to be both sharp and witty, diffusing difficult situations by a clever or deft remark. At times he seemed like a headmaster who explained things patiently and expected you to make the effort because he knew you could do it. The very opposite of patronising, this encouraged self-respect. Fortunately he also had ministers who were willing to do the rough and dirty work of government and pay for getting it wrong. But like many a premier before him, he was reluctant to make hard and unpleasant decisions that did not become less so for being pushed aside.

Carr's announcement on 27 July 2005 that he was stepping down as premier and leaving parliament the next week closely resembled Wran's unexpected departure, though whereas Wran claimed to have made his decision over a bottle of chardonnay, Carr characteristically attributed his to beautiful weekend weather. After the event it became clearer that both he and his government had become tired. None were anywhere near as old, yet it seemed not unlike the end of the Heffron government. The neverending requirement to maintain transport, health and education services had become harder than ever to satisfy while water shortages after what had become an almost permanent drought had begun to grate. Furthermore, New South Wales was more beholden than ever to a hostile federal government for funding. With the appointment of Morris Iemma, the only son of Italian migrants who had arrived in Sydney in 1960, Sussex Street was seen to be reasserting its authority, long disguised by Bob Carr's media skills. A graduate in law and economics, Iemma had served part of his apprenticeship in politics in the office of Graham Richardson.

Carr's government had received a huge boost from the goodwill generated by 'the best ever' Olympic Games when the whole world was in love with Sydney and the trains ran on time. The sharp crack of a stockwhip opening the 2000 Games set the mood brilliantly. The world-wide television audience was not to know how that dramatic scene of men on their horses was derived from the days when former convicts and their sons eked out a living as horse and cattle thieves in the high country of the Snowy River (while the colt that got away has become an environmental nightmare). One wonders too what the critics and the Aboriginal actors in the sanitised version of Australian history paraded in 1938 would make of the dreaming fantasy produced in 2000.

Sydney's financial dominance and the increasing emphasis on tourism and associated events have tended to exacerbate the differences between the city and the rest of New South Wales. There was anger as disproportionate amounts of money and effort were poured into the Homebush Bay site and other venues for the 2000 Olympic Games and into general improvements in and around Sydney in expectation of the influx of visitors. As the main point of entry for migrants and tourists, Sydney's airport was under constant strain. For years the need to expand or relocate it was a bone of contention between local residents, state and federal governments. Privatisation in 2002 merely pushed the problem aside. A new airport for Sydney may be a federal matter, yet it has vast implications for Sydney and New South Wales.

In advertising for tourists the old debates are still replayed – whether to present New South Wales as a sophisticated society in touch with, and not unlike, the rest of the world, or as a unique place of wide-open spaces inhabited by Akubra-wearing stockmen, a landscape of bush and sea with unique flora and fauna. The only new element is the now obligatory inclusion of Aboriginal references. The contrast between the vision of Henry Lawson and Jules François Archibald in the 1890s or that of C. E. W. Bean and Lindsays in the 1920s is still relevant. Novelist David Foster who remains deeply committed to an older rural lifestyle argues that as inner Sydney has come to identify with New York or California, the metaphorical distance between the city and the bush has grown greater than ever. He thinks city people no longer even try to understand either the people or the country west of the CBD. Indeed they despise it because they are only interested in style, pace, change, modernity. Yet they continue to exploit it for advertising purposes.

The country–city divide is now coloured by an extremely green version of the conservation message that would effectively deny livelihoods in mining, pastoralism, agriculture, timber getting or fishing – the industries on which New South Wales was built. Yet by the 1980s the main river systems were showing clear signs of trouble – dying trees, derelict billabongs and rising salinity levels. The 1990s saw regular toxic blue green algal blooms in the Darling and its tributaries, aggravated by the onset of another major drought. But a decision in the late 1990s to return some water to the Snowy River showed that all damage from damming and diverting the rivers was not irreversible. In a remarkably short time with adequate water the vegetation began to return to the riverbanks, and healthy life to the stream. The rivers and dams supplying Sydney water, however, could not be so easily mended. There, increasing demands for suburban development gave rise to regular cries for new dams. Even though huge new houses eschew lawns for triple garages, family rooms and home theatres, the amount of water required by modern kitchens and bathrooms would shock any drought-conscious nineteenth-century farmer.

At the same time, it was assumed that the restaurants of Sydney would serve the most tender lamb or succulent seafood accompanied by the freshest and most unusual vegetables. By the end of the twentieth century, the production and consumption of high-quality produce and fine foods had become a major business in New South Wales. As in the nineteenth century, New South Wales continues to import manufactured goods and technology from places where they are produced cheaply. But whereas they were paid for then with exports of wool and coal, now seafood, orchids and rice are sent. In the nineteenth century, visitors to New South Wales were amazed by the quantity of meat consumed and the abundance of fruit and vegetables in the markets. The range of climates and soils in New South Wales has made it possible to grow almost anything for the table, from olives to oregano, from the finest beef to the most exotic mushrooms. Sydney chefs and restaurants have developed a worldwide reputation for their care and creativity. Most country towns now boast a good coffee shop, an excellent bakery, or some local specialty, oysters, cheese, honey, fruit, fudge, wine.

Despite the corporatising and privatising of so many former government activities, the size of the enterprise once dubbed NSW Inc. has not diminished. On winning government in 1995 Carr showed no sign of undoing the changes wrought by Greiner and his successors. Indeed, Carr recalled Ken Baxter, a former NSW public servant, who had become important in Jeff Kennett's ruthless administration of Victoria, to run his Premier's Department, though it was not a happy arrangement and did not last long. Some essential modernisation in the NSW public service was achieved, perhaps without quite the cost in trust and morale experienced in Melbourne or Canberra, but Carr's aspirations to privatise electricity in New South Wales were defeated by a union-led groundswell of popular distrust with the quality of corporatised water.

In 1987 Peter Wilenski said in an interview that the administration of New South Wales was 'about ensuring that the trains run on time, that roads are built, that there is sufficient electricity generation and so on', and that without the successful management of these fundamental services, nothing else could be accomplished. This was even more so by the beginning of the twenty-first century. It had become harder than ever for New South Wales to raise the revenue to pay for the services. Furthermore, when voters became consumers, they assumed that no expense would be spared to provide them with services comparable to the private sector's in transport, health and education. So NSW country railways began to mimic the customer service of airlines. Public utilities were required to set up 'consumer councils' and publish 'vision statements'. Unlike earlier generations who had been grateful for government services, the new consumers were quick to complain or to sue for damages. The difficulties were compounded by new employees and 'customers' for whom English is their second language. Nor were public servants trained, as most of the depression- and war-affected generations had been, to think frugally. So governing New South Wales became increasingly a matter of managing rising expectations within a budget limited in its capacity for expansion. Resources, once available for simple exploitation, now had to be managed carefully for sustainability.

If managing New South Wales became more complicated as the population became more aware and better educated, information could also be controlled and manipulated. With so much political information now collected and disseminated through polling, talkback radio, 'grabs' for television and political advertising, the power of the media continued to grow. So did opportunities for distortion, ill-considered statements, and misunderstandings. Political gossip once had a limited range along Macquarie Street. It is now the nectar of an army of radio and television bees, buzzing throughout the day. The ideas needed to govern New South Wales are still human, but the transport and health bureaucracies especially have become so elaborate that efficiencies of scale are deceptive. Effective over-sight of such large organisations is very difficult and small changes are harder to effect. Extensive insider experience is still probably as useful as theoretical training in management, but seniority has been discounted, indeed almost prevented. Nor is there evidence that performance-based contracts and higher salaries have produced better management.

The census of 2001 revealed that only 71.4 per cent of the pop-ulation of New South Wales now identified as Christian. This was not so much because of the increasing numbers of non-Christians – only 2.2 per cent were Muslim and 2.3 per cent, Buddhist – but because about 22 per cent either said they had no religion, or did not answer the question. Among the Christians, Catholics were now the largest group with 28.9 per cent, followed by Anglicans (23.8%). No longer were the Catholics mostly of Irish extraction. Their numbers now included many Italians, Vietnamese and Filipinos. The Uniting church accounted for 5.3 per cent, Presbyterians 3.7 per cent (the number of Presbyterians who had rejected the opportunity to join the Uniting church in 1977 was quite high in New South Wales) and the Orthodox church 3.2 per cent. The fastest growing group, though from a low base, were the Buddhists (up 80.4% on the 1998 census), but perhaps the most interesting aspect of the religious life of New South Wales by 2001, however, was the rising number who claimed they followed wicca/witchcraft or paganism.

The statistics, however, gave little idea of the extent to which evangelicalism had once more come to influence Christian worship. In the early twenty-first century, in the hands of the Jensen brothers (known elsewhere as 'the Sydney Taliban'), Sydney's Anglican cathe-dral was gradually being stripped of its historical accumulations and returned to the simplicities of the late nineteenth century, while the church itself was moving to adopt folksy modern American mass-market forms of worship which had proved popular in Sydney's outer suburbs and elsewhere. While American-style pentecostalism flourished in the Hillsong movement, Sydney Anglicans remained a quintessential expression of something unchanging about New South Wales – middle brow, a bit dowdy, egalitarian, pragmatic, legalistic, unimpressed by tradition or sophisticated argument. Nor did it seem likely the new Catholic Archbishop George Pell would have more success than his venerable predecessors, Vaughan or Moran, in dragging New South Wales Catholics out of their almost protestant easy-going ways.

In 2001, 20 per cent of the NSW population now spoke a language other than English at home, most commonly Arabic/Lebanese, Cantonese, Italian, Greek or Vietnamese. SBS radio in New South Wales broadcast in 68 languages. A community language programme was introduced into schools whereby native and non-native speakers studied languages together ranging from Arabic to Macedonian and Vietnamese. This diversity and its extent placed additional strains on the provision of government services, especially in such areas as health, welfare and education as well as employment. While the federal government provided funding at a certain level, it was never adequate for the complex needs of New South Wales. An Ethnic Affairs Commission was established and ethnic affairs added as a portfolio in the ministry. But racial tension provided a continuous undercurrent in the administration of the justice system. If people sometimes seemed intolerant, the truth was that many Sydney suburbs had experienced change on a scale unimaginable elsewhere in Australia. Older residents complained about the loss of familiar facilities. Some sold up and moved to the Southern Highlands, the Central or the North Coast, even to Queensland. Premier Carr was not averse to voicing his opinion that Sydney was bearing the brunt of the Commonwealth government's immigration policies at considerable cost, not only in the unwholesome spread of the city, but also because of the need for additional infrastructure and services. For example, the majority of the 27,000 Chinese students granted permanent residency by Canberra after the 1989 massacre in Tiananmen Square lived in Sydney.

The event-led economy has acquired new dimensions in recent years. With the help of the insurance industry and government disaster relief funding, storms, floods, even droughts, have become significant economic events. A hailstorm in Sydney on the evening of 14 April 1999 caused over a billion dollars worth of damage and sent a shockwave through the insurance industry. Twenty thousand homes in the south and east of the city were damaged. Tiles were suddenly in short supply. Tradesmen came from all over the state and beyond to repair the damage. Along with the pressure to complete projects in connection with the Olympic Games in 2000, building workers were highly in demand during the rest of 1999.

In 2001–02 and 2002–03, summer was dominated by drought. Subsequent bushfires required investment in fire-fighting equipment and compensation for homes lost. Legislation for the prevention or regulation of fires had begun in 1886. In 1901 during that long drought, the sale of matches other than safety matches was prohibited. Severe fires were recorded in 1926, and in 1939 fire damage was estimated at more than a million pounds. In 1930 and 1949, controls on burning off and the creation of firebreaks were tightened.[16] But in 1951–52 six lives were lost in bushfires and another six in 1968–69. From 1957 when the townships of Leura and Wentworth Falls in the Blue Mountains were subject to fire, increasingly bushfires have become a suburban hazard. By the end of the twentieth century, how and when to burn native vegetation needing fire to seed and regenerate often conflicted with a desire to maintain the appearance of the landscape yet avoid the danger always present in fires. In so many places there is no longer room for essential fire control between the bush and suburban housing. After he became chief fire commissioner in 1985, Phil Koperberg asserted his experience and influence to add urgent authority to what has become the annual campaign against bushfires. With continuing drought too, water levels in the state's many dams fell to very low levels, exposing the poignant archaeology of former farms and settlements drowned to create them. The Menindee Lakes on the Darling were officially empty by the end of 2002 and Lake Burrendong on the Cudgegong and Macquarie rivers, normally $3\frac{1}{2}$ times the size of Sydney Harbour, had shrunk so that the boating, swimming and fishing possible since its completion in 1967 had ceased.[17] The pressure to privatise or extract the maximum value from existing resources is evident in plans to translate water rights, treated traditionally as an integral part of farming and grazing land, into a tradeable commodity, and in discussion of the need to turn the 'long paddock', the 600,000 hectares set aside throughout New South Wales as stock routes, to more profitable uses.

It is still not clear whether the new partnerships between the state and the private sector, supporting and guaranteeing investors who have undertaken the building of new freeways, tunnels, rail links and so forth, have been cost effective for taxpayers. As with the big events, the return on infrastructure is hard to quantify, and the time taken to recoup the state's investment seems as indefinite as it ever was when railways, roads, and telegraphs were financed by neverending government loans. And whereas there were once calls for more transparent accounting from the state treasury, in the new world of co-operative financing, a new kind of secrecy – 'commercial-in-confidence' – has arisen in the public accounts along with new and different possibilities for corruption and exploitation of the humble taxpayer. New Loan Council rules now expose New South Wales to international capital markets – reversing 1920s arrangements when the Commonwealth assumed responsibility for state debts and state borrowing overseas. Whatever happens, the shareholders have no choice but to trust their government's economic management. NSW Inc., it seems, has come to stay.

Since the mid-twentieth century, NSW Labor governments have followed the view of J. P. Osborne in 1921, that the power to govern is more important than proper policies because power at least makes it possible to manage the delivery of employment and services to the mass of the people.[18] As well, a cynic might argue that a long training in the Byzantine workings of the NSW Labor Party is perhaps the best preparation for management, i.e. government, not only as premier but also as a minister. The hundreds of workshop (i.e. branch) meetings, the hostile AGMs (i.e. annual conferences), dissident boards (i.e. caucus) and the amount of media experience and political savvy acquired in rising to the top of the ALP in New South Wales has been unparalleled in the business world since at least the middle of the twentieth century. On the other hand, former federal Labor minister from South Australia, Neal Blewett, finds Shakespeare's Richard III, particularly 'Richard's practice of mateship – masking treachery, ambition and savagery', a good guide to the workings of the New South Wales right.[19] The consequence of such intensive training in politics, however, is the narrow experience of many of those who now graduate through the ranks, only ever having worked for politicians or unions.

Over time there have been tensions between the unions and the branches, the country and the city. Clashes between the left and right wings of the party have often seemed more significant than difference between Labor and the other parties vying for government in New South Wales. The right wing of the party has become the repository of the most traditional ideas about its role – furthering the well-being of the 'working classes' by 'whatever it takes'. The left retains something of a tradition of revolutionary idealism, hints at socialism, Marxism, anarchism. Impatient with the plodding pragmatism of the right and susceptible to conspiracy theory, the left, nevertheless, has regularly goaded the right out of complacency, conformity and very conservative views on questions that are significant to society beyond the ranks of the 'workers' and must therefore be taken seriously in government. For its part, the pragmatism of the right insists on a realistic approach to taxing and spending, while the sheer ambition of individual members keeps it in touch with the upwardly mobile aspirations of the whole society. This has also left it open to self-promotion, corruption, and the exploitation or misuse of power, which in turn makes Labor suspect for failing to live up to its idealistic self-image. On the left, those with formal higher education and a grasp of the more theoretical interpretations of the nature of society and the role of government have had more influence, interpreting and promoting questions about equity, race, gender etc., while the more worldly and ambitious right has often been closer in its values to the non-Labor parties and sceptical of the 'bleeding hearts' of the left.[20]

Though life in New South Wales has always been characterised by the struggle to climb the ladder of economic success, since about the 1960s wealth has been more created than extracted, and by cleverness as much as hard work. Maintaining wealth, however, requires skill and vigilance. Wealth based on intelligence rarely survives more than a couple of generations. There is limited time or space for soft-hearted generosity or civic engagement, so the burden of moral values has traditionally been borne by the churches and the wives of successful men. Public debate, vigorous exchanges of opinions and ideas, serious power struggles have seemed mostly to occur within the labour movement rather than between Labor and non-Labor. The role of the conservatives has been to react, reject, resist, and if possible during periods of coalition government, to reverse the actions of Labor.

The ancient aspiring aristocracy or 'establishment' of New South Wales has not been prominent in politics since Labor became a significant force. This may reflect a preference for pulling strings quietly behind the scenes, exerting influence rather than entering debate. Many networks made up of families, working through private schools, sporting clubs, churches, old university friends and business associates, operate quietly and unostentatiously, leading to a certain amount of secrecy, inbreeding, and a kind of dullness. There is still something quintessentially Georgian underlying New South Wales – plain, formal, austere – despite the superficial hedonism of Emerald City, Brett Whiteley and Ken Done, and an easy climate. Perhaps to keep incipient hedonism under control, old Sydney has always turned its back on the water and headed for the upper north shore, the Blue Mountains or the Southern Highlands. Though money buys harbour views in the eastern suburbs, Sydney's north shore is still preferred by the old families and their modern imitators. An analysis of Sydney's Stock Exchange from its founding in the 1870s to the 1960s showed that the membership was remarkably homogeneous, overwhelmingly Australian-born, educated at excellent and prestigious private schools like Shore, Grammar and King's, predominantly Anglican, Presbyterian or Congregational with hardly any Catholics and no women until 1973. The authors of the study, Stephen Salsbury and Kay Sweeney, described the exchange as an 'elite private club', inward-looking, with few overseas connections, a strong sense of tradition and a web of family ties and common school experiences.[21] Among this 'modest middle class' there has never been much style or ostentation, nor since the 1920s and the flamboyance of the New Guard, assertion of the right to rule. And in the operation of these networks nothing has changed greatly since the early twentieth century when they focused on temperance and the sectarian struggle. Parallel Catholic networks have continued evolving, now no longer looking to Labor for their influence. Sectarianism in politics was submerged during the 1960s by Askin's courting of the DLP, and clearly broken by the leadership of Greiner, Fahey and Collins. The new rich social elite that emerged during the 1960s, based in the eastern suburbs, moving to Palm Beach in the summer, the ski-fields in winter, and shopping in Double Bay is less discreet about paying for power.

Once it was radical to assert the rights of working people and to legislate to ensure them. Since the 1970s, however, it has become the role of Labor in New South Wales to preserve gains that have been made and to ensure continuing growth in the availability of resources. In this way, Labor has become the conservative party, while the non-Labor parties have tried from time to time to impose radical changes seen by most working people as against their interests. On election night, March 2004 Bob Carr was described as the best Liberal premier New South Wales has ever had. It is no accident that recent successful coalition premiers (Askin, Fahey) have closely resembled old-fashioned Labor men, while the modern businessman, Nick Greiner, who had a radical program for change, the logic of which came close to the abandonment of democratic government in favour of government by the market, was beaten by his lack of political skill. Democracy, as de Tocqueville observed of eighteenth-century America, is inherently conservative. Of all the Australian states, only New South Wales shares with the United States something of the eighteenth-century ethos. Yet there is a sense, too, in which NSW Inc. has always existed. The state enterprise begun as an experimental gaol has continued ever since as an experiment in survival for the creation of wealth.

IO

Conclusion

It is still not easy to disentangle the history of New South Wales from the history of Australia, but histories of other states show that there are differences, some strongly felt.[1] Much of Australia's early history has been derived from New South Wales with diminishing relevance as the ripples spread out. Russel Ward was not wrong in tracing some essential Australian values and qualities to our convict origins, with Irish Catholic influences, and gold rush immigrants. But the particular mix really only occurred in early New South Wales, and it might be argued that Ward's *Australian Legend* was always about New South Wales.[2] Elsewhere it was applied with less validity. The NSW ethos spread north and west with the pastoral frontier to the Darling, its tributaries, and all the rivers draining into Lake Eyre. It appeared on the frontiers of Queensland, wherever mining and droving stock were the main occupations, and where women were in short supply. But the Victorian gold fields were much richer than any in New South Wales, favouring, as Geoffrey Blainey has observed in *The Rush that Never Ended*,[3] gamblers, aspiring capitalists, and eventually, large companies. After the 1850s the Victorian gold fields produced large towns and turned successfully to agriculture and other forms of production. The NSW gold fields, by comparison, continued for longer as small claims, worked with only modest success by a man and his mate, or a small syndicate. There were no gold fields towns in New South Wales to compare with Ballarat and Bendigo. Nor was there a surge of immigrant-led enterprise in the late nineteenth century. Instead the people of New South Wales made the most of abundant natural resources, harnessing the latent ability and vitality of the native-born, ex-convict, Irish, and immigrants through education and social striving, creating a society and culture which was essentially colonial, more self-consciously working class than bourgeois and in which a small wealthy elite kept a discreet profile befitting their colonial status. No group, Catholic or protestant, labour or management, was able to dominate. Differences were managed rather than resolved.

Fundamental to the history of New South Wales has been its lucky location on the eastern coast of Australia, the range of possibilities encompassed by its climate, soil types, and mineral resources. The accident of siting the first European settlement in the middle of a rich coal basin allowed a kind of industrial development unique in Australia, though for 150 years, most of it went to supporting the production of wool and wheat in a huge hinterland made accessible by railways. Mining, rural exports and industrial development for the local market underpinned employment and supported the growth of a prosperous working class. Those same rural and mineral resources allowed a free trade economy to continue in New South Wales when other Australian colonies adopted protection. Without protection industries requiring expensive equipment, high technology and a specialised workforce did not flourish. Industries leaning heavily towards rural production and existing resources required a less-skilled workforce and less entrepreneurial more traditional management. So there ceased to be much demand for creativity, versatility or innovation, either in the education system or in society as a whole. The industries favoured by free trade had a dulling effect on the population and all forms of scientific, technological and economic creativity. Though talent, originality and innovation flowed into Sydney as the metropolitan centre of the south Pacific, all too often they ran up against existing economic strengths and the 'relaxed and comfortable' conservatism of New South Wales. Since the middle of the twentieth century, this long-term dependence on traditional sources of income has had to contemplate opening up to influences from across the Pacific and to a lesser extent from Asia to the north. Since the 1980s the need for change has become more urgent, with rising concern about water shortages, green-house gas emissions and global warming, more demanding even than the changes wrought at the end of the nineteenth century when New South Wales first tried to throw off its colonial status and reluctantly accept its place as the anchor of an Australian federation.

Far from being an embarrassing question, by 1988, fascination with family history led many individuals to confront the significance of one or more convicts among their ancestors. Likewise, many of those family history researchers discovered someone, often a great-great-grandmother who was undoubtedly Aboriginal, in the family tree. Not a little of the softening in attitudes towards both the convict past and the original inhabitants of New South Wales can be explained by this growing collective knowledge of genealogy. As well it has had the effect of differentiating old Australians from the postwar immigrants. In the interests of social harmony, however, much of NSW's history has necessarily been reduced to a kind of private family knowledge. The heritage of convict buildings, simple, solid, essentially Georgian, so suited to the sandstone from which they were constructed, can be valued simply for aesthetic reasons. Because of their sturdy functionality or their link with official, administrative or government activities, enough have survived to give parts of Sydney and some of the older towns of New South Wales an old world charm which passes for history.

In some ways, NSW's society was ideally suited to the conversion to a mass popular culture that occurred after World War II. The old aristocracy could not compete with the new rich of the consumer and entertainment industries. And the middle classes either accepted the vulgarity of the new order or retreated to their secluded suburbs. A kind of middle brow egalitarianism which is suspicious of both pretension and hypocrisy persists. But so does a high level of tolerance for the extravagance of success among the newly rich.

At the beginning of the twenty-first century NSW's strength lay in the bustling and densely populated conurbation on her eastern coastline (Newcastle, Sydney, Wollongong), linked into the world economy and looking busily to the future. Sydney, especially, towered over the coast, a glittering sight for early morning trans-Pacific travellers flying in on the sunrise. The contrast between the hustling intensity of the city and the quiet serenity of the places beyond could scarcely be greater, yet each gives greatly to the other. Without the quiet places, Sydney would be no different from cities everywhere (indeed, international filmmaking has already succeeded in portraying it as an anonymous alien city-scape). But without the coastal city towers, the quiet places would be more threatened than they are by modern international forms of environmental rape and despoliation. The battle to prevent the creation of yet another Surfers Paradise on NSW's north coast is ongoing. As it is, co-existence is the essence of New South Wales. Set in train in 1788 when the first fleet anchored in Botany Bay, an experiment which often seemed likely to falter, today there is still a balance of hope that it can work to the benefit, not merely of the original inhabitants and a few hundred convicts and settlers, but to the hundreds of thousands who have been born here since or have chosen to make their home in this place.

The good life enjoyed by most of the people in New South Wales in the past two or three generations has been predicated on economic and resource management that delivers basic services and care to all, though increasingly, the government is expected to provide these services from what it receives from Canberra. New South Wales is still expected to subsidise states with smaller populations, though the need is no longer so obvious. From the beginning it was accepted that people should not starve (though too little attention was paid to the original inhabitants), then that they should have access to education, health-care, housing, and more recently unpolluted air and reliable water supplies. The stability of the society depends on this much egalitarianism. Working people early asserted the right to retain something of the fruits of their labour and the bounty provided by natural resources. Increasingly however, as reserves of natural resources shrink, the desire to preserve things once taken for granted as free – fresh air, clean water, beautiful natural places – for the use of future generations, is becoming the new egalitarianism.

Dusk approaches. The beach is almost empty. Some adults sit on the sand, watching children splash in the water. They could be Aboriginal, Australian, Greek, Italian, Vietnamese, for they all come to this beach to play with their children. A lone walker scatters the seagulls staring out to sea. There is a man fishing off the rocks. The scene is timeless. It could be a hundred years ago, or two hundred, maybe even a thousand. They say the sea will rise here with global warming. They say too that as the tectonic plates shift,

New Zealand may be drifting closer. Perhaps it will wash ashore someday at Bondi, already a New Zealand colony.

What will this scene be a hundred years hence, or two hundred? It is not easy to know or understand the past, but it is impossible to predict the future. Who in 1770 or 1788 could possibly have imagined the changes that would take place on these shores in just over two hundred years? Yet . . .

APPENDIX 1: TIMELINE, 1770–2005

1770	Captain James Cook names New South Wales
1788	First fleet arrives
1794	Agricultural settlement begins on the Hawkesbury River
1795	Useable coal deposits found to the south at Coalcliff and to the north on the Hunter
1807	First wool export
1808	Post Office established by Isaac Nichols
1813	Blue Mountains crossed
1815	Bathurst founded; first sitting of the Supreme Court
1816	Botanic Gardens formed
1817	Bank of New South Wales (subsequently Westpac) opens for business
1819	Commissioner Bigge's inquiry into the administration of New South Wales
1821	Settlement at Port Macquarie
1822	Settlement in the Wellington Valley
1823	First constitution establishing a Legislative Council of 5 to 7 members; Surveyor McBrien finds particles of gold at Fish River near Bathurst
1824	James Busby's vineyard on the Hunter River planted
1825	Van Diemen's Land proclaimed a separate colony
1826	Australian Subscription Library founded
1828	Second Constitution enlarging the Legislative Council to 15; first census
1829	Nineteen counties proclaimed; trial by jury in civil cases

1830	Beef exported to England and horses to India
1831	*Sydney Herald* (later *Sydney Morning Herald*) founded; land grants abolished; first immigrant ship arrives
1833	Sydney Mechanics' School of Arts established
1834	Commercial Banking Company of Sydney established; settlement at Twofold Bay
1835	Port Phillip area explored and settled
1836	Australian Museum established
1837	Molesworth's committee inquiring into transportation established in London
1838	Myall Creek massacre; Australian Club founded
1840	Transportation abolished
1842	Sydney Municipal Corporation established
1843	First elections under the constitution allowing representative government
1851	Hargraves discovers payable gold near Bathurst; Victoria separated from New South Wales
1852	University of Sydney inaugurated
1856	Responsible government established
1858	Manhood suffrage and vote by ballot established
1859	Queensland separated from New South Wales
1861	Anti-Chinese riots on the Lambing Flat gold fields
1862	State aid to religion abolished; Cobb & Co. depot established at Bathurst
1864	Drought continuing till 1866
1867	Supply of liquor to Aborigines banned
1874	Local option first advocated in Orange
1878	Artesian water discovered near Bourke
1879	Royal National Park established
1880	State aid to church schools abolished; first telephone in Sydney
1881	Protector of Aborigines appointed; Broken Hill mineral field discovered; women first admitted to the University of Sydney
1882	Aborigines Protection Board established
1885	Dalley sends troops to the Sudan
1886	Greta coal seam discovered by Professor Edgeworth David

1887–88	One of the driest years yet experienced in New South Wales; Centennial Park created; Tamworth is the first city in the southern hemisphere to be lit by electricity
1890	Great strike of miners, waterside workers, draymen and shearers defeated
1891	35 labour candidates elected to the New South Wales Parliament
1892	Beginning of the banking crisis with a run on the Savings Bank of New South Wales
1893	'One man, one vote'
1895	Drought in inland New South Wales lasted to 1903; Warragamba Walking Club formed
1901	Federation
1902	Votes for women; 96 men died in a mine explosion at Mt Kembla near Wollongong
1904	Inquiry into the birthrate
1906	Central Railway Station opened; Bondi Surf-Bathers' Lifesaving Club formed; public school fees abolished
1910	Mitchell Library opened; Aboriginal girls training home established at Cootamundra
1913	Workers' Educational Association founded
1914	Milo Dunphy forms the Mountain Trails Club
1915	Newcastle steelworks begin production
1916	Six o'clock closing of hotels introduced
1919	Local Government Act
1920	School attendance made compulsory
1922	Population of Sydney passes 1 million
1924	Kinchela established near Kempsey to replace the 1917 Aboriginal boys training home at Singleton
1926	Electrification of the suburban railway network begun
1928	Steelworks at Port Kembla begin operation
1929	Compulsory voting at New South Wales state elections introduced
1931	State lotteries started
1932	Sydney Harbour Bridge opened
1940	Aborigines Protection Board becomes Aboriginal Welfare Board
1941	Pensions introduced for coalminers

1942	Open-cut mining begun; Commonwealth uniform tax replaced state income and entertainment taxes
1943	School attendance made compulsory from 6th to 13th birthday
1944	Drought, bushfires and dust storms
1945	Road bridge replaces a car ferry for crossing the Hawkesbury River
1946	Electricity Authority of New South Wales established
1947	40-hour working week introduced; compulsory voting for local government elections
1948	University of New South Wales created; Fauna Protection Act
1949	Coal strike (June–August); Snowy Mountains hydro-electricity and irrigation scheme commenced
1951	Record wool prices; long service leave under state awards
1953	Compulsory unionism in New South Wales
1954	Death penalty abolished in New South Wales
1955	10 pm liquor trading introduced
1956	First regular television transmission from Sydney
1957	First nuclear reactor in Australia at Lucas Heights; New South Wales Defamation Act passed
1961	Conveyancing (Strata Titles) Act passed; referendum to abolish the Legislative Council rejected
1962	New South Wales population reaches 4 million
1964	Macquarie University established; Totalisator Agency Board to allow off-course betting set up; 4 weeks annual leave granted to state public servants
1966	Provisional driving licences introduced; screening of films in cinemas on Sundays permitted
1967	Aboriginal Welfare Board abolished; referendum of electors in north-east New South Wales to establish a new state rejected
1971	State minimum legal age lowered from 21 to 18; the battle for Kelly's Bush
1973	Aquarius Festival, Nimbin
1975	First New South Wales Ombudsman appointed; Aboriginal Lands Trust created

1976	A state referendum in favour of daylight saving carried
1977	83 people died in a train accident at Granville
1978	A referendum for the election of the Legislative Council passed by 73% of voters
1979	State workers granted a $37^1/_2$ hour working week; eastern suburbs railway opened; blockade at Terania Creek
1981	Public funding of state elections introduced in New South Wales
1982	Random breath testing of drivers begun
1983	Aboriginal Land Rights Act transferred titles of existing reserves to local communities
1984	4-year terms for the New South Wales Legislative Assembly made possible
1986	New South Wales rainforests listed on the World Heritage Register
1989	The Independent Commission against Corruption established
1992	Sydney Harbour Tunnel opened
1993	Sydney's Olympic bid for 2000 successful
1994	January bushfires claimed 4 lives; 98% of New South Wales drought-declared; Wollemi Pine discovered in the Blue Mountains
1995	Drought continued; Sydney casino opened at Darling Harbour
1996	Airport rail link commenced
1997	December bushfires claimed the lives of 4 volunteer fire-fighters
1998	Royal Easter Show held for the first time at Homebush after its move from Moore Park
1999	Sydney's April hailstorm ranked by insurers as Australia's most expensive natural disaster; rail collision at Glenbrook kills 7
2000	In May 250,000 people walked across the Sydney Harbour Bridge in support of reconciliation with indigenous Australians; in September 10,300 athletes from 199 countries competed in the Olympic Games at Homebush

2001   On Christmas Day bushfires broke out across the state

2002   Bushfires continued through January destroying 331
         buildings and 753,000 hectares; by November 99% of
         New South Wales was drought-declared

2003   Train derailment at Waterfall kills 7; Linda Burney
         becomes the first Aboriginal MP in New South Wales;
         New South Wales population growth rate falls to 0.7%
         (compared with 1.1% nationally) and 26,900 people
         leave, most of them for Queensland

2005   In May, Bob Carr becomes the longest serving premier;
         Sydney Swans win the Australian Rules Premiership

APPENDIX 2: PREMIERS OF NEW SOUTH WALES SINCE 1856

(Derived from the *New South Wales Parliamentary Record*)

Stuart (later Sir Stuart) Alexander Donaldson	6 June – 25 Aug. 1856
Charles (later Sir Charles) Cowper	26 Aug. – 2 Oct. 1856; 7 Sept. 1857 – 26 Oct. 1859; 10 Jan. 1861 – 15 Oct. 1863; 3 Feb. 1865 – 21 Jan. 1866; 13 Jan. – 15 Dec. 1870
Henry (later Sir Henry) Watson Parker	3 Oct. 1856 – 7 Sept. 1857
William Forster	27 Oct. 1859 – 8 March 1860
John (later Sir John) Robertson	9 March 1860 – 9 Jan. 1861; 27 Oct. 1868 – 12 Jan. 1870; 9 Feb. 1875 – 21 March 1877; 17 Aug. – 17 Dec. 1877; 22 Dec. 1885 – 25 Feb. 1886
James (later Sir James) Martin	16 Oct. 1863 – 2 Feb. 1865; 22 Jan. 1866 – 26 Oct. 1868; 16 Dec. 1870 – 13 May 1872
Henry (later Sir Henry) Parkes	14 May 1872 – 8 Feb. 1875; 22 March – 16 Aug. 1877; 21 Dec. 1878 – 4 Jan. 1883; 25 Jan. 1887 – 16 Jan. 1889; 8 March 1889 – 22 Oct. 1891

James Squire Farnell	18 Dec. 1877 – 20 Dec. 1878
Alexander (later Sir Alexander) Stuart	5 Jan. 1883 – 5 Oct. 1885
George (later Sir George) Richard Dibbs	7–9 Oct. 1885; 10 Oct. – 21 Dec. 1885; 17 Jan. – 7 March 1889; 23 Oct. 1891 – 2 Aug. 1894
Patrick (later Sir Patrick) Alfred Jennings	25 Feb. 1886 – 19 Jan. 1887
George (later Sir George) Houston Reid (Free Trade)	3 Aug. 1894 – 13 Sept. 1899
William (later Sir William) John Lyne (Protectionist)	15 Sept. 1899 – 20 March 1901
John (later Sir John) See (Progressive)[a]	28 March 1901 – 14 June 1904
Thomas Waddell (Ministerialist)	15 June – 29 Aug. 1904
Joseph (later Sir Joseph) Hector Carruthers (Liberal Reform)	30 Aug. 1904 – 1 Oct. 1907
Charles (later Sir Charles) Gregory Wade (Liberal)	2 Oct. 1907 – 20 Oct. 1910
James Sinclair Taylor McGowen (ALP)	21 Oct. 1910 – 29 June 1913
William Arthur Holman (ALP)	30 June 1913 – 15 Nov. 1916
William Arthur Holman (Nationalist)	15 Nov. 1916 – 12 April 1920
John Storey (ALP)	13 April 1920 – 5 Oct. 1921
James Dooley (ALP)	5 Oct. 1921 – 20 Dec. 1921; 20 Dec. 1921 – 13 April 1922
Sir George Warburton Fuller (Nationalist)	20 Dec. 1921; 13 April 1922 – 17 June 1925

[a] The party title given is that in use when the election that brought that particular group to office was held. Thus 'Liberal' and 'Progressive' are used in preference to 'Free Trade' and 'Protectionist'.

John Thomas Lang (ALP)	17 June 1925 – 18 Oct. 1927; 4 Nov. 1930 – 13 May 1932
Thomas (later Sir Thomas) Rainsford Bavin (Nationalist)	18 Oct. 1927 – 3 Nov. 1930
Bertram (later Sir Bertram) Sydney Barnsdale Stevens (UAP)	13 May 1932 – 5 Aug. 1939
Alexander Mair (UAP)	5 Aug. 1939 – 16 May 1941
William (later Sir William) John McKell (ALP)	16 May 1941 – 6 Feb. 1947
James McGirr (ALP)	6 Feb. 1947 – 2 April 1952
John Joseph Cahill (ALP)	2 April 1952 – 22 Oct. 1959
Robert James Heffron (ALP)	23 Oct. 1959 – 30 April 1964
John Brophy Renshaw (ALP)	30 April 1964 – 13 May 1965
Robin (later Sir Robert) William Askin[b] (Liberal)	13 May 1965 – 3 Jan. 1975
Thomas Lancelot Lewis (Liberal)	3 Jan. 1975 – 23 Jan. 1976
Sir Eric Archibald Willis (Liberal)	23 Jan. – 14 May 1976
Neville Kenneth Wran (ALP)	14 May 1976 – 4 July 1986
Laurie John Ferguson[c] (ALP)	16 May – 29 July 1983
Barrie John Unsworth (ALP)	4 July 1986 – 25 March 1988
Nicholas Frank Greiner (Liberal)	25 March 1988 – 24 June 1992
John Joseph Fahey (Liberal)	3 July 1992 – 4 April 1995
Robert John Carr (ALP)	4 April 1995 – 3 Aug. 2005
Morris Iemma (ALP)	3 Aug. 2005 –

[b] Name changed to Robert William Askin by deed poll 14 December 1971; knighted (KCMG) 1 January 1972.
[c] Acting Premier while Premier Wran stood down during Street Royal Commission.

NOTES

I INTRODUCTION

1. J. C. Beaglehole, ed., *The Journals of Captain James Cook on his Voyages of Discovery*, vol. I, *The Voyage of the Endeavour 1768–1771*, 1955, p. 304.
2. For a more detailed discussion see G. Arnold Wood, *The Discovery of Australia*, revised by J. C. Beaglehole, Macmillan, Melbourne, 1969, pp. 306, 318–19.
3. Based on the *Official Year Book of Australia*, no. 59, 1973, pp. 3–5.
4. Beaglehole, ed., *The Journals of Captain James Cook*, p. 399, quoted by Glyndwr Williams, 'Reactions on Cook's Voyage', in I. Donaldson and T. Donaldson, eds, *Seeing the First Australians*, Allen & Unwin, Sydney, 1985, p. 35.
5. Some are listed in the section on Sources.

2 1788–1840, THE CONVICT COLONY

1. Brian Fletcher's *Colonial Australia before 1850*, 1976, pp. 17–21 is an excellent summary of the arguments for settling New South Wales.
2. Based on Frank Crowley, *A Documentary History of Australia*, vol. I, *Colonial Australia 1788–1840*, 1980, p. 1.
3. Alan Atkinson, *The Europeans in Australia: A History*, vol. I, 1997, examines this context in detail.
4. J. B. Hirst, *Convict Society and its Enemies: A History of Early New South Wales*, 1983.
5. Babette Smith, *A Cargo of Women: Susannah Watson and the Convicts of the* Princess Royal, 1988, gives a good picture of the detail in some of the records and the uses to which it can be put by a modern historian.
6. See Deborah Oxley, *Convict Maids: The Forced Migration of Women to Australia*, 1996, pp. 137–45; also Stephen Nicholas, ed., *Convict Workers. Reinterpreting Australia's Past*, 1988.

7. Alan Atkinson, *Camden*, 1988.

8. See Atkinson's Appendix 4 on The Camden Aborigines; also Mark Hannah, 'Aboriginal workers in the Australian Agricultural Company, 1824–1857', *Labour History*, no. 82, May 2002, pp. 17–33; Richard Broome, 'Aboriginal workers on southeastern frontiers', *Australian Historical Studies*, vol. 26, no. 103, 1994, pp. 203–7.

9. Alward Wyndham and Frances McInherny, eds, *The Diary of George Wyndham of Dalwood 1830–1840*, Dalwood Restoration Association, 1987.

10. Based on Merval Hoare, *Norfolk Island: An Outline of its History 1774–1977*, 1978, pp. 1–2.

11. Jean Edgecombe, *Norfolk Island – South Pacific: Island of History and Many Delights*, pub. by the author, Thornleigh, 1999, p. 14.

12. Anne Salmond, *Between Worlds: Early Exchanges Between Maori and Europeans 1773–1815*, University of Hawai'i Press, Honolulu, 1997, p. 53.

13. See Peter N. Grabosky, *Sydney in Ferment: Crime, Dissent and Official Reaction 1788–1973*, 1977, especially for Mt Rennie.

14. See Michael Sturma, *Vice in a Vicious Society: Crime and Convicts In Mid-nineteenth Century New South Wales*, University of Queensland Press, St Lucia, 1983, ch. 7.

15. R. Therry, *Reminiscences of Thirty Years' Residence in New South Wales and Victoria*, facsimile edition, RAHS and Sydney University Press, 1974 (first published 1863), pp. 41–2.

16. In Hirst, *Convict Society and its Enemies*.

17. See Ray and Richard Beckett, *Hangman: The Life and Times of Alexander Green Public Executioner to the Colony of New South Wales*, 1980, p. 4 for 3.5 million lashes.

18. B. J. Bridges, The Church of England and the Aborigines of New South Wales, PhD thesis, UNSW, 1978.

19. See Carol Liston, *Sarah Wentworth, Mistress of Vaucluse*, 1988.

20. See James Maclehose, *Picture of Sydney and Strangers' Guide in New South Wales for 1839*, reissued by John Ferguson in association with the RAHS, Sydney, 1977.

21. Brian H. Fletcher, *Ralph Darling: A Governor Maligned*, 1984, pp. 214–16.

22. C. H. Currey, *The Brothers Bent: Judge-Advocate Ellis Bent and Judge Jeffrey Hart Bent*, Sydney University Press, 1968, ch. 1.

23. Stephen Judd and Kenneth Cable, *Sydney Anglicans: A History of the Diocese*, Anglican Information Office, Sydney, 1987, p. 8.

24. W. D. Borrie, *The European Peopling of Australasia. A demographic history, 1788–1988*, 1994, p. 24. The classic rehabilitation of the reputation of the Irish convicts was Eris O'Brien, *The Foundation of Australia (1786–1800)* first published in 1937 by Sheed and Ward in Great Britain, reprinted Angus & Robertson, Sydney, 1950.

25. Margaret Kiddle, *Caroline Chisholm*, 1950, pp. 71–8; also R. B. Madgwick, *Immigration into Eastern Australia 1788–1851*, 1969, ch. V.
26. D. W. A. Baker, *Days of Wrath: A Life of John Dunmore Lang*, 1983, p. 246.
27. Michael Roe, *Quest for Authority in Eastern Australia 1835–1851*, Melbourne University Press in association with the Australian National University, Melbourne, 1965, p. 23.
28. John N. Molony, *An Architect of Freedom: John Herbert Plunkett in New South Wales 1832–1869*, 1973, p. 5.
29. James Waldersee, *Catholic Society in New South Wales 1788–1860*, 1974.
30. Michael Roe's description from his article on Duncan in the *ADB*, vol. 1, p. 336.
31. Patrick O'Farrell, *The Irish in Australia*, 1987, pp. 31–2.
32. See Malcolm Campbell, *The Kingdom of the Ryans: The Irish in Southwest New South Wales 1816–1890*, 1997.
33. Waldersee, *Catholic Society in New South Wales*, pp.121–2.
34. John Molony, *The Native-Born: The First White Australians*, 2000.
35. Charles M'Donald, *An Address on the Fiftieth Anniversary of New South Wales and Other Poems*, Mulini Press, Canberra, 1980.

3 1841–1864, HORIZONS AND BOUNDARIES

1. Frank Crowley, *A Documentary History of Australia*, vol. 1, *Colonial Australia 1788–1840*, Nelson, Melbourne, 1980, p. 564.
2. Marion Diamond, *Ben Boyd of Boydtown*, 1995, ch. 7.
3. Leila Thomas, The Development of the Labour Movement in the Sydney District of New South Wales, MA thesis, Sydney, 1919, p. 43.
4. Gwen Dundon, *The Shipbuilders of Brisbane Water*, Gwen Dundon, East Gosford, 1997, has a detailed account.
5. D. R. Hainsworth, *The Sydney Traders. Simeon Lord and his Contemporaries 1788–1821*, Cassell, Sydney, 1971; also Gwyneth M. Dow, *Samuel Terry: The Botany Bay Rothschild*, Sydney University Press, Sydney, 1974.
6. G. P. Walsh, 'Manufacturing', in G. J. Abbott and N. B. Nairn (eds), *Economic Growth in Australia 1788–1821*, Melbourne University Press, Sydney, 1969, pp. 245–66.
7. G. B. Earp, *The Gold Colonies of Australia . . . with every advice to emigrants*, Geo. Routledge, London, 1852, p. 68.
8. M. Barnard Eldershaw, *A House is Built*, Harrap & Co., London, 1929, is a classic fictionalised account.
9. Michael Christie, *The Sydney Markets 1788–1988*, 1988.
10. S. G. Forster, *Colonial Improver, Edward Deas Thomson 1800–1879*, 1978.

11. Andrew Houison, *History of the Post Office*, Charles Potter, Government Printer and Inspector of Stamps, Sydney, 1890, pp. 25, 548.
12. R. D. Collison Black and Rosamond Könekamp, eds, *Papers and Correspondence of William Stanley Jevons*, vol. 1, pp. 123–30.
13. Lucille M. Quinlan, *Here My Home: The Life and Times of Captain John Stuart Hepburn 1803–1860, Master Mariner, Overlander, and Founder of Smeaton Hill, Victoria*, OUP, Melbourne, 1967, pp. 60, 62, 64, 72, 81.
14. K. A. Austin, *The Lights of Cobb and Co: The Story of the Frontier Coaches, 1854–1924*, 1967, workshops, p. 110.
15. Based on Robert Lee, *The Greatest Public Work: The New South Wales Railways 1848–1889*, 1988, ch. 1.
16. *Government Gazette*, 21 May 1839, p. 606, quoted R. H. W. Reece, *Aborigines and Colonists: Aborigines and Colonial Society in New South Wales in the 1830s and 1840s*, 1974, pp. 176–7.
17. NSW *Votes & Proceedings*, 1862, vol. 5, p. 1171.
18. Michael Roe, *Quest for Authority in Eastern Australia 1835–1851*, 1965, p. 205.
19. Michael Sturma, *Vice in a Vicious Society. Crime and Convicts in Mid-nineteenth Century New South Wales*, 1983, ch. 8.
20. *In Southern Lights and Shadows: Being Brief Notes of Three Years' Experience of Social, Literary and Political Life in Australia*, London, 1859, p. 22, facsimile edition, introduced by R. G. Geering, Sydney University Press, Sydney 1975.
21. Earp, *The Gold Colonies of Australia*, pp. 101, 73; see also Paula J. Byrne, *Criminal Law and Colonial Subject: New South Wales 1810–1830*, Cambridge University Press, Cambridge, 1993.
22. Sturma, *Vice in a Vicious Society*, p. 185.
23. Francis Low, comp., *The City of Sydney Directory for MDCCCXLIV–V*, F. Alcock, Sydney, 1844, pp. 157–65, 173–91.
24. *Sydney Commercial Directory* for the year 1851, compiled with the greatest care, W. & F. Ford, Sydney, 1851.
25. See John Molony, *The Native-born: The First White Australians*, Melbourne University Press, Melbourne, 2000, pp. 178–9.
26. In addition to the *ADB* for all these names, see Ann-Mari Jordens, *The Stenhouse Circle: Literary Life in Mid-nineteenth Century Sydney*, Melbourne University Press, Melbourne, 1979; Cyril Pearl, *Brilliant Dan Deniehy: A Forgotten Genius*, Thomas Nelson, Melbourne, 1972.
27. On its foundation see George Nadel, *Australia's Colonial Culture: Ideas, Men and Institutions in Mid-nineteenth Century Eastern Australia*, 1957, Part IV.
28. A Lady (Mrs A. Macpherson), *My Experiences in Australia*, J. F. Hope, London, 1860, p. 28.

29. H. S. Russell, *The Genesis of Queensland*, Turner and Henderson, Sydney, 1888, p. 446.

30. Geoffrey Blainey, *Our Side of the Country: The Story of Victoria*, Methuen Haynes, North Ryde, NSW, 1984, p. 36.

31. See John M. Ward, *Earl Grey and the Australian Colonies 1846–1857*, 1958.

32. Charles Bateson, *Gold Fleet for California: Forty-Niners from Australia and New Zealand*, 1963, p. 142.

33. W. P. Morrell, *The Gold Rushes*, 1968 (first edn 1940), p. 202.

34. Nancy Keesing, ed., *History of the Australian Gold Rushes by Those Who Were There*, 1971 (first published as *Gold Fever* by Angus & Robertson in 1967), p. 27.

35. R. Therry, *Reminiscences of Thirty Years' Residence in New South Wales and Victoria*, facsimile edition, RAHS in conjunction with Sydney University Press, Sydney, 1974, pp. 459–61.

36. J. B. Hirst, *The Strange Birth of Liberal Democracy, New South Wales 1848–1884*, 1988, p. 100.

37. See Alan Powell, *Patrician Democrat: The Political Life of Charles Cowper 1843–1870*, 1977.

38. For a survey of the historiography of the free selection legislation see Bill Gammage, 'Who gained, and who was meant to gain, from land selection in New South Wales?', *Historical Studies*, vol. 24, no. 94, April 1990, pp. 104–22.

39. W. G. McMinn, *A Constitutional History of Australia*, Oxford University Press, Melbourne, 1979, pp. 74–6.

40. Sturma, *Vice in a Vicious Society*, Appendix II.

41. Alan Barcan, *A Short History of Education in New South Wales*, Martindale Press, Sydney, 1965, ch. IX.

4 1865–1889, FREETRADING

1. See K. T. H. Farrer, *A Settlement Amply Supplied: Food Technology in Nineteenth Century Australia*, 1980, chs. 6 and 10.

2. See Alan Barnard, *Visions and Profits: Studies in the Business Career of Thomas Sutcliffe Mort*, 1961, pp. 102–3, 200–2.

3. See A. T. Yarwood, *Walers: Australian Horses Abroad*, 1989.

4. Shirley Fitzgerald, *Rising Damp: Sydney 1870–90*, 1987, p. 9.

5. The phrase is Rolf Boldrewood's from *In Bad Company and Other Stories*, Macmillan & Co., London, 1901, p. 412.

6. Charles Lyne, *The Industries of New South Wales*, Thomas Richards Govt Printer, Sydney, 1882, p. 233.

7. J. B. Hirst, *The Strange Birth of Colonial Democracy: New South Wales 1848–1884*, Allen & Unwin, Sydney, 1988, ch. 11, esp. p. 175.

8. Discussed in detail by Hilary Golder in *Politics, Patronage and Public Works: The Administration of New South Wales*, vol. 1, *1842–1900*, UNSW Press, Sydney, 2005.

9. Bede Nairn, *Civilising Capitalism: The Labor Movement in New South Wales 1870–1900*, 1973, pp. 2–3.
10. Bede Nairn on Robertson in *ADB*, vol. 6, p. 39.
11. G. J. R. Linge, *Industrial Awakening: A Geography of Australian Manufacturing 1788–1890*, 1979, pp. 574–8.
12. K. T. Livingston, *The Wired Nation Continent: The Communication Revolution and Federating Australia*, 1996, pp. 47–8.
13. Henry Lawson, A Fragment of Autobiography. MSS 1903–6 VI Sydney, in *A Camp-Fire Yarn: Henry Lawson Complete Works 1885–1900*, compiled and edited by Leonard Cronin, 1984, p. 29.
14. Based on Dan Huon Coward, *Out of Sight . . . Sydney's Environmental History 1851–1891*, 1988, pp. 99–100.
15. *Wealth and Progress of NSW 1890–91*, pp. 421–3.
16. *Under the Southern Cross*, Higginbotham & Co., Madras, 1880, republished Penguin Books, Ringwood, Vic., 1975, pp. 254–5.
17. Elena Grainger, *Martin of Martin Place . . . A Biography of Sir James Martin (1820–1886)*, Alpha Books, Sydney, 1970, pp. 75, 132.
18. Peter Proudfoot, Roslyn Maquire and Robert Firestone, eds, *Colonial City, Global City: Sydney's International Exhibition 1879*, 2000.
19. Anthony Trollope, *Australia*, edited by P. D. Edwards and R. B. Joyce, University of Queensland Press, St Lucia, 1967, p. 240.
20. Quoted Geoffrey Bolton, *Edmund Barton*, 2000, p. 27.
21. Sir Henry Parkes, *Fifty Years in the Making of Australian History*, Longmans Green & Co., London, 1892, vol. 2, p. 3.
22. Based on K. S. Inglis, *The Rehearsal: Australians at War in the Sudan 1885*, Rigby, Adelaide, 1985; also Zita Denholm, *T.Y.S.O.N.*, Triple D Books, Wagga Wagga, 2002.
23. Craig Wilcox, *Australia's Boer War: The War in South Africa 1899–1902*, Oxford University Press, Melbourne, 2002, p. 21.
24. Inglis, *The Rehearsal*, pp. 151–3.
25. See Patricia Rolfe, *The Journalistic Javelin: An Illustrated History of the* Bulletin, 1979.
26. Brian Fletcher, *Australian History in New South Wales 1888–1938*, UNSW Press, 1993, pp. 18–19.
27. See Barry Andrews, *Price Warung (William Astley)*, 1976, for a detailed analysis of Astley's research methods and influence on convict historiography.
28. See Paul De Serville, *Rolf Boldrewood: A Life*, 2000.
29. See Paul Ashton, *Waving the Waratah: Bicentenary New South Wales*, New South Wales Bicentennial Council, Sydney, 1989, pp. 13–20.
30. *Bulletin*, 28 January 1888, p. 5; and 4 February 1888, p. 2.
31. T. A. Coghlan, *The Wealth and Progress of New South Wales*, 1890–91, p. 689.

32. Graeme Davison and Shirley Constantine, eds, *Out of Work Again: The Autobiographical Narrative of Thomas Dobeson 1885–1891*, Monash Publications in History, 6, 1990.
33. Brian Kiernan's Introduction to *A Camp-Fire Yarn: Henry Lawson Complete Works 1885–1900*, compiled and edited by Leonard Cronin, 1984, p. iii.

5   1890–1914, THE CHALLENGE OF FEDERATION

1. T. A. Coghlan, *The Wealth and Progress of New South Wales*, Government Printer, Sydney, 1890–91, p. 676.
2. Bede Nairn, *Civilising Capitalism: The Labor Movement in New South Wales 1870–1900*, 1973, p. 8.
3. Coghlan, *The Wealth and Progress of New South Wales*, 1890–91, pp. 723–4.
4. See John Rickard, *Class and Politics: New South Wales, Victoria and the Early Commonwealth, 1890–1910*, 1976, pp. 38–9.
5. Based on *ADB*, vol. 4, pp. 65–9, but see T. W. Campbell, *George Richard Dibbs: Politician, Premier, Patriot, Paradox*, 1999, and L. F. Crisp, *Federation Fathers*, 1990, ch. 2.
6. Ian Evans, *The Lithgow Pottery*, 1981.
7. In R. S. Parker, *The Government of New South Wales*, University of Queensland Press, St Lucia, 1978, p. 303.
8. G. J. R. Linge, *Industrial Awakening: A Geography of Australian Manufacturing 1788–1890*, ANU Press, Canberra, 1979, p. 542.
9. Based on C. T. Wood, *Sugar Country: A Short History of the Raw Sugar Industry of Australia 1864–1964*, Queensland Cane Growers' Council, Brisbane, 1965, pp. 34–51.
10. From C. J. King on Campbell quoted in *ADB*, vol. 7, p. 553.
11. C. W. Wrigley on William James Farrer, *ADB*, vol. 8, pp. 471–3 and Frederick Bickell on Guthrie, *ADB*, vol. 9, pp. 143–4.
12. Based on C. E. W. Bean, *The Dreadnought of the Darling*, A & R, Sydney, 1956 (first published London, 1911) p. 247, and George F. Shoebridge's Preface to A. E. Bowmaker, comp., *A Brief History of Leeton*, Rotary Club of Leeton, 1968; also the British Association for the Advancement of Science, *Handbook for New South Wales*, Edward Lee & Co., Sydney, 1914, ch. VII.
13. See Geoffrey Hawker, *Politicians All: The Candidates for the Australian Commonwealth Election 1901, A Collective Biography*, 2002.
14. Christopher Cunneen, *Kings' Men: Australia's Governors-General from Hopetoun to Isaacs*, pp. 97–103.
15. In 'New South Wales' in *The Oxford Companion to Australian History*, Oxford University Press, Melbourne, 1998, p. 464.
16. Marian Sawer, 'The ethical state: Social liberalism and the critique of contract', *Australian Historical Studies*, vol. 31, no. 114, April 2000, pp. 67–90.

17. Geoffrey Blainey, *Our Side of the Country: The Story of Victoria*, 1984, p. 225.
18. See Neville Hicks, *'This sin and scandal': Australia's Population Debate 1891–1911*, 1978.
19. *Official Year Book of New South Wales*, 1913, pp. 110–11.
20. Stephen Judd and Kenneth Cable, *Sydney Anglicans: A History of the Diocese*, Anglican Information Office, Sydney, 1987, p. 73.
21. On Jones see William James Lawton, *The Better Time to Be: Utopian Attitudes to Society among Sydney Anglicans 1885–1914*, 1990.
22. Bruce Mitchell, *Teachers, Education, and Politics: A History of Organizations of Public School Teachers in New South Wales*, 1975, p. 16.
23. Quoted by Jeff Kildea, *Tearing the Fabric: Sectarianism in Australia 1910–1925*, p. 29.
24. J. P. Osborne, *Nine Crowded Years*, George A. Jones, Printer, Sydney, 1921, p. 36.

6 1915–1940, DIVISION AND DEPRESSION

1. E. M. Johnston-Liik, George Liik, and R. G. Ward, *A Measure of Greatness. The Origins of the Australian Iron and Steel Industry*, 1998.
2. Dorothy M. Catts, comp., *James Howard Catts MHR*, Ure Smith, Sydney, 1953–4, p. 56.
3. A classic account, *How Labour Governs. A Study of Workers' Representation in Australia*, was written in 1923 by Vere Gordon Childe who had been John Storey's private secretary before embarking on a distinguished career as a pre-historian.
4. Ian Turner, *Sydney's Burning*, Alpha Books Sydney, 1967, p. 15.
5. Based on Dan Coward, 'Crime and Punishment: The Great Strike in New South Wales, August to October 1917' in John Iremonger, John Merritt and Graeme Osborne, eds, *Strikes: Studies in Twentieth Century Australian Social History*, Angus & Robertson in association with the Australian Society for the Study of Labour History, Sydney, 1973, pp. 51–80.
6. Stuart Macintyre, *The Reds*, 1998, p. 25.
7. Adapted from David Day, *Chifley*, HarperCollins, Sydney, 2001, pp. 168–9.
8. Based on *The Roadmakers: A History of Main Roads in New South Wales,* 1976, pp. 116–23.
9. First published as *Tomorrow and Tomorrow* by Georgian House, Melbourne, 1947; also Jill Ker Conway, *The Road from Coorain*, William Heinemann, London, 1989.
10. See Don Aitkin, *The Colonel: A Political Biography of Sir Michael Bruxner*, Australian National University Press, Canberra, 1969.
11. Shirley Walker, *Roundabout at Bangalow. An Intimate Chronicle*, University of Queensland Press, St Lucia, 2001, pp. 17–19.

12. Jim Hagan and Ken Turner, *A History of the Labor Party in New South Wales 1891–1991*, Longman Cheshire, Melbourne, 1991, p. 120.

13. Patrick O'Farrell, *The Catholic Church and Community in Australia*, 1977, p. 351.

14. See Sir John Cramer, *Pioneers, Politics and People: A Political Memoir*, Allen & Unwin, Sydney, 1989.

15. Alan Barcan, *Radical Students: The Old Left at Sydney University*, 2002, pp. 35–6.

16. See Peter Kirkpatrick, *The Sea Coast of Bohemia: Literary Life in Sydney's Roaring Twenties*, 1992.

17. Maslyn Williams, *His Mother's Country*, Melbourne University Press, 1988, pp. 10–11.

18. *Commonwealth Yearbook*, no. 27, 1934, pp. 318, 785.

19. Wray Vamplew, *Historical Statistics*, Fairfax, Syme & Weldon Associates, Sydney, 1987, p. 152.

20. Alan Walker, *Coaltown: A Social Survey of Cessnock, New South Wales*, Melbourne University Press, 1945; see also Len Richardson, *The Bitter Years: Wollongong during the Great Depression*, Hale & Iremonger, Sydney, 1984.

21. Eric Campbell, *The Rallying Point: My Story of the New Guard*, Melbourne University Press, 1965, p. 13.

22. Ibid., p. 158.

23. Bruce Mitchell, *Teachers, Education, and Politics. A History of Organizations of Public School Teachers in New South Wales*, 1975, p. 130.

24. *Commonwealth Yearbook*, 1934, p. 77.

25. Based on Gavin Souter, 'Skeleton at the Feast' and Jack Horner and Marcia Langton, 'The Day of Mourning' in Bill Gammage and Peter Spearritt, eds, *Australians 1938*, Fairfax, Syme & Weldon Associates, Sydney, 1987; Jack Horner, *Bill Ferguson. Fighter for Aboriginal Freedom*, the author, Dickson, ACT, 1994; Bobbie Hardy, *Lament for the Barkindji*, Rigby, Adelaide, 1976, p. 222.

7 1941–1965, LABOR'S LONG HAUL

1. Based on Jim Hagan and Ken Turner, *A History of the Labor Party in New South Wales 1891–1991*, Longman Cheshire, Melbourne, 1991, Part 3.

2. See John Ramsland, '"Silver pencils of light": Fragments of remembered and forgotten space in wartime Newcastle', pp. 160–6 in R. John Moore and Michael J. Ostwald, *Hidden Newcastle: Urban Memories and Architectural Imaginaries*, Gadfly Media Pty Ltd, Ultimo, 1997.

3. See Christopher Cunneen, *William John McKell*, 2000.

4. Cunneen, *William John McKell*, pp. 156–8.

5. Based on David Day, *Chifley*, HarperCollins, Sydney, 2001, pp. 478, 484.
6. Lionel Wigmore, *Struggle for the Snowy. The Background of the Snowy Mountains Scheme*, 1968, p. 171.
7. See Mary Rose Liverani, *The Winter Sparrows*, Nelson, Melbourne, 1975, for an account of life in a migrant hostel in Wollongong.
8. See T. Brennan, *New Community: Problems and Policies*, 1973.
9. Peter Kirkpatrick, *The Sea Coast of Bohemia. Literary Life in Sydney's Roaring Twenties*, University of Queensland Press, St Lucia, 1992, p. 307.
10. Denis Winston, *Sydney's Great Experiment, The Progress of the Cumberland County Plan*, 1957, pp. 66–7.
11. Loosely based on Ann Curthoys, *Freedom Ride: A Freedom Rider Remembers*, 2002, p. 85.
12. Heather Goodall, *Invasion to Embassy: Land in Aboriginal Politics in New South Wales, 1770–1972*, 1996, pp. 330–32.
13. Ruby Langford, *Don't take your love to town*, Penguin Books, Ringwood, Vic., 1988.
14. Peter Read, *Charles Perkins: A Biography*, 1990, 2nd edn, 2001.
15. Brian Kennedy, *A Passion to Oppose: John Anderson, Philosopher*, 1995, p. 99.
16. See Alan Barcan, *Radical Students: The Old Left at Sydney University*, Melbourne University Press, 2002; also Anne Coombs, *Sex and Anarchy: The Life and Death of the Sydney Push*, 1996.
17. Based on Ava Hubble, *More than an Opera House*, Lansdowne Press, Sydney, 1983, pp. 24–5; 59–60; see also John Douglas Pringle's essay on 'The Opera House' in *On Second Thoughts: Australian Essays*, Angus & Robertson, Sydney, 1971.
18. Bob Ellis, *So it goes: Essays, Broadcasts, Speeches 1987–1999*, Viking/Penguin, Ringwood, Vic., 2000, p. 309.
19. *Year Books, NSW*, 1974 and 1988.
20. From Edmund Campion, *Rockchoppers*, 1982, p. 70.
21. Donald Horne, *Into the Open*, 2000, pp. 96–9.

8 1966–1987, EVERYONE'S DOING IT

1. M. T. Daly, *Sydney Boom Sydney Bust: The City and its Property Market 1850–1981*, 1982, p. 5.
2. Ibid., p. 2.
3. Drew Hutton and Libby Connors, *A History of the Australian Environment Movement*, 1999, pp. 112–14.
4. David Hickie, *The Prince and the Premier*, 1985, pp. 333–6.
5. According to Mike Steketee and Milton Cockburn, *Wran: An Unauthorised Biography*, 1986.

6. See Hilary Golder, *High and Responsible Office: A History of the NSW Magistracy*, 1991.
7. Chris Puplick (1965) in Michael Hogan and David Clune, *The People's Choice, Electoral Politics in 20th Century New South Wales*, 2001, vol. 2, p. 435.
8. Hickie, *The Prince and the Premier*, p. 88.
9. Geoffrey Reading, *High Climbers: Askin and Others*, 1989.
10. Freudenberg, Graham, *Cause for Power. The Official History of the New South Wales Branch of the Australian Labor Party*, 1991, p. 252.
11. Richard Alaba, *Inside Bureaucratic Power: The Wilenski Review of New South Wales Government Administration*, 1994, p. 138.
12. Ibid., p. 79.
13. Ibid., p. 174.
14. In V. G. Childe, *How Labour Governs: A Study of Workers' Representation in Australia*, 1923, reprinted MUP, 1964, p. ix.
15. See Brian Kiernan, *David Williamson: A Writer's Career*, William Heinemann Australia, Melbourne, 1990.
16. David Williamson, *Emerald City*, Currency Press, Sydney, p. 2.

9 1988–2005, THE EVENT-LED ECONOMY

1. Robert Hughes, *The Fatal Shore*, Alfred A. Knopf, New York, 1987; Mollie Gillen, *The Founders of Australia*, Library of Australian History, Sydney, 1989.
2. By Peter Spearritt, 'Celebration of a nation: The triumph of spectacle', in Susan Janson and Stuart Macintyre, eds, *Making the Bicentenary*, *Australian Historical Studies*, vol. 23, no. 91, October 1988, p. 5.
3. *New South Wales Year Book*, 2001, p. 280.
4. On tourism see Jim Davidson and Peter Spearritt, *Holiday Business: Tourism in Australia since 1870*, 2000.
5. Quoted in the *Sydney Morning Herald (SMH)*, 19–20 June 2004, Spectrum, p. 3.
6. J. A. Froude, *Oceana or England and Her Colonies*, Longmans, Green and Co., London, 1886, p. 191.
7. *SMH*, 1–2 May 2004, Domain, p. 8H.
8. Ross Gittins, 'Answers are useful to hide the problems', *SMH*, 5 May 2004, p. 13.
9. J. C. Docherty, *Newcastle: The making of an Australian city*, 1983, pp. 164–6.
10. Martin Laffin and Martin Painter, eds, *Reform and Reversal: Lessons from the Coalition Government in New South Wales 1988–95*, 1995, p. 91.
11. For a detailed account of the crisis see Christopher Sheil, *Water's Fall: Running the Risks with Economic Rationalism*, 2000.
12. Laffin and Painter, eds, *Reform and Reversal*, p. 7.

13. See Sue Williams, *Peter Ryan: The Inside Story*, 2002.
14. Nancy Viviani, *The Long Journey. Vietnamese Migration and Settlement in Australia*, Melbourne University Press, 1984, p. 282.
15. Peter Collins, *The Bear Pit: A Life in Politics*, 2000, pp. 155–6.
16. H. E. Maiden, *The History of Local Government in New South Wales*, 1966, ch. XIX on fire protection.
17. *SMH*, 25 February 2003.
18. J. P. Osborne, *Nine Crowded Years*, George A. Jones, Printer, Sydney, 1921, p. 36.
19. Neal Blewett, *A Cabinet Diary*, Wakefield Press, Adelaide, 1999, p. 182.
20. Based on Tom Wheelwright, 'New South Wales: The dominant right', in A. Parkin and J. Warhurst, eds, *Machine Politics in the Australian Labor Party*, Allen & Unwin, Sydney, 1983.
21. Stephen Salsbury and Kay Sweeney, *Sydney Stockbrokers. Biographies of Members of the Sydney Stock Exchange 1871–1987*, Hale & Iremonger, Sydney, 1992, p. 16.

10 CONCLUSION

1. Notably in Geoffrey Blainey's competitive *Our Side of the Country: The Story of Victoria*, Methuen Haynes, North Ryde, NSW, 1984.
2. Russel Ward, *The Australian Legend*, Oxford University Press, Melbourne, 1958.
3. Geoffrey Blainey, *The Rush that Never Ended: A History of Australian Mining*, first published 1963, 5th edn, 2003.

SOURCES AND FURTHER READING

Apart from brief accounts in yearbooks, guidebooks and encyclopaedias, there is no general history of New South Wales covering the two centuries and more since the beginning of white settlement. There are, however, some excellent studies of major periods and themes listed here according to the chapters for which they are most relevant.

In 1970 I was sent to deputise for Professor Frank Crowley on the New South Wales Working Party of the *Australian Dictionary of Biography*. Ever since, the experience of drawing up lists of names for inclusion, searching for suitable authors, then researching, writing and reading the entries has given me a particular insight into the history of New South Wales. Not surprisingly, the *Australian Dictionary of Biography* (16 vols) (Melbourne University Press, Melbourne, 1966 to 2002) has been used extensively for this work. Additional information on most individuals mentioned here, so long as they died before 1990, will be found in the *ADB*. Biographies and autobiographies of significant figures still living have been listed for the later chapters. Other basic works of reference include *The Australian Encyclopaedia* (various editions), the New South Wales yearbook prior to 1901 (published as *The Wealth and Progress of New South Wales*), and after 1901, both the Australian and New South Wales yearbooks. Statistics unless otherwise noted have been taken from these sources.

The preceding pages reflect the magpie habits of a great many years reading, researching and thinking about Australian history in general. The lists below are far from definitive but contain a selection of classic works of special relevance to New South Wales, items of likely interest not mentioned in the notes, and some of the more accessible popular contemporary accounts of events and personalities.

GENERAL REFERENCE

Aitkin, Don, *The Country Party in New South Wales: A Study of Organisation and Survival*, Australian University Press, Canberra, 1972.

Barcan, Alan, *Two Centuries of Education in New South Wales*, UNSW Press, Sydney, 1988.

Barnard, Alan, *The Australian Wool Market 1840–1900*, Melbourne University Press, Melbourne, 1958.

Blainey, Geoffrey, *Our Side of the Country: The Story of Victoria*, Methuen Haynes, North Ryde, 1984.

Blainey, Geoffrey, *The Rush that Never Ended: A History of Australian Mining*, Melbourne University Press, Melbourne, 1963.

Coghlan, T. A., *Labour and Industry in Australia*, 4 vols, Macmillan, Melbourne, 1969.

Connolly, C. N., *Biographical Register of the New South Wales Parliament 1856–1901*, Australian University Press, Canberra, 1983.

Crowley, Frank, *A Documentary History of Australia, 1788–1900*, 3 vols, Nelson, Melbourne, 1980.

Crowley, F. K., *Modern Australia in Documents, 1901–1970*, 2 vols, Wren, Melbourne, 1973.

Deacon, Desley, *Managing Gender: The State, the New Middle Class and Women Workers 1839–1930*, Oxford University Press, Melbourne, 1989.

Golder, Hilary, *Politics, Patronage and Public Works: The Administration of New South Wales*, vol. 1: 1842–1900, UNSW Press, Sydney, 2005.

Gunn, John, *Along Parallel Lines: A History of the Railways of New South Wales*, Melbourne University Press, Melbourne, 1989.

Hancock, W. K., *Discovering Monaro: A Study of Man's Impact on His Environment*, Cambridge University Press, Cambridge, 1972.

Hogan, Michael, *The Sectarian Strand: Religion in Australian History*, Penguin Books, Ringwood, Vic., 1987.

Hogan, Michael, and Clune, David, *The People's Choice: Electoral Politics in 20th Century New South Wales, 1901–1999*, 3 vols, The Parliament of New South Wales and the University of Sydney with the assistance of the National Council for the Centenary of Federation, Sydney, 2001.

Judd, Stephen, and Cable, Kenneth, *Sydney Anglicans: A History of the Diocese*, Anglican Information Office, Sydney, 1987.

Jupp, James, ed., *The Australian People: An Encyclopedia of the Nation, its People and their Origins*, Angus & Robertson, Sydney, 1988.

Lloyd, C. J., *Either Drought or Plenty: Water Development and Management in New South Wales*, Department of Water Resources New South Wales, 1988.

Maiden, H. E., *The History of Local Government in New South Wales*, Angus & Robertson, Sydney, 1966.

McMartin, Arthur, *Public Servants and Patronage: The Foundation and Rise of the New South Wales Public Service, 1786–1859*, Sydney University Press, Sydney, 1983.

McMinn, W. G., *A Constitutional History of Australia*, Oxford University Press, Melbourne, 1979.

Mulvaney, D. J., and White, Peter, *Australians to 1788*, Fairfax, Syme and Weldon Associates, Broadway, NSW, 1987.

Parker, R. S., *The Government of New South Wales*, University of Queensland Press, St Lucia, 1978.

Radi, Heather, Spearritt, Peter, and Hinton, Elizabeth, *Biographical Register of the New South Wales Parliament 1901–1970*, Australian National University Press, Canberra, 1979.

The Roadmakers, A history of Main Roads in New South Wales, Department of Main Roads New South Wales, Sydney, 1976.

Robson, Lloyd and Roe, Michael, *A Short History of Tasmania*, Oxford University Press, Melbourne, 1997.

Souter, Gavin, *Company of Heralds: A Century and a Half of Australian Publishing by John Fairfax Limited and its Predecessors 1831–1981*, Melbourne University Press, Melbourne, 1981.

Spearritt, Peter, *Sydney's Century: A History*, UNSW Press, Sydney, 2000.

I   INTRODUCTION

Beaglehole, J. C., ed., *The Journals of Captain James Cook on his Voyages of Discovery*, vol. 1: *The Voyage of the Endeavour 1768–1771*, Hakluyt Society, London, 1955.

Clendinnen, Inga, *Dancing with Strangers*, Text Publishing, Melbourne, 2003.

Flood, Josephine, *Archaeology of the Dreamtime: The Story of Prehistoric Australia and its People*, Angus & Robertson, Sydney, 1995.

Horton, D., ed., *The Encyclopedia of Aboriginal Australia*, Australian Institute of Aboriginal and Torres Strait Islander Studies Press, Canberra, 1994.

Jeans, D. N., *The Historical Geography of New South Wales to 1901*, Reed Educational, Sydney, 1972.

Johnson, David, *The Geology of Australia*, Cambridge University Press, Cambridge, 2004.

Turbet, Peter, *The Aborigines of the Sydney District before 1788*, Kangaroo Press, Sydney, 2001.

Willey, Keith, *When the Sky Fell Down: The Destruction of the Tribes of the Sydney Region, 1788–1850s*, Collins, Sydney, 1979.

2   1788–1840, THE CONVICT COLONY

Abbott, G. J., and Nairn, N. B., eds, *Economic Growth of Australia 1788–1821*, Melbourne University Press, Melbourne, 1969.

Atkinson, Alan, *Camden*, Oxford University Press, Melbourne, 1988.

Atkinson, Alan, *The Europeans in Australia: A History*, vol. 1, Oxford University Press, Melbourne, 1997.

Baker, D. W. A., *Days of Wrath: A Life of John Dunmore Lang*, Melbourne University Press, Melbourne, 1983.

Beckett, Ray and Richard, *Hangman, The Life and Times of Alexander Green, Public Executioner to the Colony of New South Wales*, Nelson, Melbourne, 1980.

Borrie, W. D., *The European Peopling of Australasia: A Demographic History, 1788–1988*, Demography Program, RSSS, Australian National University, Canberra, 1994.

Byrne, Paula J., *Criminal Law and Colonial Subject: New South Wales 1810–1830*, Cambridge University Press, Cambridge, 1993.

Campbell, Malcolm, *The Kingdom of the Ryans: The Irish in South-west New South Wales 1816–1890*, UNSW Press, Kensington, NSW, 1997.

Cleverley, John C., *The First Generation: School and Society in Early Australia*, Sydney University Press, Sydney, 1971.

Currey, C. H., *The Brothers Bent: Judge-Advocate Ellis Bent and Judge Jeffrey Hart Bent*, Sydney University Press, Sydney, 1968.

Fletcher, Brian H., *Ralph Darling: A Governor Maligned*, Oxford University Press, Melbourne, 1984.

Fletcher, Brian, *Colonial Australia before 1850*, Nelson, Melbourne, 1976.

Fletcher, Brian, *Landed Enterprise and Penal Society: A History of Farming and Grazing in New South Wales before 1821*, Sydney University Press, Sydney, 1976.

Garran, J. C., and White, L., *Merinos, Myths and Macarthurs: Australian Graziers and their Sheep, 1788–1900*, Australian National University Press/Pergamon, Rushcutters Bay, NSW, 1985.

Grabosky, Peter N., *Sydney in Ferment: Crime, Dissent and Official Reaction 1788–1973*, Australian National University Press, Canberra, 1977.

Hirst, J. B., *Convict Society and its Enemies: A History of Early New South Wales*, George Allen & Unwin, Sydney, 1983.

Hoare, Merval, *Norfolk Island: An Outline of its History 1774–1977*, University of Queensland Press, St Lucia, Qld, 1978.

Kiddle, Margaret, *Caroline Chisholm*, Melbourne University Press, Melbourne, 1950.

King, Hazel, *Richard Bourke*, Oxford University Press, Melbourne, 1971.

Liston, Carol, *Sarah Wentworth, Mistress of Vaucluse*, Historic Houses Trust, Glebe, NSW, 1988.

Madgwick, R. B., *Immigration into Eastern Australia 1788–1851*, Sydney University Press, Sydney, 1969.

Molony, John N., *An Architect of Freedom: John Herbert Plunkett in New South Wales 1832–1869*, Australian National University Press, Canberra, 1973.

Molony, John, *The Native-Born: The First White Australians*, Melbourne University Press, Melbourne, 2000.

Nicholas, Stephen, ed., *Convict Workers: Reinterpreting Australia's Past*, Cambridge University Press, Cambridge, 1988.

O'Farrell, Patrick, *The Irish in Australia*, UNSW Press, Kensington, NSW, 1987.

Oxley, Deborah, *Convict Maids: The Forced Migration of Women to Australia*, Cambridge University Press, Cambridge, 1996.

Rude, George, *Protest and Punishment: The Story of the Social and Political Protestors Transported to Australia 1788–1868*, Oxford University Press, Oxford, 1978.

Smith, Babette, *A Cargo of Women: Susannah Watson & the Convicts of the Princess Royal*, UNSW Press, Sydney, 1988.

Waldersee, James, *Catholic Society in New South Wales 1788–1860*, Sydney University Press, Sydney, 1974.

Whitaker, Anne-Maree, *Joseph Foveaux Power and Patronage in Early New South Wales*, UNSW Press, Sydney, 2000.

Yarwood, A. T., *Samuel Marsden: The Great Survivor*, Melbourne University Press, Melbourne, 1977.

3   1841–1864, HORIZONS AND BOUNDARIES

Austin, K. A., *The Lights of Cobb and Co: The Story of the Frontier Coaches, 1854–1924*, Rigby, Adelaide, 1967.

Barnard Eldershaw, M., *A House is Built*, Harrap & Co, London, 1929.

Bateson, Charles, *Gold Fleet for California: Forty-Niners from Australia and New Zealand*, Ure Smith, Sydney, 1963.

Blainey, Geoffrey, *The Rush that Never Ended: A History of Australian Mining*, Melbourne University Press, Melbourne, 1963.

Burroughs, Peter, *Britain and Australia 1831–1855: A Study in Imperial Relations and Church Land Administration*, Oxford University Press, Clarendon, 1967.

Christie, Michael, *The Sydney Markets 1788–1988*, Sydney Market Authority, Sydney, 1988.

Diamond, Marion, *Ben Boyd of Boydtown*, Melbourne University Press, Melbourne, 1995.

Dow, Gwyneth M., *Samuel Terry: The Botany Bay Rothschild*, Sydney University Press, Sydney, 1974.

Forster, S. G., *Colonial Improver, Edward Deas Thomson 1800–1879*, Melbourne University Press, Melbourne, 1978.

Hainsworth, D. R., *The Sydney Traders: Simeon Lord and his Contemporaries 1788–1821*, Cassell, Sydney, 1971.

Hirst, J. B., *The Strange Birth of Colonial Democracy: New South Wales 1848–1884*, Allen & Unwin, Sydney, 1988.

Jordens, Ann-Mari, *The Stenhouse Circle: Literary Life in Mid-nineteenth Century Sydney*, Melbourne University Press, Melbourne, 1979.

Keesing, Nancy, ed., *History of the Australian Gold Rushes by Those who were There*, Lloyd O'Neil, Hawthorn Vic., 1971 (first published as *Gold Fever* by Angus & Robertson in 1967).

Lee, Robert, *The Greatest Public Work: The New South Wales Railways 1848–1889*, Hale & Iremonger, Sydney, 1988.

Morrell, W. P., *The Gold Rushes*, Adam & Charles Black, London, 1968 (first edn 1940).

Nadel, George, *Australia's Colonial Culture: Ideas, Men and Institutions in Mid-nineteenth Century Eastern Australia*, F. W. Cheshire, Melbourne, 1957.

Pearl, Cyril, *Brilliant Dan Deniehy: A Forgotten Genius*, Thomas Nelson, Melbourne, 1972.

Powell, Alan, *Patrician Democrat: The Political Life of Charles Cowper 1843–1870*, Melbourne University Press, Melbourne, 1977.

Reece, R. H. W., *Aborigines and Colonists: Aborigines and Colonial Society in New South Wales in the 1830s and 1840s*, Sydney University Press, Sydney, 1974.

Roe, Michael, *Quest for Authority in Eastern Australia 1835–1851*, Melbourne University Press in association with the Australian National University, 1965.

Sturma, Michael, *Vice in a Vicious Society: Crime and Convicts in Mid-Nineteenth Century New South Wales*, University of Queensland Press, St Lucia, 1983.

Ward, John M., *Earl Grey and the Australian Colonies 1846–1857*, Melbourne University Press, Melbourne, 1958.

4 1865–1889, FREETRADING

Andrews, Barry, *Price Warung (William Astley)*, Twayne Publishers, Boston, 1976.

Barnard, Alan, *Visions and Profits: Studies in the Business Career of Thomas Sutcliffe Mort*, Melbourne University Press, Melbourne, 1961.

Bolton, Geoffrey, *Edmund Barton*, Allen & Unwin, St Leonards, NSW, 2000.

Coward, Dan Huon, *Out of Sight: Sydney's Environmental History 1851–
    1891*, Department of Economic History, Australian National Univer-
    sity, Canberra, 1988.
Cronin, Leonard, comp. and ed., *Henry Lawson Complete Works 1885–
    1900*, Lansdowne Press, Sydney, 1984.
De Serville, Paul, *Rolf Boldrewood: A Life*, Melbourne University Press,
    Melbourne, 2000.
Dickey, Brian, *Politics in New South Wales 1856–1900*, Cassell Australia,
    North Melbourne, 1969.
Farrer, K. T. H., *A Settlement Amply Supplied: Food Technology in Nine-
    teenth Century Australia*, Melbourne University Press, Melbourne,
    1980.
Fitzgerald, Shirley, *Rising Damp: Sydney 1870–90*, Oxford University
    Press, Melbourne, 1987.
Hawker, G. N., *The Parliament of New South Wales 1856–1965*, Govern-
    ment Printer, Ultimo, NSW, 1971.
Inglis, K. S., *The Rehearsal: Australians at War in the Sudan 1885*, Rigby,
    Adelaide, 1985.
Linge, G. J. R., *Industrial Awakening: A Geography of Australian Manu-
    facturing 1788–1890*, Australian National University Press, Canberra,
    1979.
Livingston, K. T., *The Wired Nation Continent: The Communication Rev-
    olution and Federating Australia*, Oxford University Press, Melbourne,
    1996.
Martin, Alan, and Loveday, Peter, *Parliament Factions and Parties:
    The First Thirty Years of Responsible Government in New
    South Wales, 1856–1889*, Melbourne University Press, Melbourne,
    1966.
Proudfoot, Peter, Maquire, Roslyn, and Firestone, Robert, eds, *Colonial
    City, Global City: Sydney's International Exhibition 1879*, Crossing
    Press, Darlinghurst NSW, 2000.
Rolfe, Patricia, *The Journalistic Javelin: An Illustrated History of the Bul-
    letin*, Wildcat Press, Sydney, 1979.
Rolls, Eric, *They All Ran Wild: The Animals and Plants that Plague
    Australia*, Angus & Robertson, Sydney, 1984.
Yarwood, A. T., *Walers: Australian Horses Abroad*, Melbourne University
    Press, Melbourne, 1989.

5   1890–1914, THE CHALLENGE OF FEDERATION
Bean, C. E. W., *The Dreadnought of the Darling*, Angus & Robertson,
    Sydney, 1956 (first edn London, 1911).
Bollen, J. D., *Protestantism and Social Reform in NSW 1890–1910*,
    Melbourne University Press, Melbourne, 1972.

Broome, Richard, *Treasure in Earthen Vessels: Protestant Christianity in NSW 1900–1914*, University of Queensland Press, St Lucia, Qld, 1980.

Campbell, T. W., *George Richard Dibbs: Politician, Premier, Patriot, Paradox*, published by the author, Canberra, 1999.

Crisp, L. F., *Federation Fathers*, Melbourne University Press, Melbourne, 1990.

Cunneen, Christopher, *Kings' Men: Australia's Governors-General from Hopetoun to Isaacs*, George Allen & Unwin, Sydney, 1983.

Evans, Ian, *The Lithgow Pottery*, The Flannel Flower Press, Sydney, 1981.

Ford, Patrick, *Cardinal Moran and the ALP*, Melbourne University Press, Melbourne, 1966.

Grattan, Michelle, *Back on the Wool Track*, Vintage, Sydney, 2004.

Hawker, Geoffrey, *Politicians All: The Candidates for the Australian Commonwealth Election 1901, A Collective Biography*, Australian Institute of Political Science, Sydney, 2002.

Hicks, Neville, *'This sin and scandal': Australia's Population Debate 1891–1911*, Australian National University Press, Canberra, 1978.

Kildea, Jeff, *Tearing the Fabric: Sectarianism in Australia 1910–1925*, Citadel Books, Sydney, 2000.

Lawton, William James, *The Better Time to Be: Utopian Attitudes to Society among Sydney Anglicans 1885–1914*, UNSW Press, Sydney, 1990.

McMinn, W. G., *George Reid*, Melbourne University Press, Melbourne, 1989.

Nairn, Bede, *Civilising Capitalism: The Labor Movement in New South Wales 1870–1900*, Australian National University Press, Canberra, 1973.

Pearl, Cyril, *Wild Men of Sydney*, W. H. Allen, London, 1958.

Phillips, Walter, *Defending 'A Christian Country': Churchmen and society in New South Wales in the 1890s and After*, University of Queensland Press, St Lucia, Qld, 1981.

Piggin, Stuart, and Lee, Henry, *Mt Kembla, The Mt Kembla Disaster*, Oxford University Press, Melbourne, 1992.

Rickard, John, *Class and Politics, New South Wales, Victoria and the Early Commonwealth, 1890–1910*, Australian National University Press, Canberra, 1976.

Roberts, Jan, *Maybanke Anderson: Sex, Suffrage and Social Reform*, Hale & Iremonger, Sydney, 1993.

Townsend, Norma, *Valley of the Crooked River: European Settlement on the Nambucca*, UNSW Press, Sydney, 1993.

Wilcox, Craig, *Australia's Boer War: The War in South Africa 1899–1902*, Oxford University Press, Melbourne, 2002.

6   1915–1940, DIVISION AND DEPRESSION

Ashton, Paul, *Waving the Waratah: Bicentenary New South Wales*, New South Wales Bicentennial Council, 1989.

Barcan, Alan, *Radical Students: The Old Left at Sydney University*, Melbourne University Press, Melbourne, 2002.

Bayley, William A., *History of the Farmers and Settlers' Association of New South Wales*, Farmers and Settlers' Association, Sydney, 1957.

Fletcher, Brian H., *Australian History in New South Wales 1888–1938*, UNSW Press, Kensington, NSW, 1993.

Horne, Donald, *The Education of Young Donald*, Angus & Robertson, Sydney, 1967.

Horner, Jack, *Bill Ferguson: Fighter for Aboriginal Freedom*, the author, Dickson, ACT, 1994.

Horner, Jack, *Seeking Racial Justice: An Insider's Memoir of the Movement for Aboriginal Advancement, 1938–1978*, Aboriginal Studies Press, Canberra, 2004.

Johnston-Liik, E. M., Liik, George, and Ward, R. G., *A Measure of Greatness: The Origins of the Australian Iron and Steel industry*, Melbourne University Press, Melbourne, 1998.

Kirkpatrick, Peter, *The Sea Coast of Bohemia: Literary Life in Sydney's Roaring Twenties*, University of Queensland Press, St Lucia, Qld, 1992.

Macintyre, Stuart, *The Reds*, Allen & Unwin, Sydney, 1998.

Mitchell, Bruce, *Teachers, Education, and Politics: A History of Organizations of Public School Teachers in New South Wales*, University of Queensland Press, St Lucia, Qld, 1975.

Moore, Andrew, *The Secret Army and the Premier: Conservative Paramilitary Organisations in New South Wales 1930–32*, UNSW Press, Sydney, 1989.

Nairn, Bede, *The Big Fella: Jack Lang and the Australian Labor Party 1891–1949*, Melbourne University Press, Melbourne, 1986.

O'Farrell, Patrick, *The Catholic Church and Community in Australia*, Nelson, Melbourne, 1977.

Richardson, Len, *The Bitter Years: Wollongong during the Great Depression*, Hale & Iremonger, Sydney, 1984.

7   1941–1965, LABOR'S LONG HAUL

Brennan, T., *New Community: Problems and Policies*, Angus & Robertson, Sydney, 1973.

Campion, Edmund, *Rockchoppers*, Penguin Books, Ringwood Vic., 1982.

Collins, Diane, *Sounds from the Stables: The Story of Sydney's Conservatorium*, Allen & Unwin, Sydney, 2001.

Coombs, Anne, *Sex and Anarchy: The Life and Death of the Sydney Push*, Viking/Penguin, Ringwood, Vic., 1996.

Cunneen, Christopher, *William John McKell*, UNSW Press, Sydney, 2000.

Curthoys, Ann, *Freedom Ride: A Freedom Rider Remembers*, Allen & Unwin, Sydney, 2002.

Ginibi, Ruby Langford, *Don't take your love to town*, Penguin, Ringwood, Vic., 1988.

Gollan, Robin, *The Coalminers of New South Wales: A History of the Union, 1860–1960*, Melbourne University Press in association with Australian National University, 1963.

Goodall, Heather, *Invasion to Embassy: Land in Aboriginal Politics in New South Wales, 1770–1972*, Allen & Unwin, St Leonards, NSW, 1996.

Hagan, Jim, and Turner, Ken, *A History of the Labor Party in New South Wales 1891–1991*, Longman Cheshire, Melbourne, 1991.

Horne, Donald, *Into the Open*, Harper Collins, Sydney, 2000.

Hubble, Ava, *More than an Opera House*, Lansdowne Press, Sydney, 1983.

Kennedy, Brian, *A Passion to Oppose: John Anderson, Philosopher*, Melbourne University Press, Melbourne, 1995.

McHugh, Siobhan, *The Snowy: The People behind the Power*, Angus & Robertson, Sydney, 1995.

Read, Peter, *Charles Perkins: A Biography*, Penguin Books, Ringwood, Vic., 2001.

Short, Susanna, *Laurie Short: A Political Life*, Allen & Unwin, Sydney, 1992.

Wigmore, Lionel, *Struggle for the Snowy: The Background of the Snowy Mountains Scheme*, Oxford University Press, Melbourne, 1968.

Winston, Denis, *Sydney's Great Experiment: The Progress of the Cumberland County Plan*, Angus & Robertson, Sydney, 1957.

8   1966–1987, EVERYONE'S DOING IT

Alaba, Richard, *Inside Bureaucratic Power: The Wilenski Review of New South Wales Government Administration*, Hale & Iremonger, Sydney, 1994.

Barry, Paul, *The Rise and Rise of Kerry Packer*, Bantam/ABC Books, Sydney, 1993.

Chaples, Ernie, Nelson, Helen, and Turner, Ken, *The Wran Model: Electoral Politics in New South Wales 1981 and 1984*, Oxford University Press, Melbourne, 1985.

Crowley, Frank, *Tough Times: Australia in the Seventies*, Heinemann, Melbourne, 1986.

Cumming, Fia, *Mates: Five Champions of the Labor Right*, Allen & Unwin, Sydney, 1991.

Dale, Brian, *Ascent to Power*, Allen & Unwin, Sydney, 1985.

Daly, M. T., *Sydney Boom Sydney Bust: The City and its Property Market 1850–1981*, George Allen & Unwin, Sydney, 1982.

Franklin, James, *Corrupting the Youth: A History of Philosophy in Australia*, Macleay Press, Sydney, 2003.

Freudenberg, Graham, *Cause for Power: The Official History of the New South Wales Branch of the Australian Labor Party*, Pluto Press, Leichhardt, NSW, 1991.

Golder, Hilary, *High and Responsible Office: A History of the NSW Magistracy*, Sydney University Press in association with Oxford University Press, Melbourne, 1991.

Golder, Hilary, *Sacked: Removing and Remaking the Sydney City Council 1853–1988*, City of Sydney, 2004.

Griffin-Foley, Bridget, *Sir Frank Packer: The Young Master*, HarperCollins, Sydney, 2000.

Griffin-Foley, Bridget, *The House of Packer: The Making of a Media Empire*, Allen & Unwin, Sydney, 1999.

Harvey, S. D., *The Ghost of Ludwig Gertsch*, Pan Macmillan, Sydney, 2000.

Hickie, David, *The Prince and the Premier*, Angus & Robertson, Sydney, 1985.

Hutton, Drew, and Connors, Libby, *A History of the Australian Environment Movement*, Cambridge University Press, Cambridge, 1999.

Kiernan, Brian, *David Williamson: A Writer's Career*, William Heinemann, Melbourne, 1990.

Lyons, John, *John Laws: A Life of Power*, Random House, Sydney, 1991.

Masters, Chris, *Inside Story*, Angus & Robertson, Sydney, 1992.

McCoy, Alfred, *Drug Traffic*, Harper & Row, Sydney, 1980.

McKenna, Mark, *Looking for Blackfellas' Point: An Australian History of Place*, UNSW Press, Sydney, 2002.

Margo, Jill, *Frank Lowy: Pushing the Limits*, Harper Collins, Sydney, 2000.

Reading, Geoffrey, *High Climbers: Askin and Others*, John Ferguson, Sydney, 1989.

Rees, Peter, *Killing Juanita: A True Story of Murder and Corruption*, Allen & Unwin, Sydney, 2004.

Richardson, Graham, *Whatever It Takes*, Transworld, Sydney, 1994.

Singleton, John, *True Confessions*, Cassell Aust., Stanmore, NSW, 1979.

Steketee, Mike, and Cockburn, Milton, *Wran: An Unauthorised Biography*, Allen & Unwin, Sydney, 1986.

Turner, Ken, *House of Review? The New South Wales Legislative Council, 1934–68*, Sydney University Press, Sydney, 1969.

Wild, R. A., *Bradstow: A Study of Status, Class and Power in a Small Australian Town*, Angus & Robertson, Sydney, 1974.

Wilkinson, Marian, *The Fixer: The Untold Story of Graham Richardson*, William Heinemann, Melbourne, 1996.

9   1988–2005, THE EVENT-LED ECONOMY

Arantz, Philip, *A Collusion of Powers*, published by the author, Dunedoo, NSW, 1993.

Arena, Franca, *My Story*, Simon & Schuster, Sydney, 2002.

Carr, Bob, *Thoughtlines: Reflections of a Public Man*, Viking, Camberwell, Vic., 2002.

Collins, Peter, *The Bear Pit: A life in politics*, Allen & Unwin, Sydney, 2000.

Costar, Brian, and Economou, Nicholas, eds, *The Kennett Revolution, Victorian politics in the 1990s*, UNSW Press, Sydney, 1999.

Davidson, Jim, and Spearritt, Peter, *Holiday Business: Tourism in Australia since 1870*, Melbourne University Press, Melbourne, 2000.

Docherty, J. C., *Newcastle: The Making of an Australian City*, Hale & Iremonger, Sydney, 1983.

Dodkin, Marilyn, *Bob Carr: The Reluctant Leader with Extracts from Carr's Private Diaries*, UNSW Press, Sydney, 2003.

Laffin, Martin, and Painter, Martin, eds, *Reform and Reversal: Lessons from the Coalition Government in New South Wales 1988–95*, Macmillan, Melbourne, 1995.

Lagan, Bernard, *Loner: Inside a Labor Tragedy*, Allen & Unwin, Sydney, 2005.

Marr, David, *The High Price of Heaven*, Allen & Unwin, St Leonards, NSW, 1999.

Marsden, John, *I am what I am: My life and Curious Times*, Viking/Penguin, Camberwell, Vic., 2004.

Sheil, Christopher, *Water's Fall: Running the Risks with Economic Rationalism*, Pluto Press, Annandale, NSW, 2000.

Souter, Gavin, *Heralds and Angels: The House of Fairfax 1841–1990*, Melbourne University Press, Melbourne, 1991.

Wang, Lucy, *Blood Price*, William Heinemann Australia, Melbourne, 1996.

West, Andrew, and Morris, Rachel, *Bob Carr: A Self-made Man*, Harper Collins, Sydney, 2003.

Williams, Sue, *Peter Ryan: The Inside Story*, Viking, Ringwood, Vic., 2002.

INDEX